Murder
in
Little
Egypt

Books by Darcy O'Brien

Murder in Little Egypt (1989)

Two of a Kind (1985)

The Silver Spooner (1981)

A Way of Life, Like Any Other (1978)

Patrick Kavanagh (1975)

W. R. Rodgers (1970)

The Conscience of James Joyce (1968)

Murder
in
Little
Egypt

Darcy O'Brien

William Morrow
and Company, Inc.
New York

Death Sends for the Doctor by Eugene Heltai—adapted from the Hungarian by John Ward Bayly. Copyright 1938 by Samuel French, in *One-Act Plays for Stage and Study, Ninth Series*. Reprinted by permission of Samuel French, Inc.

Library of Congress Cataloging-in-Publication Data

O'Brien, Darcy.
    Murder in Little Egypt / Darcy O'Brien.
        p.   cm.
    ISBN 0-688-07137-6
    1. Murder—Illinois—Saline County.   I. Title.
HV6533.I4027 1989
364.1 '523' 097739—dc19   88-13229
                                                                                            CIP

Printed in the United States of America

First Edition

1 2 3 4 5 6 7 8 9 10

To
Suzanne
who went down to Egypt

"Pap warn't in a good mood that morning—so
he was his natural self."
—Huck Finn

CHICAGO

PEORIA   URBANA

ILLINOIS R.

SPRINGFIELD   DECATUR

EMBARRAS R.

ALTON

LITTLE WABASH

ST. LOUIS

I L L I N O I S

KASKASKIA R.

MISSISSIPPI R.

SALINE R.

MURPHYSBORO   BENTON
                   ELDORADO
                   HARRISBURG
                   CARBONDALE
                   MARION

LITTLE MUDDY R.

WABASH R.

OHIO R.

KASKASKIA

MAKANDA
          STONEFORT

SHAWNEETOWN
EQUALITY

CAVE IN ROCK

GRAND
TOWER

BIG MUDDY R.

E G Y P T

L I T T L E   E G Y P T

ELIZABETHTOWN
ROSICLARE

GOLCONDA

CAPE GIRARDEAU

CACHE CREEK

GALE   JONESBORO
THEBES   MOUND CITY
          CAIRO

BAY CREEK

METROPOLIS

HAMLETSBURG

OHIO R.

BROOKPORT

CUMBERLAND R.

PADUCAH

TENNESSEE R.

JAYE ZIMET

1

SOUTHERN ILLINOIS, CALLED EGYPT BY ITS NATIVES, IS THAT inverted triangle bounded by the Wabash, the Ohio, and the Mississippi, bordered by Kentucky on the south and by an indeterminate line drawn east from St. Louis on the north. In this land between the rivers, people lead lives that are self-contained, known only to themselves, cut off, if it were not for television, from the rest of the country. Down there they know that Chicago is up north, but they seldom think about it, and they know that the people in Chicago rarely think about them. A joke has it that in southern Illinois, mothers frighten their children not with the bogeyman but with the threat of never going to St. Louis. This Egypt is a secret and a secretive sort of place, an outback and a throwback to earlier, murkier times.

The rare visitor to this other Illinois may seize on the word surreal to describe the landscape: peaceful-looking small farms, white churches, little brick-faced towns, lakes where Canada geese spend the autumn and winter, the big muddy rivers, the Ozark hills that, covered in hardwoods, rise in the Shawnee National Forest—a reassuring prospect, idyllic if you care for isolation, but disrupted every few miles by enormous coal pits, strip mines scarring the land with their huge power shovels several stories high, tearing up the ground, leaving behind black heaps where not even weeds can grow. Local children call the shovels monsters and ask to be taken on Sunday drives to see them. Their great booms reaching skyward, they look like giant mechanical insects rooting in the earth. At night the coal dust, lying in gob piles, sometimes spontaneously ignites, lighting the air with a weird orange flicker. Southern Illinois gets its share of sunshine, but night and gray, gloomy days seem to fit the place, its black mines, and its obscurity.

It has been called Egypt since the rugged winters of 1824 and 1831–1832, when northerners journeyed south to buy corn and seed, imagining themselves as the sons of Jacob, who went "down to Egypt to buy corn" in Genesis 42. After 1832 the term Egypt came into general use, as people enjoyed thinking that they had settled in a land of plenty sanctioned by Scripture, though the soil was actually thin compared to the rest of Illinois. In 1837 the town of Cairo (pronounced Kerro) was chartered at the Nile-like delta where the Ohio joins the Mississippi; Karnak and Thebes followed, and many Biblical names, Palestine, Lebanon, Mt. Carmel, Eden, Goshen, Olive Branch, Herod, even a Sodom that vanished early in this century.

In the heart of Egypt, often called Little Egypt, lie Eldorado and Harrisburg, coal towns that have not changed much from sixty or seventy years ago, except for the K marts and Wal-Marts and Huck's Convenience Food Stores that line the highways on their outskirts. They stand seven miles apart on Route 45 about thirty miles west of the Ohio, separated by Muddy, which is mostly just the Gateway motel, restaurant and liquor store, formerly a Holiday Inn, still the major social center for both towns, the site of Peggy Ozment's annual Christmas party, to which four hundred of the local business and social elite get invited. 5200 FRIENDLY PEOPLE says the sign on Route 45 outside Eldorado, AND ONE OL' SORE-HEAD, with a cartoon of a sour-faced man in overalls; Harrisburg has twice as many people, equally friendly, though not to strangers.

A stranger in Eldorado (pronounced Elder-RAY-dough) feels uneasy, as in any small town where everybody knows everybody and an out-of-state license plate provokes stares. Except for the hunters who come in for the geese or the deer in the Shawnee forest, this has never been a big tourist area in spite of the beauties of the Ohio, and the people are unused to dealing with outsiders. State your business, the silence asks as you pay for a Hershey bar at Terry's Market. The sense of not belonging, and of not being wanted particularly, haunts the stranger as it does in parts of Arkansas and in the hills of Kentucky and Tennessee. Family ties and local associations matter here, one can sense, and nothing else.

You can tour Eldorado in half an hour. Once the town had the only railroad station in Saline County; now that there are none, it has the Depot Inn restaurant, which serves ham and eggs and chicken-fried steak in part of the abandoned station. Downtown the new First State Bank building, right angles of red brick and glass, stands out among the old, weathered red-brick structures, the boarded-up movie theater, the pool hall, Bertis Herrmann's tin shop, and the Jet Set beauty parlor, located in a trailer that needs paint. The Ferrell Hospital on Pine Street, with its green awnings and clearly marked emergency entrance, appears prosperous, more so than the Pearce Hospital over on Organ Street, a rectangular, bunkerlike building of thin, pink-purplish brick that brings to mind a large veterinary clinic. The number of churches impresses, sixteen in all, twelve of them Baptist, fundamentalist, or charismatic of one kind or another.

Eldorado's neighborhoods range from neat little white frame houses on hilly, tree-lined streets to shacks in irregular rows that straggle out along and beyond the railroad tracks. In the tidy areas pride and industry are everywhere apparent in the trimmed lawns and shrubs, the garden furniture ranged around the outdoor grill, the pots of flowers and plaster statuary—toads, deer, flamingoes, the rare nymph—and the polished automobiles, mostly Fords and Chevys, many pickups, a few vans. Emblems of the season, pumpkins or Christmas wreaths and lights, never fail to appear here. Elsewhere rusty trailers and pickups get parked in yards along with other junk. Tiny houses look patched together. Eldorado seems about half proud and half given up. In a ramshackle area a portable sign, the kind with stick-on plastic letters, stands beside a Laundromat and tells a story:

LAUNERY
WE DO MINING CLOTHES.

Harrisburg has more enterprise and more money. Several of the houses in the two-hundred block on Walnut Street approach elegance, many of them nicely landscaped, two and three stories high with porticoes reminiscent of the Old South. The Bar-B-Q Barn on Main Street, lately spruced up and decorated with old farm and kitchen implements, also feels southern, offering different kinds of pickled vegetables and fried okra along with the ribs. The accents of the diners sound southern, too, indistinguishable from those of neighboring western Kentucky except for an "ar" sound for "or," as in "barn again" for born again, "park roast" for pork roast.

The families of most of the people of southern Illinois migrated from the Carolinas, Tennessee, and Kentucky before and immediately after the Civil War. A coal boom early in this century brought in Italians, Czechs, and Poles to work the mines, but the Anglo-Saxon and Scotch-Irish southern strain still predominates. These are white southerners. You can spend all day in Eldorado or Harrisburg without seeing a black person. Eldorado has no black families, Harrisburg only a handful.

"Poor, shiftless, and ignorant outcasts," a writer from northern Illinois called the immigrant southerners in 1871. "Of the humbler class," a sympathetic, local historian described them in 1875, adding that "there were no half-breeds, neither of Indians nor other obnoxious races. In private life they lived with austerity, and in society moved with chivalrous spirit." But by the turn of the century the phrases "worthless as an Egyptian" and "scabby as an Egyptian" were in common use, and it was said that to call a man a "son of Egypt" was considered an affront and meant "a fight or a foot race." In the early days of the nineteenth century, southern Illinois had been the commercial center of the state, but it declined into poverty after the Civil War, inviting the northerners' contempt. Today incomes remain low, unemployment is perennially between thirteen and twenty percent, dependence on public relief double that in central and northern Illinois. Over fifty percent of the people of Eldorado have for decades relied on public assistance of one kind or another, a rate matched or exceeded only in the Chicago ghettoes.

In the town square of Harrisburg, however, sometimes called Shawnee Square, people move about with a certain determination, something short of a bustle but businesslike. They have been here a long time and intend to stay, no matter what the rest of the state thinks. The word Chicago can provoke an epithet and the wish that that city be shoved into Lake Michigan with a bulldozer. In the center of the square stands the almost windowless, modern Saline County Courthouse, brick and concrete, not beautiful but new and substantial. On a corner of the square the Harrisburg National Bank, founded 1876, occupies the town's tallest building, a seven-story red-brick tower with ornate cornices, built during the coal boom.

Over at the First Bank and Trust on Walnut, you can receive a two-gun set of Smith & Wesson automatic pistols on purchasing special certificates of deposit, a promotional gimmick so successful that the Associated Press carried a story about it in 1986, attracting money from as far away as San Francisco, as the bank's officers will tell you proudly.

The free pistols epitomize certain aspects of the character of Egypt. To understand this, and the vague sense of apprehension a visitor feels, it helps to know that Saline County, like the entire eleven-county area known as Little Egypt, is one of the most violent places in America, with a murder rate per capita comparable to or exceeding in any given year that of Chicago or New York City. Compared to the United States as a whole, the annual murder rate in Little Egypt is nearly double, about 10.1 per 100,000 inhabitants, 6.6 for the rest of the country. Of rural and semi-rural areas, only Harlan County, Kentucky, rivals it for violence.

Many Egyptian murders have a special, local flavor to them, as with the wife who shot her husband to death, cut him up, and fed him to the hogs; or the thirty-year-old son who loved his mother so much that he laced his daddy's iced tea with antifreeze. Bar fights ending in shoot-outs take their toll.

This violence has been an unbroken tradition for nearly two hundred years.

"There's not a lot of murderers and cutthroats in southern Illinois," Will Rogers told a reporter for the Marion *Daily Republican* in 1926. "They are real people, congenial and hospitable. But instead of being like a lot of committees, fussing and arguing, calling each other names, they just shoot it out if it's necessary."

Will Rogers was reacting to the gangsters who were shooting each other with impunity all over Little Egypt in the mid-twenties. But before them the Ku Klux Klansmen ruled, murdering at least fifty people in two years, all in the cause of Americanism, which

13

in southern Illinois meant temperance: There were not enough blacks in the region for even a white supremacist to worry about, so the Klan united against Italian and Irish Catholics in defense of Prohibition, with the Klan's contributions to local Protestant ministers assuring their support. And in 1922, twenty strikebreakers were shot to death, mutilated, and their corpses spat on by a union mob in what became known as the Herrin Massacre, a labor dispute at a strip mine, the culmination of a thirty years' war between union and management. Nine men went on trial after the Herrin Massacre. All nine gained acquittal, and the state gave up on further prosecutions, accepting that local loyalties made convictions impossible.

From 1868 to 1876 the Bloody Vendetta, a feud involving four prominent families, took the lives of at least six men and terrorized the countryside. When local authorities seemed unable or unwilling to gain indictments, let alone convictions, the *Chicago Tribune* thundered from the north, "The feud is a disgrace to the whole State of Illinois—a disgrace to the courts of the State, to the government of the State, to the Governor of the State, and to the people of the State."

Southern Illinois was notorious for violence long before the *Tribune* was founded, back in the days when Shawneetown, twenty-five miles east of Harrisburg on the Ohio, was a commercial and banking power and could turn down a request for a ten-thousand-dollar loan from the village of Chicago with the message, "You are too far from Shawneetown ever to amount to anything." Some historians have suggested that Cave-in-Rock, a cavern overlooking the Ohio below Shawneetown, was the birthplace of organized crime in the United States. Robbers, counterfeiters and murderers used the cave as a headquarters and a place to store booty plundered from immigrant families floating down the river in flatboats.

Cave-in-Rock's bloodiest tenants were Big Harpe and Little Harpe, Micijah and Wiley, brothers who killed for the pleasure of it, attacking travelers with the terrible cry "We are the Harpes!" and slaughtering their victims with knives and tomahawks, then slicing them open, tearing out the innards, and filling the bodies with stones to sink them in the river. They ranged about accompanied by antecedents of Charles Manson's followers, three women who shared the brothers sexually and bore them three children. Big Harpe's infant daughter irritated him one day with her crying, so he bashed out her brains against a tree. The Harpes' documented victims number in the forties, but they killed many more than that, until Big Harpe was finally cornered, shot, and decapitated by the father of one of his victims, who lodged the head in the crotch of a tree as a warning. Little Harpe was hanged in 1804. They were serial murderers before the term was coined.

More recently Charlie Birger, a bootlegger and gangster who virtually ruled Little Egypt from 1925 to 1927, brought a brief, national notoriety to southern Illinois and created of himself an enduring legend that says much about the place. Named Sachna Itzik Birger at his birth in Lithuania in 1882, Charlie emigrated with his family to New York in 1887 and moved on to St. Louis. By 1913, after a stint in the 13th U.S. Cavalry, he was selling beer and whiskey to coal miners in southern Illinois. When the Klan interfered with his bootlegging, Charlie engineered the murder of its leader in a shoot-out at the Canary Cigar Store at the European Hotel in Marion in January 1925.

Charlie Birger was popular. Even today, local cynics say, the people of Harrisburg would erect a statue to him if they could get away with it. He won their affection by protecting them from the rival Shelton brothers' gang and by well-publicized acts of charity, donations to church building funds, gifts of candy and ice cream to children, bags of groceries left on the doorsteps of the poor. Harrisburg was where he lived and educated his children, as he said in a radio broadcast over station WEBQ (We Entertain Beyond Question) in 1926. Nor were folks on the highways in any danger, "because a gangster's bullet in this instance will be aimed at an enemy gangster." He liked to parade the town square in his big Lincoln, armored and decked out with firing chairs and gun slits, a couple of his men perched on top with machine guns.

"Baron of Egypt, America's Robin Hood," a writer for H. L. Mencken's *American Mercury* called him, noting that Charlie often dressed the part with his soft brown leather coat, riding breeches, leather hunting cap, bright yellow cavalry boots, and jingling spurs. His tailor, recalling Charlie's fondness for a large beer stein decorated with portraits of King Arthur and Queen Guinevere, called him "a knight of another sort." He was the local killer made good. People looked up to this Robin Hood, this protector who kept the booze flowing and dispensed gifts. His was a time of relative prosperity in Egypt. The coal mines were at full tilt, everyone had a job, but nobody was getting rich, because the mine owners, like the railroad owners, were all absentee. The big money ended up in Chicago or left the state. Only Charlie Birger appeared to have whipped the system, with a flair that made him the darling of reporters from St. Louis, Chicago, and the East.

"Live and let live is my motto," Charlie liked to say. And "I don't know what in the hell's the matter with me. Every time I kill a man it makes me sick afterwards. I guess it's my stomach."

In 1928 he was hanged for the murder of the mayor of West City. Five hundred ticket-holding spectators filled the courtyard of the Benton jail for the event; others jammed the street outside and peered from the windows of buildings across the way.

"It's a beautiful world," Charlie Birger said just before he dropped. It made wonderful copy.

After Charlie Birger's hanging, the region grew somnolent. The Great Depression came early, hit hard, and lingered until the middle of World War II. The coal mines never fully recovered; southern Illinois missed out on the postwar economic boom. People stayed on, attached to the land between the rivers, used to the old ways, working sporadically in the mines, growing corn and peaches, talking of new industries that never appeared, cashing relief checks, hunting and fishing and going to church. Many of the educated young cleared out, so the population remained about the same in 1984 as it had been in 1934. Violence was frequent but less dramatic than before, accepted merely as the way things were. As if longing for the glamorous, wild old days, county officials put up a historical marker in 1976 on the site of Shady Rest, Charlie Birger's road-house and arsenal, where a man could buy a drink and a woman and bet on a cockfight or a dogfight. Quickly the marker vanished, shot up and blown up by ancient enemies or kids on a lark, nobody knew which.

Then in mid-December of 1984, something happened on a lonely road outside of St. Louis that woke Little Egypt up. A farmer, out to feed his horses at dawn, discovered the body of a young man. It looked like an execution: two shots to the head; dumped and abandoned.

Within a day the news reached Eldorado and Harrisburg and set people talking. The murdered young man was Sean Cavaness, twenty-two years old, the son of Dr. John Dale Cavaness, who was then living in Harrisburg and practicing at Pearce Hospital in Eldorado, as he had since 1955. Citizens of the two towns immediately recalled that Dr. Cavaness's firstborn son, Mark, had also died of gunshot wounds several years before. Mark had been found lying near his truck on a farm Dr. Cavaness owned near Galatia, in Saline County. Most people believed that Mark had accidentally shot himself to death; there had been a lengthy investigation but never any arrests, nor even any known suspects; and people had pretty much forgotten about Mark until now. It seemed an unbearably cruel blow for the doctor to have to suffer, losing a second son like this. His wife had left him in 1971, taking all four of their sons with her. Then Mark had returned to Egypt, only to die, and now Sean was dead in St. Louis. Another boy, married, was living in St. Louis; and the fourth son was with his mother and her new husband somewhere up in Wisconsin. But the people of Eldorado and Harrisburg did not give too much thought to the distant ex-wife and the surviving sons. They grieved for their doctor.

No man in Little Egypt was more admired than Dr. John Dale Cavaness, or Dr. Dale, as he was affectionately called. He had a reputation for being the most skillful physician and surgeon in the region and the most kindly. He understood people, not only their illnesses, and he never asked those to pay who could not afford his services, but treated them for free, sometimes not even bothering to send a bill. His patients regarded him as a medical genius, as one of their own, and as a kind of Robin Hood. Religious folk wondered why God would have singled out this good man to bear such a heavy cross.

Then the unimaginable happened. After his son's funeral in St. Louis, which had been attended by friends of the doctor from Little Egypt, detectives arrested Dr. Cavaness for Sean's murder. The news tore through southern Illinois like a twister. Within days St. Louis homicide detectives were arriving armed with search warrants, nosing around Harrisburg and Eldorado like foreign agents. Not since the Herrin Massacre had anything like this happened to people used to minding their own business and telling outsiders to mind theirs. The story hit front pages and television news programs in Chicago and St. Louis.

These big-city sensationalists did not understand the doctor, local people insisted, nor the devotion of his patients and friends, nor the character of Little Egypt itself. Everybody knew that Sean had been unstable. Probably he had been killed by drug dealers—

17

possibly he had committed suicide—the St. Louis police needed a scapegoat—the people of St. Louis wanted a hanging—so the rumors multiplied.

The doctor's hometown supporters, organizing for his defense, began to attract attention throughout the Midwest and Upper South and in national publications. They set out to show the world what Dr. Dale Cavaness was really like.

2

IT MUST HAVE BEEN IN HIM FROM THE BEGINNING—THE fighting instinct, the intensity of will.

"He was breech birth," his mother liked to say of him, "and he's been doing things the hard way ever since."

She often reminded her son and others of how she had nearly lost her own life, or so she said, giving him his. She talked about the event almost as if it had been a survival contest between mother and son that ended in a draw on October 15, 1925, when John Dale Cavaness battered his way into the world buttocks first.

He was Noma and Clarence Mark "Peck" Cavaness's only child. After him, as Noma never tired of saying, she could not bear another.

She did not wish her son to forget her importance to him. When he was still very young, only three or four years old, she devised a new sort of contest with him. She would let him crawl up onto her bed with her to chatter and laugh and snuggle. In the middle of the giggling and maternal teasing Noma would pretend to die. All of a sudden, she would expel her breath, roll up her eyes and shut them, muttering, "I'm dying," and lie there motionless.

It was the death game.

As she described it, Dale would crawl up to her face and touch it. "Mommy! Mommy!" he would begin to cry. "No, Mommy! Don't die, Mommy! Are you dead? No!"

Soon he would be wailing hysterically, pounding at her with little fists. She would stay still.

Then, just as he was ready to hurl himself onto the floor in agony, Noma would pretend to revive. She would open her eyes and laugh. And the boy would cling to her, reprieved.

The remarkable thing about the death game, Noma Cavaness always said, was how frightened little Dale became. She dared not let the game last too long, not even as long as she could hold her breath. He might have gone berserk with terror and grief.

His mother's hold on him remained strong for the first ten years or so. His father worked as a brakeman on what was then the Louisville and Nashville railroad. The L&N ran southeast from St. Louis to Eldorado, over toward Shawneetown and across the Ohio into Kentucky and beyond, so Peck Cavaness was often away for days at a time and never had regular working hours. Noma was ever present and watchful. They called the boy Dale after Noma's father's family. Her mother and father lived in the house next door on Maple Street in Eldorado, just across from the Ferrell Hospital, with her aunt and uncle next door on the other side. Dales set the tone of daily life.

Of the Dales (English in origin) and the Cavanesses (Scotch-Irish), the Dales were the older, more established family in the area, along with the Wards, Noma's mother's people. The Dales had been in southern Illinois since before the Civil War, migrating up from the South, establishing the settlement of Dale in Little Egypt as a timber town in the days when pioneers were still clearing the great forests. The town remained a point of family pride, although by the 1930s it had dwindled to scarcely a village on the road between Eldorado and McLeansboro, where the Dales and the Cavanesses shared a common graveyard. The social gap between the two families was not large; but in their regional longevity the Dales had acquired bits of property here and there and the respectability that land bestowed. They were not rich, but they were middle class. As a working man, Peck Cavaness had married a smidgen above himself.

Noma wanted all the Dales' respectability, and then some, passed on to her son, and she wanted him to rise in the world. It was she who insisted on his finishing his homework every night and prodded him about his grades, which were excellent from the start. It was she who told him that he was smarter and better than the other boys and that she and his father would sacrifice to get him places. And it was she who took him to Sunday school and to services every Sunday at the First Presbyterian Church in Eldorado, where young Dale heard sermons in the gloomy, strict Calvinist mode of those days, with emphasis on predestination and the unknowable nature of God's chosen, the elect. You could never be sure whether you were saved or damned; all you knew was that the matter had already been decided. It was a hopeful sign to be successful in this life. Achieving respectability might possibly mean that, through God's mysterious grace, you had been saved, even as not being able to pay your way might indicate that you were headed for perdition. So you always wore your new shoes to church; they squeaked, and everyone could hear that you could afford new ones. But only God knew your fate. The best you could do was to work hard, hope, and pray, as the hymn said:

> *Few are thy days and full of woe,*
> *O man of woman born!*
> *Thy doom is written, "Dust thou art,*
> *And shalt to dust return!"*
>
> *Cheered by this hope, with patient mind*
> *I'll wait heaven's high decree,*
> *Till the appointed period come*
> *When death shall set us free. Amen.*

Whatever her sternness, Noma made the best peach cobbler in the world, and nobody could match her fried chicken or chicken and dumplings. But the way she made Dale dress for school increased the tension between mother and son. She insisted that he wear fancy corduroy knickerbockers when the other boys all ran about free in bib overalls ordered once a year from the Sears catalog. Those knickers set Dale apart, as Noma wanted and as he hated. He was not allowed to get dirty. On the rare occasions when Dale did come home with mud on his knickers, Noma would throw a fit. He had gotten dirty just to spite her, she told him. He had run off "wallering" in the mud just to infuriate her.

21

She also forced Dale to study the violin, a radical choice in a place where a baseball bat or a shotgun, or at worst a country fiddle, was the preferred instrument. Soon he was getting beaten up all the time. Mother Noma complained to the teacher and the principal, but other boys continued to waylay and pummel him, calling him a priss and a mama's boy.

Peck Cavaness knew and worried about the beatings. If he could not tell Noma how to be a mother, he knew he would have to help his son become a man. One afternoon when he was off work from the railroad, Peck stood in the backyard near the run where he kept his two hunting dogs and watched Dale come home from the sixth grade. Up the graveled alley he saw his son running from a crowd of bigger boys who shouted after him and chased him until they noticed his father and retreated.

"Don't you ever let me catch you running away like that again," Peck told Dale. "The next time that happens, you stand your ground, hear?"

Peck let his son know about the time a couple of old boys from the Charlie Birger gang had tried to intimidate him. Peck had been standing on the Eldorado platform waiting for Noma to return from visiting relatives. These gangsters had ordered him to move on. They said they were clearing the platform for somebody important. Peck told them they could go to hell, there wasn't anybody more important than his wife. One of them started to reach inside his coat for his pistol, but Peck decked him with a quick right cross. While the other one stood there like a dummy, stunned for a moment, Peck lit out, ran home, and fetched his shotgun. When he made it back to the station, the gangsters were gone and Noma was waiting for him, wondering why he had shown up to meet her carrying his gun.

"I wasn't about to let some two-bit gangsters push me around," Peck said, "and they knew it. You stand and fight or don't bother coming home."

For the rest of his life Dale spoke of that moment as a turning point. The next day he faced his tormentors and fought. He found that he could fight like hell. He was a small boy but he used his feet as well as his fists and, when he had to, his teeth. The word got around that if you got into a scrap with Curly Cavaness, as he was called, you remembered it. He could pick his own opponents and found that he could take punishment without giving ground, could endure pain, and that not giving up and not caring if you got hurt meant more than how big you were.

The knickerbockers gave way to jeans. The violin was left behind. He kept up with his studies, but he began spending more time on sports, and Noma had to relent when her boy came home as dirty as the next kid.

Dale had not really needed the knickers to know that he and his family were better off than most of the people in Eldorado. Throughout the Depression, six out of ten men were out of work and on relief in Little Egypt. Few could pay taxes, and running water was cut off in most towns by 1932. People dug wells in their yards and reverted to outdoor privies. Many lost their electricity and saw their houses fall apart for lack of paint and other maintenance.

Southern Illinois depended on coal, and the mines shut down one after another. In 1925, twenty-five mines in Saline County had been operating; by 1939 the number was down to ten, some of these strip mines requiring few workers. In Eldorado—called one of *Seven Stranded Coal Towns* in a report by the Works Projects Administration—the typical family of four, taking into account all available forms of relief, averaged about forty dollars a month in income. Half of this went for food. People ate a lot of water gravy—bacon dripping, flour, salt, and water, poured over bread if they had it. When lodges and churches distributed surplus government food, people lined up for it, humiliated but starving. In the hot summers, if a family had a nickel to spare, they could make a twelve-and-a-half-pound block of precious ice, wrapped in rags and stowed under the house, last for three or four days, meaning the magic of iced tea and lemonade. A man might find a day's work now and then in a mine, if he could get transportation to the job. He could pick peaches for a few days a year, getting paid mostly in fruit. He could collect scrap metal and coat hangers, make flower pots out of tin cans, or clean tombstones in an effort to create goods and services no one wanted or could afford.

Through all these years Peck Cavaness was able to bring home his paycheck, and Noma kept house meticulously and could afford the materials to do so. Her hardwood floors shone; her pots and pans gleamed; no cobweb lasted through a day. It was a modest, white frame house, two bedrooms and a porch; but Peck and Noma cared for it religiously. Peck could repair just about anything, and if he wanted a rest, he could get the whole house painted for five dollars, with scores of men desperate for the work.

On December 3, 1932, Dale wrote a letter:

Dear Santa Clause,
   I have been a fairly good boy. . . .

He asked for a football and a bathrobe, a desk and a watch. His mother, he told Santa Claus, wanted a dress and a new floor lamp. His daddy wanted a billfold, a new tie, and a bird dog. That was quite a Christmas list for any Eldorado family that year, when the last thing most local men needed was a new billfold. A typical Christmas present was a pair of those overalls from Sears, and many families saved every penny they had for the spring, when they could buy some chicks from the Otis Carter Hatchery at a dollar apiece. A few White Leghorns and Rhode Island Reds in your yard meant eggs and the occasional fryer throughout the year. Every morning at six A.M. over station WEBQ in Harrisburg, Otis Carter broadcast the virtues of his chicks "direct by remote control" from his Eldorado hatchery on a country-music program which was followed at seven by *The Baptist Hour*. Carter's sales took off, chickens being about the only thriving business in Egypt then.

If Peck Cavaness had been a religious man, which he was not, leaving the praying to his wife, he would have thanked the Lord at grace before Sunday dinner of chicken or pork roast. He was grateful that he and his family were spared the hunger and misery so many of their neighbors were suffering. The Cavanesses had many other advantages. Because Peck had a car and could afford gasoline, he was able to take his son fishing and hunting all over Egypt. By the time Dale was twelve they would head for the woods on a free autumn Saturday to get some quail, which Noma would fry up with her special brown gravy rich with pan juices. Dale quickly became an ace with a shotgun. He learned from his father how to imagine an invisible line between the gunsight and the target, and he had terrific eyesight and reflexes. He went after birds like a soldier stalking the enemy. Before long he had his own gun and was outshooting his dad.

Dale wanted to win at everything. When there was no one around, he practiced sports by himself, shooting baskets and throwing balls and running wind sprints to improve speed and stamina. He would challenge anybody to a race and was always surprising boys bigger and supposedly faster than he by beating them in the last few steps.

In the summers he and his dad, sometimes with a couple of Dale's schoolmates along, would take drives together, expeditions over to Shawneetown to swim off the levee and eat fried catfish, or to one of the county fairs. Peck would point out places of interest. Along Route 13 near Crab Orchard, Peck would stop to explore the burned-out shell of Charlie Birger's cabin, Shady Rest. Men still gathered in a clearing in the woods behind the cabin to throw dice, stage cockfights and reminisce about the famous gangster. It was fun to search for spent cartridges buried under leaves or in the earth and imagine what gangster or lawman had been the target of the bullet.

There was so much in Little Egypt to appeal to the contrary in a boy, enough story, myth, legend, and history to inspire a Huck Finn or a Dracula. Everybody knew about Mike Fink the river rat who was so tough that he called himself half man and half alligator. Down at Cave-in-Rock you could play at river pirates and search for bloodstains left by the outlaws on the walls of the big cavern. There were bloodstains too at the Old Slave House off the Harrisburg-Shawneetown road, a colonial mansion on a hill where runaway slaves had been held for resale before the Emancipation Proclamation. Under the eaves on the third floor, tiny cells with wooden bunks, chain anchors embedded in the floor, bars on the doorframes, and a torture rack made of rough timbers evoked the pro-slavery sentiments of Egypt and the peculiarly legal presence of slaves in this southeastern corner of the supposedly free state of Illinois. At the rear of the house a double-door carriage entrance permitted a cargo of runaways to be delivered discreetly, unloaded out of sight, and hurried up a winding stair to the prison above. The owner, John Crenshaw, an Englishman, entertained grandly on the ground floor with profits from his upstairs trade and from the nearby salt works, manned by slaves brought in under a special loophole enacted by the Illinois Constitutional Convention in 1819. It was said that after dark at the Old Slave House you could hear strange cries emanating from the upper rooms and the mournful strains of spirituals.

Until 1938 Potts' Inn still stood on a hill between Cave-in-Rock and Shawneetown. More bloodstains there, more nightmares. Everyone knew its grisly story, and it remained a popular spot to visit after the original building was torn down. There in the 1830s Billy Potts and his wife had kept a tavern. They were in league with James Ford, called Satan's Ferryman, who either robbed and murdered travelers crossing the Ohio or sent them along Ford's Ferry Road to Potts' Inn. Mr. and Mrs. Potts would feed their guests and fill them with drink and then slice them up in their beds or stab them in the back as they stooped to drink from a clear spring on the hill. At first light they chopped their victims into pieces and buried them in the yard.

One day their son, Billy junior, returned home after a long absence. His parents did not know him with his long black beard, and he delighted in fooling them. They fed him and got him drunk. At midnight as the young man bent over the spring to drink, Billy Potts stabbed his son in the back, the spring ran red with his blood, and Mrs. Potts cut him into pieces and buried him.

In the morning Billy junior's friends came looking for him. Mr. and Mrs. Potts said no man of that description had visited the inn. They had not seen their son for ten years, they said. But when the friends left, Billy Potts and his wife dug up the remains. Under a shoulder blade, beside the fatal wound, they saw their son's black birthmark, shaped like a four-leaf clover.

On Potts' Hill, near the spring that runs clear again, a sign stands to remind the visitor of the boy who was marked for death and of the father who killed his son.

3

IF VINCE LOMBARDI HAD NOT SAID THAT WINNING ISN'T everything, it's the only thing, Dale Cavaness might have said it; he certainly believed it. By the time he entered Eldorado Township High School in 1939, Dale was what sportswriters used to call a real scrapper. Winning by intimidation was another phrase he might have coined, making up for what he lacked in height and weight with a fierce aggressiveness. He would challenge anybody to arm wrestle or Indian wrestle, the veins standing out on his temples and neck, breaking the other fellow down by force of will. Strong arms and shoulders made him more powerful than he appeared. He worked on building up his strength. At home he did push-ups and chinned himself from a doorsill every morning and evening.

He also made a lot of noise. In a different environment Dale would have been called a loudmouth, but the rugged atmosphere of southern Illinois, where most men earned their living through their sweat, suited his style. "Hey, Rudie!" Dale would shout to a buddy, or, "Let's get all the Rudies together and have a game!" It was a term he had picked up from a carney at a county fair. Nobody knew exactly what a Rudie was, but the name conveyed what Dale liked best, rough-and-tumble, rowdy times with plenty of shouting and shoving and competition.

Dale was a great one for practical jokes, the thumbtack left on the chair seat or pennies rolled down the classroom aisle to drive the teacher to distraction. Once in a while somebody would think that Dale had gone too far, as when he asked to see a girl's new watch and then dropped it and stepped on it accidentally on purpose. He made himself a lifelong enemy with that one. The laughter he provoked could quickly sour into a fistfight; but as a good student and a school leader he was above suspicion from authorities and could get away with pranks other boys could not afford to dare, making him of the crowd and yet above it.

He was always near the top of his class in grades, science and mathematics coming most easily to him. In his senior year he earned a certificate of merit as one of the fifteen best students in a class of a hundred and nineteen. Other students sought his help, which he willingly gave, unless the fellow having trouble was too thick to understand. Dale did not mind telling the slow-witted not to waste his time. Only his history teacher seemed indifferent to his brilliance, giving him consistent B's and earning Dale's resentment. Dale publicly vowed revenge.

The other students admired him enough to elect him president of the Latin Club and president of the Hi-Y, a service club sponsored by the YMCA and stressing leadership and clean, Christian virtues. He became sophomore-class president and then junior-class president. No other student during his time at Eldorado High School quite matched his combination of brains, popularity, and athletic accomplishment.

As a junior in the fall of 1941, Dale made the varsity football squad. Since he weighed only about a hundred and thirty-five pounds and was barely five feet five, he did not see much action that year. That winter and spring, however, he lettered in basketball as a guard and as a miler led the track team to an undefeated conference record. "Dale 'Curly' Cavaness was impressive with his 4:42.5 mile," the Eldorado *Daily Journal* commented after the Eagles had defeated Carrier Mills and Vienna (pronounced Vy-anna) in a triangular meet. Timed on his own, he was less impressive; against competition he managed the final kick to win.

In April Dale and two other Eagles, a discus thrower and a low hurdler, entered the southern-Illinois invitational at Cairo to compete against entrants from thirty-four other high schools. Winners would go on to the state championships. Dale's Eldorado teammates did not place, and his own grit was not enough for him to win; but he finished third in the mile, twenty-five yards behind the winner, who was clocked at 4:37. (The best mile in the state that year was run by an Urbana boy at 4:28.8, twelve seconds better than Dale's best time.) Dale's coach told his teammates that they should look to Cavaness as an example of someone who was making the best of his ability. It was effort like his that would take a boy far in life.

His drive paid off in his senior football season. He had by then reached his full height of about five feet seven. He went out for left halfback, but at a hundred and fifty pounds, he had to battle for a starting position. There was no free substitution in those days. Players went the full sixty minutes on offense and defense. Dale would have to show that he could bring down bigger boys in the open field.

In the opening game against the Marion Wildcats, Dale received a punt on his own forty-five-yard line and took off, streaking fifty-five yards down the sideline for the only Eagle touchdown in a 7–6 loss and earning himself a permanent starting berth. Against Anna the Eldorado Purple and Gold lost again, and Dale was hurt. He came back in a 26–0 victory over Carterville, scoring an extra point on a plunge through center and intercepting a pass on the twenty-three, zigzagging his way in for the score with seconds left to play.

After the Eagles defeated Johnston City 19–0, the *Journal* singled out "Dale Cavaness, star passer and runner. . . . His brilliant performances in the backfield for the Eagles have sparkplugged his team throughout the season, and his presence has meant the difference between victory and defeat." Eldorado fans were counting on Dale to bring them their first victory since 1934 against archrival Harrisburg.

Harrisburg versus Eldorado was the local equivalent of Harvard versus Yale or Notre Dame versus U.S.C. The other high school games were played on Friday nights under lights, but traditionally the Eagles faced the Harrisburg Bulldogs on Thanksgiving Day. Families saved the turkey until after the final gun. It was the event of the year for both towns, bigger than the Fourth of July or the Saline County fair. In 1942, because of war shortages and rationing, the game was moved up to Armistice Day afternoon as part of an abbreviated season.

The big game was tense from the start as the favored Bulldogs and the Eagles traded touchdowns. Dale brought the crowd to its feet in the first quarter by heaving a fifty-yard touchdown pass. The Eagles used the old Notre Dame box formation. More and more as the season progressed, the center snapped the ball directly to Dale at left half, and it was anybody's guess whether he would run or pass. In the fourth quarter he hit his left end eighteen yards downfield for another touchdown. Eldorado lost, 26–25, a heartbreaker, but the Eagles had made twelve first downs to the Bulldogs' four and felt they should have won.

In a subsequent 12–7 loss to Carmi, Dale tossed a twelve-yard pass for the lone Eldorado touchdown. The Eagles played their final game of the season against DuQuoin in the rain and mud. With the score tied 6–6, Dale faded back to his left and then flipped a pass cross-field to his right for the winning extra point.

The Eagles ended up with three wins against six defeats, but they had scored a hundred points to their opponents' hundred and twelve, with Dale responsible for nearly half the Eldorado scores. He had proved such a threat that the coach had adapted his offensive strategy to Dale's talents, and Dale led the Eagles in yards gained on the ground. It was murder trying to bring the little guy down, and he tackled like a freight train. Some of the admiring Harrisburg Bulldogs gave him a new nickname, Toughie.

In Little Egypt no one received as much attention as the star high school athlete. Dale's performance in basketball during the 1942–43 season equaled his football feats. For a while it looked as if the season would have to be canceled because of wartime fuel restrictions, but parents pooled their allotments of six gallons of gasoline a week to drive the boys to their games. Dale's father never missed one of his son's performances unless the railroad kept him at work.

The Eagles captured the Goshen Trail Conference championship with a perfect 20–0 record, and overall they were 23–4. The sweetest win came against Harrisburg, 38–37, to take the Christmas Holiday Tournament crown on Eldorado's home court. That low score was typical of basketball in the 1940s, when it was more of a defensive contest, featuring ball control and set shots. Although height was less of a factor then, Dale was still the shortest player on his team, and as a guard, his role was primarily defensive. Even so, he managed to score as many as nine points in several games, and he averaged six—enough, when combined with his tenacious defending, to make him a star and the Eagles' leader. Undoubtedly he would have improved his times in the mile run that spring, but pulled ligaments kept him on the sidelines during most of the track season.

As graduation approached, war was on everyone's mind. Military training had begun at the high school. Boys could learn commando techniques, how to scale a wall and thrust a bayonet. The government announced its goal of an army of seven million by the autumn. Families that had not strayed from Little Egypt for generations saw their sons shipped off to mysterious places on the other side of the world. Every day the local newspapers printed letters home from sons abroad, almost every one of them expressions of longing for home cooking, the voices of parents, a walk in the southern Illinois woods. One boy wrote that he wished he could write a poem called "These Things I Miss," listing apple pie, Eldorado's tree-lined streets, "a date with a pretty American girl. . . . When you are denied so much, you come to expect very little." Some letters included descriptions of ships blown up and comrades lost; none indicated the exact location of the absent son. Many boys from Little Egypt were sent to Northern Ireland in preparation for D-Day. Families would sit around reading the letters in the paper and talking about them, cherishing Eldorado's blessings, for all its poverty. Local loyalties and patriotism ran high.

Dale decided that he would join the navy after graduation, instead of waiting to be drafted that summer. As for life after the war, if he made it through, he had his mind set on becoming a doctor.

There was never any question that Dale Cavaness would go to college and rise above his father's status as a working man. If there was one boy in Eldorado who had ambition, it was Dale, and with his mother urging him on, nobody doubted that he had the will to achieve whatever he wanted. By the eighth grade he had begun talking about becoming a doctor.

To a degree, seeing his neighbors suffer through the Depression influenced his choice of medicine. He learned how important doctors were when so many people could not afford one. All around

31

him signs of medical neglect were manifest. Malnutrition and the anxieties of long unemployment caused a variety of illnesses. Fathers leaned on WPA shovels while children scrounged in empty lots for dandelion and poke weeds their mothers could boil up with a little vinegar. It was not lost on Dale that the Cavanesses stayed well while other families averaged weeks of debilitating illness during the year, minor complaints turning major through lack of proper attention. A classmate had to stay out of school for a year because he had broken his eyeglasses and his parents could not afford a new pair. Toothaches had to be endured, since dental care was out of the question. When teeth fell out, false ones were a pricey vanity.

People relied on folk remedies common in Egypt. Pick an aching tooth with a hickory splinter, then stick the splinter into a freshly dug grave. For measles, tea made from sheep droppings was supposed to speed recovery. A dirty sock tied around the throat cured tonsilitis, while sassafras tea thinned the blood at the end of winter. A drop of buttermilk poured into the ear soothed an earache.

In this gloom Noma Cavaness developed a fondness for attending funerals. No matter what the church, Noma would be there, usually accompanied by a lady friend with similar impulses, singing and praying and joining the procession to the graveyard. Back home she would tell Dale and Peck about the service, about what the minister had said and which hymns had been sung, and often she would draw her moral: If only the deceased had been able to afford medical care, death might have been avoided. Noma had no truck with home remedies. Wasn't Dale lucky, she would remind him, that when he got sick, they could send for the doctor right away. Otherwise he might be dead. If she had not had a good doctor helping her to give birth to him, she wouldn't be going to other people's funerals now. She'd be long under the sod.

Late in January of 1937 the worst Ohio River flood ever recorded swamped the farmlands of Little Egypt, pouring millions of gallons down mine shafts and driving people from their homes all the way from Shawneetown to Harrisburg. A million and a half acres in southern Illinois went under. Thousands who had endured collapsed farm prices, years of unemployment, and the drought of 1936 now lost whatever they had left. Army engineers had to dynamite the levee above Shawneetown to let the waters flow in before they rampaged over the top. At its height the flood stood fifty feet deep in Shawneetown's Main Street. Most of its citizens reluctantly abandoned historic Old Shawneetown forever to live in tents and eventually to build New Shawneetown four miles inland. As the mayor said, the lives of two generations had been ruined; they owed it to their children to relocate.

Throughout the countryside villages went under, automobiles and farm equipment swirled away and sank, permanently wrecked beneath the flood. Houses caved in, floated off. Some people, refusing to leave, chopped holes in their ceilings and frantically tried to store furniture in their attics before huddling on rooftops to be rescued—if they were lucky. Livestock swam until dead, their carcases caught in trees.

Although Harrisburg was more than twenty miles from the Ohio, backwaters seeped into the town, rising an inch an hour for several days, inundating eighty percent of the area and sending its citizens into refugee centers. Harrisburg's water and gas plants shut down; lumps of coal became precious; water had to be sent in five-gallon containers from Marion and Eldorado.

It was an economic disaster and a medical one. Women gave birth in schoolrooms, even in boats. Fears of cholera and typhoid epidemics spread, and exposure led to scores of pneumonia cases. Because Eldorado had eight physicians and was the closest town to the flood safe from the waters—Muddy, only four miles away, had to be evacuated—the Red Cross, the Salvation Army, the National Guard, and the U.S. Naval Reserve made it their headquarters. The Red Cross set up headquarters in the city hall and in the American Legion hall, and the mayor of Eldorado issued a proclamation asking people to open their homes to the refugees and to donate to the relief fund. Twelve hundred refugees poured into Eldorado, filling churches, lodges, the bank, the Cinderella Ballroom. They arrived in boats on the outskirts of town, soaked and helpless. The First Christian Church became a kitchen and a dining hall, with volunteer women cooking three meals a day for the homeless. Steamers put in at Shawneetown to take people out on the swollen river. Motorboats arrived by train from Chicago and from as far away as Boston for the rescue effort, which was frustrated by a freeze that followed the rains. Men had to dynamite the ice to free the boats, and the weather made the medical situation more dangerous. Eldorado doctors offered free vaccination against typhoid, diphtheria, and smallpox.

Like everyone else in Eldorado, Dale and his parents worked to aid the refugees. Noma cooked. Peck was out with L&N railroad crews rescuing people and providing boxcars for shelter. Dale's Sunday-school class donated eight dollars to the relief fund, and his grammar school welcomed refugee children and their teachers during the nearly two months that it took for the waters to subside.

The flood became a decisive influence on Dale's vision of his personal future. In this spectacle of human dependancy, everyone praised the Eldorado doctors whose work, Illinois Governor Henry Horner among others said, prevented epidemics and kept the death toll in Little Egypt to around forty. Prominent among these doctors was Lee Pearce, whose father had founded and run the Eldorado Hospital before turning it over to his son. It was after the '37 flood that Dale began talking about becoming a doctor and started paying attention to Dr. Pearce's daughter, Helen Jean, who was just Dale's age and in school with him. By the time the two entered high school, Dale was seeing a lot of Helen Jean. She followed his athletic feats, they went to the movies together—there were three picture shows in Eldorado then—and he began dropping by the Pearces' house regularly.

Helen Jean was a small, pretty girl with short brown hair—kewpie-doll-cute was how some people described her. She was neither as hard-driving nor as successful as Dale in school—as a doctor's daughter, she did not have to be—and socially she was above him, but with his brains and ambition they were a natural match. Noma Cavaness was jealous of her but could hardly disapprove of so irrefutably respectable a girl. As for Helen Jean's parents, Lee and Irma Pearce took to Dale from the start. What Eldorado parent would not have welcomed Dale Cavaness as a daughter's beau and prospective son-in-law? By senior year, Dale and Helen Jean came to be considered sweethearts, marriage a possibility. Most of the other boys had nothing but the coal mines in their futures.

Like Dale, Helen Jean was an only child. Dr. Pearce, a garrulous, homespun man who had tried schoolteaching before following his father into medicine, treated Dale like a son. He showed him the hospital and took the boy on his rounds, explaining various illnesses and their treatment. The more Dale learned about medicine, the more it appealed to him.

Here was a different sort of contest, a competition that pitted the doctor against disease and death. It was also a battle against ignorance. People knew nothing about their bodies. They inclined in Little Egypt to let Jesus do the healing and to regard a cure as a miracle. Dale noticed the awe in which Dr. Pearce was held and the power he wielded over those in his hands.

Power well-compensated. The Pearces did not lack for money. Just as Dale knew that his own family was better off than most in Eldorado, the Pearces were clearly more prosperous than the Cavanesses. By the time Dale was a senior and certain that he wanted to become a doctor once the war was over, Dr. Pearce would invite him over to the house, show him an article in a medical journal, fix himself a highball, and talk about the length and rigor of medical study and the rewards that followed it. Dale would succeed in medical school, Dr. Pearce would tell him over a steak dinner. He had an aptitude for science and a curious mind, and he retained facts. In addition, he had the respect of others, his teachers and his fellow students. Commanding respect was an important quality in a doctor.

Dr. Pearce confided to Dale that he had plans to replace the Eldorado Hospital with a new building after the war, a modern and efficient place with all the latest equipment. There would be opportunities. After medical school, Dale might even decide to come back to Eldorado.

Graduation approached; Dale prepared to join the navy. As the final event before commencement exercises, Dale's English teacher happened to choose a melodrama about a doctor as the senior-class play. The teacher came across the piece in a volume called *One Act Plays for Stage and Study* and thought it suitable in spite of its morbid theme. Dale did not try out for a part. He was too busy with basketball and getting himself into shape for running the mile, but he and Helen Jean were in the audience for its Friday night performance. The play, written by a Hungarian, Eugene Heltai, was called *Death Sends for the Doctor*.

The action takes place in a low-arched room of the Castle of Death in "an undiscovered country" resembling Transylvania. The time is the present; and the dark, dusty room, filled floor to ceiling with filing cabinets and shelves holding file folders, suggests a bureaucratic government office.

Principal characters include the Doctor and his young male Assistant, Death himself and Death's Secretary, another young man. Death, also called His Grace, has not been feeling well and has summoned the Doctor. The Doctor and his Assistant at first do not recognize His Grace as Death. They look around the room and notice at one end a clock which has neither hands nor numerals. Its pendulum bears a crest composed of two scythes crossed. Their own watches have stopped at midnight; they begin to catch on.

"There's something about this place," the Assistant says. "It smells of death."

"You mustn't be afraid of death, my son," says the Doctor. "A physician must never fear death. It's always at his side, watching and waiting. We fight death. Sometimes we drive it away . . . for a while. But we always fight it. A physician need not fear so old an enemy as death."

The Doctor examines his patient and realizes that the sick man is actually Death himself and that he is suffering from a malignant tumor. The Doctor decides to operate.

"You mean to save Death?" the Assistant asks.

"No—to destroy Death," the Doctor replies. "I am going to kill him."

"You can't."

"Yes, I can. . . . Now he has science against him. For the first time men are learning how to outwit him. I myself have held him at bay a good many times. And he is afraid. We have not yet overcome him. We have not yet won a clear, decisive victory. But he is afraid. We have made progress, and he fears that some day we may destroy his power. . . . This is my opportunity."

"You must be insane," the Assistant objects, but on reflection suggests that there might be a lot of money in killing Death.

"Money?" the Doctor says. "No, I may become a murderer, but I shall not be a usurer. These murderer's hands will bestow health and peace—life. They won't reach for gold."

"But to kill! Aren't you afraid? You, who believe in God—"

"God will help me."

Offstage the Doctor places Death under the knife and kills him. Thunderclap. The Doctor returns rubbing his hands, feeling proud of himself. Boasting of the power of modern science, the Doctor suggests to Death's Secretary that immortality would be an appropriate fee.

But Death's Secretary has a surprise in store for the Doctor.

"I am no longer the Secretary," he announces.

"Who are you?"

"I am now—His Grace."

"His Grace?"

"He was my father."

The Doctor and his Assistant step back, dismayed. The ticking of the clock grows louder.

"This pendulum swings on forever," Death's son says. "Life and Death exist together, but Death is the stronger. . . . His power lies in my hands, Doctor. Take care that I do not use it."

The Doctor offers a handshake. Death's son refuses it "with an ironic smile."

"I no longer fear you," the Doctor insists, alluding to his scientific knowledge. His hands tremble.

"I don't fear you, either," the Assistant chimes in.

"Time enough, Doctor," Death's son snickers. "We shall meet again, all of us."

The curtain falls.

No one in the audience that night was required to take the play seriously. *Death Sends for the Doctor*, with its theme of murder and death and scientific arrogance, was familiar stuff to a crowd raised on Frankenstein movies. Only in retrospect did it seem a peculiarly appropriate choice for the senior play at Eldorado High that year.

4

AT FIRST EVERYTHING WENT ACCORDING TO PLAN. DALE SPENT
two years in the navy, entering Officers' Candidate School at the
University of North Carolina, where he was able to take several
courses for college credit, and then serving as an ensign aboard
the battleship *North Carolina* in the Pacific, seeing some action
during the kamikaze phase of the war. As soon as he was discharged,
he went home to marry Helen Jean.

They were both still under age, so they eloped to Arkansas.
Noma, who had wanted Dale to finish college first, capitulated
once the marriage was accomplished. Peck professed approval, and
Dr. and Mrs. Pearce were enthusiastic.

Dale entered Southern Illinois Normal University at Carbondale,
switched to the University of Illinois at Champaign-Urbana in June
1946, and with credits transferred from North Carolina and Southern Illinois received his bachelor of science degree *cum laude* in
May 1947, benefiting from the G.I. Bill and from the university's
Division of Special Services for War Veterans. He entered the
Washington University, St. Louis, Medical School in September

of that year, still a month shy of his twenty-second birthday. His quick mind and hard work had enabled him to keep on schedule toward becoming a doctor.

A private university founded by T. S. Eliot's grandfather, Washington was the most distinguished educational institution in the region, its medical school among the best in the nation. Medical students from Washington trained at Barnes Hospital, which was also highly regarded. Dr. Pearce had advised the move to St. Louis. If Dale did decide to return to Eldorado to practice, it would be useful for him to have had experience and contacts there. Dr. Pearce routinely referred difficult cases to St. Louis specialists. Dale and Helen Jean settled into a tiny apartment over a pizza parlor on Pine Street, near Barnes. She took a part-time job with the telephone company, and with the G.I. Bill and help from her parents, they were able to sustain a pleasant if frugal life, postponing having children until Dale could secure his degree.

Dale began that gradual conditioning to disease and death that every medical student experiences. He had seen some injury and death in the Pacific, but he had not stuck needles into arms and legs, into livers and bone marrow. He had not threaded tubes down noses and mouths into lungs, nor plunged his arms into a body up to his elbows. He had not confronted death in the form of old people preserved in formaldehyde and displayed on stainless steel tables perforated to permit fluids and fat to drain away as from meat in a roasting pan. Systematically cutting dead people into pieces over a semester, the medical student may gain the sense of being different from the common run of humanity, coming to regard life as a proving ground and other people as members of an opposing team. When the classwork finishes and the student goes into the hospital to deal with live patients—to whom he may speak, whom he may even get to know, whose relatives may gather—the success of a procedure or the loss of a patient may become more a matter of performance than of suffering, more a question of winning or losing than of pity.

Dale prided himself on his cleverness and efficiency. He could grasp the principles of a subject, while many others became distracted by details. He had no trouble mastering the vocabulary of body parts and processes: He had developed mnemonic tricks, he said, and his high school Latin helped.

Some of Dale's fellow students found him a blowhard and a know-it-all; others admired him. As in high school, slower students came to him for assistance. Everyone agreed that with Dale Cavaness, there was no middle ground. His country accent and folksy manner were among the points of division. He still called everybody Rudies. His brothers in his medical fraternity, Phi Beta Pi, elected him president, a sign of social rather than of academic approval. When he visited Eldorado, people there were glad to see how little he had changed, outwardly at least. They saw the same old Dale, older and smarter but, apparently, uncitified, down-to-earth.

In Eldorado Dr. Pearce built his new hospital on Organ Street. He was so pleased with his son-in-law, who from all reports was sailing through his studies in St. Louis, that he decided to make a special gesture. When he chose the cornerstone for his new building, Dr. Pearce ordered it to read: Pearce-Cavaness Hospital.

Dale's return to Eldorado now seemed a certainty. St. Louis in those days had a reputation for beer, baseball, and Buster Brown shoes. It also had the energy of its railroads and all the attractions of a long-established metropolis, a symphony and an opera company, a jazz scene, scores of Italian and other good restaurants, celebrated botanical gardens, neighborhoods of beauty and wealth. The flow of American life in this postwar period was away from small towns and into cities of promise. Yet Dale's inclinations remained homeward, toward the outdoors and scenes of his early triumphs. On holiday visits he enjoyed reminiscing about high school athletics and hearing about who was leading the Purple and Gold that year. He could draw on the past, and now people also revered him as a doctor, or as almost one, confiding in him about their ailments and regarding him with spaniel eyes. Even Noma, while she remained cool toward Helen Jean, deferred to him.

Pressed as he was by his studies and by being president of his fraternity, Dale found time to take Helen Jean to movies and sporting events. They saw a lot of another couple: Chet Williams, a medical classmate, and Marian Newberry, a nurse at Barnes who was a lot of fun. The four of them took weekend excursions together, picnics in the countryside, drives over to Champaign-Urbana to watch the Fighting Illini play football. Chet and Marian were not serious about one another; she had dates with other fellows, too. Sometimes Chet would come over to share pizza and a couple of beers with the Cavanesses by himself. Dale considered Chet one of his best friends.

* * *

One afternoon in June of 1950, Marian Newberry was working at her station in Chest Service at Barnes when Dale dropped by to chat. Dale asked her whether she would be interested in a blind date for next Saturday night.

"Oh, gee," Marian said, "no, thanks, Dale. Blind dates just aren't my cup of tea."

"You'd like this guy," Dale said.

"What's his name?"

"Elad Senavac."

"What?"

"Name's Elad Senavac."

"My God, what kind of a name is that?"

"Don't worry. You'll really like this guy."

"I'll let you know," Marian said. "Let me think about it."

That evening Marian telephoned Helen Jean to find out about this mysterious stranger. If he was a medical student, Marian could not imagine why she had never heard of him. With a name like that he would stand out.

"Who is this Elad Senavac?" Marian asked. "Dale dropped by today and asked whether I'd like a blind date with this guy. Is he a friend of yours or something?"

"Marian, I think Dale means himself," Helen Jean said.

Marian felt like an idiot, not having caught on to Dale Cavaness spelled backward. What was all this about? One of Dale's jokes, she supposed. He was always kidding around.

"We're separated," Helen Jean said. "Dale and I are no longer living together."

Marian could only mumble that she was sorry. She hadn't heard the news. She hoped the Cavanesses would reconcile soon.

"I doubt it," Helen Jean said.

Marian had not seen the Cavanesses for about a month, and she had had no inkling of troubles between them. She had thought them well-matched and had never noticed signs of friction. Helen Jean was not as jovial as Dale, but her relative quietness and seriousness had seemed to complement his constant joking. Marian thought that it was typical of Dale to have asked her out in the form of a joke—one that had misfired under the circumstances. She had no intention of accepting a date with him. She had never thought of him as anything but Helen Jean's husband: The two might be separated now, but they could get back together, and in that case, Marian knew, she would be caught in the middle and lose both of them as friends. She thought it was foolish of Dale to have asked her out.

But when Dale telephoned Marian, he apologized:

"I know I didn't handle that very well," he said. "I'm pretty upset. I'm not myself. Let's get together and I'll tell you what happened."

Marian Rose Newberry had grown up in the Webster Groves and Kirkwood sections of St. Louis, pleasant middle-class districts first settled in the 1850s and resembling small midwestern towns, with broad, tree-shaded lawns, big brick houses, white churches, and tidy little stores with colorful awnings. Her father had been a paperhanger, an amiable man but a heavy drinker whom her mother divorced in 1929, when Marian was only a year and a half old and her brother, Bill, five. Her mother received neither alimony nor child support from Harry Newberry—it would have been futile to ask; he was always broke—and she supported herself and her children by working as a housekeeper for a high school Latin teacher.

Marian's mother had started out in life under more comfortable circumstances. Her parents, the Schotts, had been successful grocers and had left money to their daughter and her brother, who managed the inheritance. But the stock-market crash wiped out the investments, and for a time during the Depression Marian had to go to live with her uncle and aunt who, she believed, did not really want her. Her mother and brother shared a one-bedroom apartment that Mrs. Newberry considered too dingy for a young girl. Once reunited, however, in a small house for which Mrs. Newberry somehow managed the down payment, the three formed a happy band; and Marian began to absorb her mother's steady emphasis on culture and education. Mrs. Newberry read aloud to her children every evening, drumming into them the importance of doing well in school, and saw that Marian got piano lessons. Every Sunday Marian and Bill traipsed off to services and to Sunday School at the Presbyterian church. Over her bed Marian hung the eight gold stars she received for being able to recite her beatitudes.

Marian rarely saw her father, but she looked forward to his visits. He would hold her on his knee and sing to her. Her mother spoke of him as a well-meaning ne'er-do-well, and that was how Marian thought of him. He was simply incapable of responsibility, Marian believed, loving her brother and her from a distance.

When Marian was thirteen, her mother suddenly died, and Marian went to live with family friends, Truman and Ella Yard. Her father continued to keep his distance, but Marian felt wanted and loved by the Yards, and her brother had become more of a father to her. When she was troubled, she confided in Bill, and she liked to remember the time when she had accidentally caught her sweater on fire and he had saved her, embracing her to smother the flames. When he joined the service in 1942, she dedicated a poem to her brother:

> *I can remember long ago*
> *When we played with our wooden blocks;*
> *I can remember my big red bow*
> *And your little horse that rocked.*
>
> *Remember the day you broke your arm,*
> *And the dreadful day I cut my hair.*
> *And remember how on Christmas morn*
> *We'd hunt for Santa everywhere?*
>
> *And remember the cave you fellows dug*
> *You wouldn't let us near?*
> *You chased us away with a big fat bug*
> *Then sent up a mighty cheer.*
>
> *Our hearts were young & gay then,*
> *The years went swiftly by.*
> *We hadn't a troubled day when*
> *We were happy, you and I.*
>
> *And then the impossible came,*
> *God took Mother away.*
> *Things will never be the same,*
> *But perhaps it's better that way.*
>
> *For you went marching off to war—*
> *Mother would worry so!*
> *But yet, no matter how near or far,*
> *She's praying for you, I know.*

And so amid the world's dark maze
Of turmoil, war, and hate,
I keep remembering our childhood days,
And leave what may to Fate!

Some day we'll be together—
You and I and Mother.
Come fair or stormy weather,
God bless you, my dear Brother.

Marian also wrote poems in memory of her mother, asking God to lend her some of her mother's loving devotion "and a bit of her heartening friendly cheer," for her mother remained to her an example of selflessness worthy of emulation. She kept a notebook filled with quotations from her favorite poets—Shakespeare, Browning, Oscar Wilde, and A. E. Housman—copying out passages about love, hope, and the soul in a small, backward-slanting hand:

> *. . . call to thought, if now*
> *you grieve a little,*
> *The days when we had rest, oh Soul,*
> *for they were long.*

She practiced the piano and attended the opera and the symphony in the city as often as she could. In October 1945, she went to a performance of the Ballet Russe de Monte Carlo at Kiel Auditorium and was so entranced that she waited by the stage door afterward to get Alexandra Danilova, Maria Tallchief, and Frederic Franklin to sign her program. Balanchine's choreography and Tchaikovsky's music for the *Ballet Imperial* moved her to write a poem wishing that when she died, her ashes could be thrown to the air, so that she could ride the wind forever.

But there was more to Marian's disposition than romantic melancholy, and her enthusiasms encompassed more than the arts. By the time she had graduated from Kirkwood High and entered the Washington University School of Nursing, she had become a lively little beauty, raven-haired with dark eyes and an olive skin, as fond of dancing and sports and silly good times as she was of the concert hall. The boys flocked to her, but she was in no hurry to marry, determined to have a profession and not to suffer as her mother had from a man's capriciousness. Her brother, too, had taken his mother's advice about education. Bill returned from the war with a Purple Heart and earned his law degree from Washington University in 1948, when Marian received hers in nursing.

When Dale Cavaness asked Marian out, she was beginning her third year working at Barnes Hospital. She had been in love once, with an Irish Catholic engineering student who had gone east for a job. They had corresponded for a while; Marian wondered whether she should have followed him, but their letters dwindled and stopped. She had been feeling restless, missing the Irishman and questioning whether nursing was right for her: Confronting suffering every day was taxing; she had no true passion for the work; no one aspect of medicine particularly fascinated her. Nursing was becoming routine, merely a job and an underpaid one. She longed to travel before it was too late and toyed with the idea of becoming an airline stewardess to see more of the world. New York appealed to her.

After Dale's apology, Marian relented and agreed to go out for coffee with him to hear his version of what had happened to his marriage. What he said floored her.

Dale told her that he was afraid that Helen Jean had fallen in love with Chet Williams. At first he had scarcely been able to believe it, Dale said. He had been too stunned, had suspected nothing. It had never occurred to him that his marriage might be in trouble. As for his friend Chet, Dale was totally surprised. If Chet had cared for anyone, Dale had thought it was Marian.

As Dale spoke, Marian saw a different person from the cocky, brash medical student she thought she had known, the fellow who had seemed to have everything in his life under control and to be destined for success. He now appeared haggard, wounded, almost pitiful. She had never thought that Dale was anybody she would ever have to feel sorry for, but she felt the urge to comfort him.

"I haven't seen Chet for a while," Marian said. "I never suspected anything either, believe me. He never said a word about Helen Jean to me, except how much he enjoyed both of you. We had fun, didn't we? Oh, Dale, you poor thing. What did you do? Did you just leave, or what?"

Dale said that he had confronted Chet, demanded to know whether he was in love with Helen Jean, even challenged him to fight. But

Chet had just stood there, hanging his head and saying he was sorry. A lot of good that did. Dale had wanted to break him in two.

Color came into Dale's face now. His clenched fists grew white-knuckled. Marian was glad that the two had not fought. Someone would have been hurt, probably Chet. She had heard that Dale had a temper, though she had never seen it. As for Chet, Marian was surprised at him. He had not seemed like the type to get involved in something like this—something so, well, passionate. He had seemed to her to have the cool temperament of a surgeon, which was what he was studying to become. You never knew about people. Not that she blamed Chet, or for that matter Helen Jean. These things happened. People did what they did. Helen Jean must have been unhappy with Dale. Probably they had married too young.

"How do you feel now?" Marian asked. Dale was looking at her with eyes that asked her to say something. To give him advice. She could not say what color those eyes were. She had thought they were a steely blue or a battleship gray. Now they looked green. They were deep-set, shadowed.

"I feel betrayed. Goddamnit, I've been betrayed."

"By Helen Jean?"

"By both of them. I thought he was my friend. Especially by Helen Jean. She's filing for divorce."

"Already?"

"It's all over. I could never trust her again. She doesn't want me anyway. She says she wants to marry Chet."

He spoke like a man who had been tricked and could not figure out a way to get back.

"Oh, Dale. Where are you living?"

"I found an apartment by myself."

"You'll get through this, you know. It's just terrible luck."

It happened quickly after that. Easily they grew close. They loved going to sports events and movies together, and Marian introduced him to classical music. She taught him to dance to big-band music, leading him around the floor, amused at the way he stayed on his toes—to appear taller, she supposed. She discovered that he was wearing lifts in his shoes, and she talked him into throwing them away. After all, she was only five feet four, so he did not have to worry about being overshadowed by her.

47

They laughed at Judy Holliday playing the dumbbell in *Born Yesterday* and afterward Dale did a hilarious imitation of Broderick Crawford as the crude, aggressive junk merchant. Marian was pleased to see Dale regain his sense of humor so quickly. He gave her a pet name, Maria, and called himself Lucky Pierre. They spent a lot of time partying at the fraternity; she enjoyed his being president there.

She introduced him to her brother and to the Yards, who had continued to care for her like parents, and to an old friend, Ed Bell, and his wife. All of these people acted protectively toward Marian; she would have found it difficult to care for someone whom they discounted or disliked. Her father, who had died just after the war, would also have approved of Dale, she thought, although she would hardly have relied on her dad's judgment.

Marian had known Ed Bell since his marriage to her first cousin, Thelma Schott, for whom Marian had been a bridesmaid. Ed had spent the war in the Pacific, had been wounded, and had never felt quite right since, although his doctors had failed to figure out what was wrong with him. Dale diagnosed Ed's symptoms as diabetic—pinpointed what was wrong with him in seconds, it seemed—and advised him to begin insulin treatment. When Dale turned out to be correct, everyone could see that Marian had latched on to a brilliant guy on the verge of a great career. All of her friends and relatives, including her brother, loved Dale, she felt, and why not? He was dynamic and funny and smart.

And, Marian thought, he seemed to have got over Helen Jean: Marian hoped that she could take some credit for that. She must be good for him.

They made no specific marriage plans, neither proposed to the other, but let matters evolve. When Dale received word that he would be interning at Union Memorial Hospital in Baltimore, Marian decided that this was just the opportunity she needed to become an airline stewardess. She would train at the American Airlines flight school in Chicago, then get herself based somewhere in the East. She and Dale would not be together all the time, but they could visit one another.

In the spring of 1951, as the two of them prepared to begin this new phase of their lives, Dale decided that it was time for Marian to meet his parents. They made plans to drive down to Eldorado one Saturday in Dale's '47 Plymouth, which they called the Green Beetle. They could have dinner with Noma and Peck, stay the night and be back in St. Louis by Sunday evening.

Like almost all St. Louisans, Marian knew nothing of southern Illinois. Unless they recalled the days of labor strife and gangster wars, St. Louisans never thought about the place called Egypt and had no idea that Egyptians considered St. Louis their city. To Marian, Illinois meant Chicago or the great central plain. At first, as they crossed the Mississippi and headed toward the center of the state, the just-planted corn and wheat fields fit her image of limitless expanses, flat and dull. After they turned south near Mt. Vernon, the landscape gradually became more hilly and wooded, the farms grew smaller, the towns—Benton, West Frankfort, Johnston City, Herrin—more run-down.

"It's not very prosperous down here, is it?" Marian observed as they headed east at Marion.

"You should've seen it ten or fifteen years ago," Dale said. "Things are picking up."

Marian decided that she would keep any other comments to herself. This was Dale's home territory, after all, and he was probably sensitive about it. As they drove east along Route 13, past Crab Orchard and Shady Rest toward Harrisburg, she noticed lakes and hills to the south. The countryside was pretty, anyway.

"Saline County," Marian read the sign aloud, pronouncing it as in saline solution.

"Sa-*lean*," Dale corrected her. "The way we say it down here. We're coming into the Jordan curve now and Dead Man's curve."

Around the second big curve, through trees to the left, an enormous black pit, acres wide and thirty or forty feet deep, came suddenly into view. A gigantic mechanical shovel stood in the pit.

"Strip mine," Dale said.

"That shovel must be five stories high," Marian said.

"Biggest in the world, they say."

"What are those fires?"

Here and there black metal pipes shot blue-orange flames into the gloom of the late, overcast afternoon, sending a weird, orange light against the sky. The pit, the great heaps of black slag, that outsized shovel, the flares—to Marian it was a peculiar and forbidding vision. She remembered Dante from high school. This was how she had imagined the *Inferno*.

49

"They're burning off the gas," Dale said. "They have to do that."

Marian said nothing more. She could only think what a strange place this was and that she would not enjoy being on this road alone at night.

Past Harrisburg, driving along Route 45 to Eldorado, Marian had the impression of descending, although the road seemed level. She began to feel closed in. The shabbiness of Eldorado's downtown—not much to notice there; in the fading light it seemed almost a ghost town—weighed on her. In no time at all they were through it and pulling up in front of the Cavanesses' on Maple Street.

"Here's where I was born and raised," Dale said. "Right in that house."

"How nice," Marian said. The trees were coming into leaf. The house looked well-kept, freshly painted white. Noma and Peck came out to greet them.

That evening Noma fixed a big dinner, pot roast and potatoes with gravy, homemade biscuits and rolls, peach cobbler made from Noma's home-canned fruit. Grandmother and Grandfather Dale came over from next door with a maiden aunt and a great-aunt. When Marian realized that she was sitting in the middle of a sort of family compound, she felt like a foreigner. I would never in my life be able to fit into this scene, she thought. It was difficult for her to believe that she was only a hundred and fifty miles from St. Louis. This was a different world.

She did not wish to be or appear to be a snob. She was sure she could manage holidays here and occasional visits. But she did not fit in, and she felt ill at ease. Her clothes were too bright and stylish; she was wearing a green cashmere pullover and a matching green tweed skirt. Now that she had her own money, however little of it, she enjoyed spending it on herself and looking attractive. Here, she could see, were people who believed in saving for a rainy day and who probably would consider her eye for fashion a vanity.

Her rapid speech sounded sharp in her ears amid the southern drawls. She noticed that Dale's accent was more southern than usual and that he was talking more loudly. Being home loosened him up.

Of all the relatives Marian liked Dale's father and grandmother the best, as Dale had predicted. Grandmother Dale was hearty and warm, compared at least to the other women; Peck seemed a kindly gentleman. Dale had warned Marian about Noma. He had even said that he did not like his mother very much.

Marian thought Noma seemed nervous, and she could understand why. Noma was testing her out. Dale had told Marian that his mother had not liked Helen Jean at all, regarding her as selfish and no good for Dale. He had also told Marian about a telephone conversation Helen Jean had supposedly had with Noma about the time of the divorce, in which Helen Jean had said that the main reason she had married Dale in the first place was to have a way of getting out of Eldorado. Dale did not know whether to believe that Helen Jean had actually said that. Noma could well have made it up. It may have been, Marian considered, that Noma was simply the sort of mother to whom no woman was good enough for her son, but Marian did her best to be friendly. She did not have to lie about the cobbler; it was wonderful, and Marian said so, she hoped not too fulsomely. She had to be enthusiastic about something.

After dinner everyone gathered in the sitting room with their coffee. When conversation dragged, Peck told a couple of stories. He mentioned how well Dale had always done in school, not like the young man over in Rudement who had come home from Southern Illinois Normal one day and announced to his father that he was quitting school. The father invited the boy out to the barn.

"You see these here lines—" Peck paused to ask Marian whether she knew what lines were. She did not, so Peck explained that the lines were what you drove the horse with when you hitched him to the plow.

"Reins?" Marian said.

"Yes. So the boy's father said, 'Do you see these here lines? Well, if these lines and your ass hold out, I figure you'll be back in school by tomorrow morning.' "

Only Noma didn't seem to think that was funny. Marian laughed, and she didn't mind Peck's using a slightly vulgar word in front of her. It seemed a kind of welcome. He told another story about a farmer over in Raleigh who had been paying too much attention to a sweet young thing who was the new schoolteacher. The schoolteacher complained to the farmer's wife, who said that she would take care of the matter. Her husband wouldn't be bothering the schoolteacher anymore. The next morning when the farmer was

51

out in the cornfield, his wife brought him a jug of water, and she wouldn't go back to the house until he had satisfied his marital obligations. She brought him another jug of water that afternoon, another one the next morning and the next afternoon, until pretty soon the poor old boy was hollering "No more water! No more water!" and he never did bother that schoolteacher again. That cornfield over in Raleigh had been famous ever since.

Marian took the front bedroom that night. Dale slept on a bed on the back porch. On Sunday morning Marian wriggled out of Noma's invitation to go to church with her, and after breakfast Peck, Dale, and Marian took the two bird dogs out for a walk around town and into the woods. Everybody knew everybody in Eldorado, that was clear. On the way back they passed by the new hospital. Dale pointed out the cornerstone. It read simply Pearce Hospital now, no longer Pearce-Cavaness.

Marian said nothing. She reflected that perhaps Helen Jean had done Dale a big favor by leaving him. If she had stayed with him, he might have been stuck in Eldorado forever.

5

ONCE DURING THE NEXT YEAR MARIAN CAUGHT A GLIMPSE OF Dale's temper. Peck and Noma, who had never before been farther from southern Illinois than St. Louis, came to New York to visit. Marian was based in the city as a stewardess for American Airlines; Dale drove up from Baltimore and stayed with his parents at their hotel. It was a pleasant few days, with plenty of sightseeing, including an excursion down to Williamsburg. Everyone was saying good-bye in front of the hotel, when Noma reached into her purse and produced a check for a hundred dollars and handed it to her son. Dale took it, mumbling thanks, when Noma said:

"Don't go spending this on something foolish. Your father works hard for his money. You know how we have sacrificed for you. You know how important we think your education is. I don't want you going and—"

"Goddamnit!" Dale shouted and tore the check to pieces in his teeth, spitting it out on the sidewalk. "Don't talk to me! Just don't ever talk to me!" He spat out the last few shreds of the check like poison.

Marian retreated down the block. She flinched as Dale screamed at Noma, waving his arms, his head thrust toward her in fury. Marian heard Peck and Noma trying to placate him. "Now, Dale, don't be that way," Peck pleaded. "Please don't be that way," Noma begged him.

Marian did understand how Dale felt. He was scratching out an existence then, well aware that he depended on checks from his parents, now that Helen Jean was gone, to supplement his meager salary: That Union Memorial was a prosperous hospital serving a relatively well-to-do clientele did not mean that it paid more than the usual minimum to interns. His nerves were raw from overwork. But she did think his reaction extreme. Noma could not help being preachy—that was how Marian saw her. She was compelled to make Dale feel guilty for taking the money. She was simply that kind of person, and you had to humor her. The thing to do was to pocket the check and keep quiet, paying Noma's little interest charge in silence. Peck had learned how to handle her. Still, Marian could not blame Dale: Part of her admired him for standing up to his mother.

Dale was so strapped for money in Baltimore that he often resorted to selling his own blood at five dollars a pint. He was not alone in this—several of the poorer interns did it—but as in everything, Dale pushed himself to the limit. One evening after skipping dinner and selling two pints, he fainted in the hospital elevator. He had been up for thirty hours on one of the brutal shifts interns had to endure, and for once his willpower failed him.

Whatever extra money Dale had, he spent running up to New York to see Marian. She was making more than he, and she chipped in what she could. Once in a while they splurged, dinner out and drinks and music afterward at Birdland or Club 181, a place on lower Second Avenue they liked, where Dale could forget his work and be funny and a little wild.

When they were apart he sent love letters saying that he could see her dark hair and eyes before him, that thinking of her made the miserable room he was renting bearable, that he lived for the next time he could see her. Sometimes he included a verse from Omar Khayyám—

> *Ah, make the best of what we yet may spend,*
> *Before we too into the Dust descend;*

Dust unto Dust, and under Dust, to lie,
Sans Wine, sans Song, sans Singer, and—sans End!

When, at her request, the airline agreed to transfer Marian to Washington, D.C., she moved there to be closer to Dale, flying Convairs and DC-6's on what they called the milk run to Philadelphia, Boston and back. She loved the travel and being on her own. In Washington she shared an apartment with two other stewardesses, one of whom quickly became engaged to a young advertising man from St. Louis who was often at the apartment for one of the frequent bashes the girls liked to throw. They were evicted from one building after a party became too noisy for too long. Marian acquired the nickname Skipper or Skip, which seemed to fit her fun-loving nature. Dale drove over from Baltimore often to see her, partying all night and heading back to Union Memorial in time for the morning shift.

When Marian visited Dale on her days off, they bought fresh crabs at the wharf and took them to share with a couple of nurses whom Dale had befriended. Marian would toss the crabs into a big pot with plenty of pepper, spread newspapers over the nurses' kitchen table, and they would all eat the crabs and corn on the cob right off the paper and drink cold beer. With a record on the machine everything was simple and nobody was ever in a bad mood.

One long weekend Dale said that he had heard about a place in the Maryland countryside called Candlewood Lake.

"We could drive out there and spend a couple of days," he said. "I hear they have boats."

"Where will we stay?"

"I don't know. We'll find some place. Don't worry. I'll just say we're married."

When they reached the lake on a warm afternoon in late spring it was beautiful. They drove around for a while in the Plymouth, not quite sure how to go about getting a room. It was exciting feeling illegal.

Dale spotted a line of cabins by the lake shore. He pulled up beside one that had a hand-painted sign on it saying office, vacancy. A big old dog drowsed in the sun on the cabin's steps.

"What're you going to say?" Marian asked.

"I don't know. First thing, I'm going to say hello to that dog. Leave it to me."

Dale got out and went over to the dog, hunkering down and talking to him, scratching his ears. A man who was a lot older than the dog opened the office door and watched for a minute as the dog rolled over to get his belly scratched. Dale looked up and said that he'd like to rent a cabin for a couple of days for himself and his wife.

"Sure," the man said.

"Fine dog you got here."

"He's a good one. You can take Number Four. It's got a toilet works. Everything you want."

Marian told Dale she was positive they didn't look married. You could tell when people were married, couldn't you? She was sure that the only reason the man had rented them the cabin was because Dale had been so good with that dog.

"Maybe so," Dale said. "We always had dogs."

"I know. It's because you're a country boy and because you look so All-American."

"Come on."

"But you do! You're my All-American boy."

"I am?"

"Sure you are. You're my own Jack Armstrong."

"Okay. But does Jack Armstrong go on a weekend with somebody he's not married to?"

"Once in a while. If they're engaged. We are engaged, aren't we?"

"I guess we must be. We better be," Dale said, laughing.

They bought some beer and cheese and crackers and had the best time doing nothing but making love and floating around in a rowboat. Dale, who was very fair, took too much sun one afternoon, and Marian had to nurse him, but nothing spoiled their time at Candlewood Lake. At night they sat on the shore feeling the breeze and listening to the water.

One of Dale's supervising physicians at Union Memorial, an internist, invited him to stay in Baltimore, offering him a place in an already successful practice. It was quite a vote of confidence in a new intern. Dale considered the position, and Marian urged him to go ahead and accept it. She had come to love the East and could not understand when, after not much deliberation, Dale refused what would have assured a fast start in his profession. He would not discuss the matter with her. He said that he had already decided to complete further interning at St. Louis Maternity Hospital. She did not argue with him. She could see that he had his mind made up. She figured that he must know what he was doing.

They returned to St. Louis and were married on October 3, 1952, in the Webster Hills Methodist Church, where Marian's aunt and uncle were members. Truman Yard gave Marian away. She wore a long gown of ivory satin trimmed with Chantilly lace, Dale white tie and tails. Her brother, Bill, served as one of the ushers, and the two nurses from Baltimore flew out to be bridesmaids. Peck and Noma and friends of Dale's from medical school and from southern Illinois were among the more than a hundred guests.

After a two-week honeymoon at a lake in northern Minnesota, they settled into an apartment at Canterbury Gardens, in the University City section of St. Louis. Marian returned to nursing, working in a doctor's office. She found the routine tedious after the freedom of flying, but she knew that the job was temporary.

Marian assumed that once Dale completed his internship at St. Louis Maternity Hospital, he would become a resident there or at some other city hospital. As usual he was taking on as much as anyone could, learning surgery as well as obstetrics and gynecology, and acquiring advanced techniques in anesthesiology. He would end up so well qualified that he would have his pick of jobs anywhere, she believed; he might even think better of his rejection of the Baltimore offer and return East, a prospect Marian would still have welcomed, although she loved St. Louis as always. Any city in the Midwest or East appealed to her, any place with energy and cultural attractions.

When in June 1954 Dale abruptly announced to her that they would be moving to southern Illinois in September, Marian was dumbfounded. There was a small hospital in McLeansboro, Dale said. The town's main doctor was retiring, leaving a ready-made practice behind. Dale and another young St. Louis doctor, Ed Everson, were going to take everything over. It would be like having his own hospital. He would have total control. It was a great opportunity.

"Where is it?" Marian asked.

"Where's what?"

"McLeansboro. What's it near?"

"It's just a few miles north of Eldorado. You'll like it."

If Marian seemed unenthusiastic, and she tried not to be, Dale ignored it. He was so excited about the position, and he presented it so forcefully as an accomplished fact, that she could hardly register objections. Nor did she believe, in spite of her misgivings, that it was her place as a wife to argue with Dale about his professional decisions. But she did a lot of thinking.

She tried to understand Dale's reasoning. There must have been a great deal going on inside of him that she had failed to notice. There had never been so much as a hint, that she had picked up on anyway, of his desire to return to southern Illinois. She had taken the change in the cornerstone at Pearce Hospital as a symbol, and an unambiguous one, that the Eldorado chapter of Dale's life had closed along with his first marriage.

Why had he not confided in her? Had he been afraid that she would object, throw a fit, even threaten to leave him? That was absurd. She felt wholly committed to him. His experience with Helen Jean must have scarred him. He was probably still unable to trust any woman. Whether it was true or not that Helen Jean had married him only to get out of Eldorado—and Marian doubted this—Dale must still have suspected as much. Helen Jean had gone on to marry Chet Williams; they had moved to a large city in the Southwest. It would not do for Dale to suspect that Marian had married him only on condition that they live in a big city. If he thought that, he would never trust her.

Marian decided that somehow she would have to try to overcome Dale's doubts by being absolutely loyal and unquestioning. He was still at the outset of his career; he must be full of misgivings in spite of his outward self-confidence. He was human; time would take care of his skittishness. She found his frailty endearing, even amid her deep disappointment at the prospect of southern Illinois, which she had thought depressing the moment she had laid eyes on it. The idea of actually living there!

The more she ruminated, the more signs Marian recognized of Dale's having made up his mind long ago to return home. Why else would he have refused the Baltimore offer? And his specializing in obstetrics and gynecology and basic surgery—that fit in as well. Those would be exactly the skills required of a country doctor. Most of his practice would consist of delivering babies, diagnosing routine ailments, performing appendectomies, that sort of thing.

He must have known what he was going to do from the start. He had simply been awaiting an opportunity to return.

Marian sought to discover some fault in herself, some selfish lack of understanding that might have contributed to Dale's secretiveness about his plans. Maybe she had enjoyed New York and Washington too much. Maybe she had been too obviously enthusiastic about things like the Muni Opera in St. Louis. But she could only conclude that the circumstances of Dale's divorce outweighed any other possible factors behind his silence. In some obscure way, he was returning to southern Illinois to prove something: that he could succeed there without Helen Jean and without Dr. Pearce's help.

Marian chose to believe that once he had established himself down there, Dale would no longer have anything to prove and would feel free to move on again. After a couple of years, three or four at the most, they would be able to return to St. Louis or go on to some other city. Surely Dale would eventually chafe at the limitations of southern Illinois. She had never imagined him as a man content with low horizons. She would try to make the best of the move and to count on the future. She decided to draw on some of her mother's cheerfulness: How lucky she felt compared to what her mother had faced with never a complaint!

Marian did not visit McLeansboro before moving there. Dale said that he would take care of everything. He made several trips down to secure a house and make it ready for her. His mother was eager to help. He and Noma would fix the place up, hang new wallpaper, lay in the essentials.

Marian appreciated Dale's apparent eagerness to please, but as September approached she had to struggle to conceal her sadness at leaving St. Louis and the friends and relatives she loved. To her brother, to Uncle Eddie Bell and the Yards she spoke only of the excitement of a new life and the challenge of Dale's having his first practice and a hospital to run, but the hundred and fifty miles to southern Illinois began to seem a thousand. She could not get the coal pits out of her mind, and it was as if the streets and parks and tall buildings of St. Louis were begging her to stay.

It had been a long time since she had written any poetry, but one night when Dale was down in southern Illinois she sat at her kitchen table and this came to her:

The night is cool.
The soft summer air comes through the window
brushes my hair,
and is gone.

I watch the city.
Its lights throw shining beams
like a million stars
each undisturbed
by the city's din.

I see smokestacks.
Silhouetted against the brightness
the smoke curls,
lingers and drifts away.

A train goes by.
Its lonely whistle,
Its monotonous roll presses onward.
The sound fades.
Listen! The wind.

My eyelids droop.
The night's characters blur
To dreams that won't come true.
But there's tomorrow—

It was a common saying among the men of Little Egypt that if you wanted to give the state of Illinois an enema, you would inject the nozzle at McLeansboro. Half the size of Eldorado and with fewer trees, the town had lost whatever point it might once have had, a remnant without so much as a bar to enliven it. In all of Hamilton County, which in area was bigger than St. Louis County and of which McLeansboro was the seat, there were only nine thousand people; the county courthouse in the middle of the town was McLeansboro's principal attraction. Oil had been discovered in the county in 1939, and a few farmers had profited with their one-eighth royalties from leases on their land; but because most of the money, like that from the coal mines, went to absentee owners, who brought in skilled workers from Oklahoma and Texas to do the drilling and maintain the rigs, oil had not meant the prosperity McLeansboro had dreamed of when the local newspaper had cheered in a headline running across the front page:

HURRAH! WE'LL ALL WEAR DIAMONDS!

The house Dale selected was out in the country on a hill, about three miles from town. Marian was glad of that, after seeing McLeansboro. If she was going to make a life here for herself and Dale and their children, for they were ready to start a family, better to be able to do it on her own without worrying about the customs and opinions of neighbors. And out in the country she would not have to contend with Noma and other in-laws next door. Noma made herself felt as it was, dropping by unexpectedly at any hour for what seemed to Marian an inspection.

One morning, before she had been able to settle in, Marian was in jeans on her hands and knees scrubbing the kitchen floor when Noma entered without a knock, accompanied by three other ladies from Eldorado wearing little mink stoles. They were on their way to a funeral. They stood in the kitchen doorway, peering down, Noma advising on the proper proportions of ammonia and vinegar and recommending her preferred brand of floor wax. Noma was playing so much the classic mother-in-law, Marian didn't know whether to laugh or scream. She suggested that the ladies return at a more appropriate time, when she would be prepared and delighted to give them a decent welcome.

"We didn't mean to intrude," Noma said. "I just wanted to see how you were getting on, dear."

With Noma, Marian adhered to a strict no-comment policy. Even when Noma criticized her clothes—"Do you really think Bermuda shorts and knee socks are appropriate for a doctor's wife? Is that what young women are wearing in St. Louis these days? Married women?"—Marian kept her mouth shut. She would just smile. She enjoyed thumbing through copies of *Vogue* or *Harper's Bazaar* in front of Noma and feeling the disapproval drift across the room like a breeze off a snowdrift.

Dale threw himself into his work at Hamilton Memorial Hospital, which had forty-eight beds but usually needed no more than twenty. His friend from St. Louis, Dr. Everson, quickly tired of McLeansboro and departed for a bigger town, so Dale had his hands full. His patients grew in number as his reputation spread. People were delighted to have a bright, energetic young doctor available. He kept office hours well into the evening, so that patients would not have to lose pay from work to visit him, and he made house calls when someone who could not get into town needed him. Marian sometimes went with him to keep him company.

She got to know Little Egypt well, better than she would have preferred, driving around with Dale. The poverty depressed her, and she decided that she had never been cut out to be a nurse, because she permitted herself to become too much affected by disease and death. It was worse seeing people suffering in their own houses: A big, impersonal place like Barnes Hospital separated illness from daily life and made it easier to forget when you went home.

One house call in particular got to her. They visited an old woman dying of cancer in the village of Macedonia. She had retreated to the basement of her decaying house, lying on a cot in the damp and the dark, her head swathed in dirty rags. The stench was terrible. When Dale urged her to let him remove the rags from around her head, she refused, throwing her hands up to protect herself, rocking back and forth and moaning, "No! No!" He took her pulse, listened to her heart, gave her some pills.

Afterward Marian wanted to know why the woman had clung so adamantly to those old rags. Dale said that she had lost all her hair, not from radiation treatment, she was too far gone for that, but from the disease itself. The rags were her last vanity.

"Can't she be moved someplace? Doesn't she have any relatives?"

"I won't charge her for the visit," Dale said. "She couldn't pay me anyway. She's got nothing. Don't worry, she won't last long. I give her another week or two."

It took Marian days to get over that scene. She envied Dale his ability to move on to the next case, to put unpleasant things behind him, to forget about one patient because another always needed him. The memory of the woman in the basement never left her.

In the middle of one night Dale got an emergency call from the hospital. A young man had been brought in badly injured from an automobile accident.

"You come, too," Dale said. "You be the E.R. tonight. There's no one on duty. I won't have to get anyone up."

"You know I'm no good in emergency," Marian said. "I get flustered. It's too hectic."

"Come on. You'll be fine."

Marian monitored the vital signs as Dale tried to attend to the boy, who could not have been more than twenty or twenty-two at the outside. His face had been obliterated, his skull crushed. They hadn't the equipment or the staff to deal with such a traumatic case. Dale said that the boy was already brain-dead. There was nothing to do but prepare him for the ambulance ride over to Evansville, Indiana, the nearest major hospital.

Marian begged off emergencies after that.

During their time in McLeansboro, only one incident marred Dale's practice. A baby girl on whom he had performed a hernia operation seemed to be recovering normally. Dale sent her home. A week later she was back in the hospital with a fever, and she died.

Dale was beside himself for losing her. He begged the parents to permit an autopsy to see what, if anything, had gone wrong with the operation. They were furious with him, and they refused to allow him to open up their daughter again. The irony, as Dale said, was that only an autopsy could have proved malpractice. He had been willing to take that risk.

This misfortune did nothing to reduce people's trust in their new doctor. In the press of performing other, successful operations, delivering babies and making his rounds, Dale forgot about his failure to save the girl, or at least stopped berating himself over it. Such things happened to every doctor, he knew, and would probably happen to him again.

Although McLeansboro was a dry and by any standards a socially limited town, Marian discovered people who were congenial to her, as she would have anywhere with her natural desire to make the best of things. Drinks were available only at the Elks Club, and the doctor and his wife could not, they thought, permit themselves more than a mild degree of exuberance, for fear of raising eyebrows. They were in great demand as dinner guests, Dale from his position and his personable manner, Marian as his wife and because of her beauty and warmth: She could counter the ill effects of her good looks on other women by her friendliness and ready laugh.

They attended church most Sundays because Dale thought it was expected of him; the religion of his youth was something he would have preferred to forget. Peck and Noma came up for dinner regularly, and Peck and Dale went hunting. Dale taught Marian how to use a shotgun; and she went along occasionally, enjoying the woods and being with Dale, sharing in his pleasure at his shooting skills.

On their first wedding anniversary Marian bought big steaks for Dale to cook out on the grill—a treat then, for they still had little money. She baked a cake and put flowers and candles on the table. Dale opened a bottle of champagne.

They sat alone together, toasting each other, talking of how they had met and fallen in love. He told her she looked ravishing in candlelight.

"We should go dancing, Maria," he said with a Latin accent. "Maria and Lucky Pierre should samba at the Copa tonight."

"Remember Candlewood Lake? Remember how you got sunburned and we had so much fun and the little cabin? You fooled that man. I know you did."

"Sure."

"That was the most beautiful place of all."

"It was nice all right. We're doing okay, though. We're making good progress."

"I didn't mean that. You know how proud of you I am. But that was the most beautiful weekend, don't you think? I don't think two people have ever been happier. Oh, Dale, I hope neither of us dies first. Wouldn't it be too awful to be without each other?"

"I know what you mean," Dale said, taking her hand across the table.

"I wish when we get old we could die together. And have our ashes scattered together over Candlewood Lake."

"I wish so, too," Dale said. "Let's have some more champagne."

Dale opened another bottle and pretended to be a waiter, draping a dishcloth over his arm and bowing deeply to her and clicking his heels. They went into the living room to talk some more. Marian sat in the easy chair and Dale sprawled on the couch humming tunelessly.

"I'm getting to like it here," Marian said. "There are some very dear people. And I love living in the country and this little house and being with you. Will it be cold in the winter?"

"Not too bad. The winters aren't too cold here."

Marian was surprised when the second bottle was finished. They didn't usually drink that much.

"I didn't know you had another one," Marian said as Dale began to uncork a third bottle. "Hey, don't point that thing at me! Devil. What the heck, it's our anniversary. Let's hope you don't get a call."

"I can handle it." He poured her glass half full and filled his too rapidly, so that the foam slopped over the sides.

"This is so beautiful," Marian said. She began to feel giddy and bold. "I think we're going to have the best life ever, don't you? You can never tell what we might do. I mean, we might do anything."

"What do you mean?"

"Oh, I don't know. We might end up anywhere."

"What do you mean by that?"

"Well . . ." She giggled. "Somehow I can't see us staying here forever, can you?" Dale did not respond. "I mean, it is sort of the ends of the earth, after all."

Marian contemplated the bubbles in her glass and remembered New York. She sighed and tried to imagine Paris. She sensed Dale getting up from the couch and coming over to her, but she did not look up at him. For a second she thought he was going to kiss her and how nice that would be.

Then he was beside her and the last thing she saw out of the corner of her eye was his balled-up fist coming at her. She felt it crack into the side of her jaw. She went over the side of the chair and down. She lay on the floor until the pain came. Groaning, she crumpled up and cried out. She made it to her feet, stumbled into the bathroom and closed the door behind her, locking it.

Marian stayed in the bathroom a long time, hanging on to the sink with both hands. She could not comprehend what had happened. Wasn't he going to come in and say something? She held a washcloth under the tap and put the cool cloth to her face. She was afraid to look in the mirror.

When she stopped crying, the only sound she heard from the living room was the clink of a glass against a bottle. After what seemed like an hour, she heard Dale get up and go into their bedroom.

Marian slept in the spare bedroom that night. At dawn she woke up with a terrific pain in her jaw, wondered what had happened, why it had happened, what it meant. What had she said? Done? No man had ever hit her before. It had never occurred to her that a man would hit her, not just a slap but a sock with his fist. What was he thinking? She tried to remember everything and dozed off again hoping that the pain and everything would be gone when she awakened again.

Dale stood over her, touching her shoulder.

"It's almost nine o'clock," she heard him saying. "What are you doing in here? Why did you sleep in here last night?"

"You hit me." She started to cry again.

"I what?"

He was profuse in his apologies. He said he remembered nothing. By that evening the bruise was a dark purple.

6

MARIAN STAYED CLOSE TO HOME UNTIL HER BRUISE HEALED. SHE did not belabor the incident, letting it rest as an aberration, blaming it on the champagne. When Dale forgot her twenty-sixth birthday in November, she was not sure what to think. She did not want to be childish and pout. She kidded him about being absentminded and concealed her sadness, feeling a little foolish when, alone, she shed a few tears. Dale was trying so hard to get established, it was no wonder that he was distracted. He gives so much of himself emotionally to his patients, she thought, that he must be drained. At Christmas when she set the table with the mother-of-pearl dishes she had inherited from her maternal grandmother and the West-morland silver she had been collecting piece by piece since her days as a student nurse, Dale said nothing.

Marian's misgivings dimmed when they made love. Sexually she felt she had nothing to complain of—not that sex was something they discussed at all, even in bed. It simply happened, and she felt no desire for more than Dale gave her. She took it for granted: That they did not have to discuss it was to her a good sign. She assumed that as long as she kept herself attractive and they cared for one another, sex would be there.

By February 1954 she was pregnant, and Dale seemed, if not overjoyed, then pleased. The pregnancy was no surprise; they had stopped using contraceptives shortly after settling in McLeansboro. Dale instructed her not to gain more than twenty pounds, and she never came close. She quit drinking and smoking, took prenatal vitamins, drank lots of milk. She began a three-mile walk every morning along the highway that passed by their house; truck drivers making deliveries into town came to recognize her, honking and waving. Dale said that she was overdoing the preparations, that nature would take care of the process, but she enjoyed her regime.

Dale himself delivered the boy without complications on August 13. They named him Mark, Peck's middle name, and gave him Dale for his middle name, which pleased Noma.

Marian was so entranced by the baby that it was months before she noticed that Dale took little interest in Mark, except to tell her not to keep picking him up every time he cried. She could not bear to let the infant cry himself to exhaustion, as Dale said she would have to do unless she wanted a spoiled brat around. He rarely picked Mark up himself unless it was to pose for snapshots, which Dale disliked anyway, always handing the baby over as soon as the picture-taking was done. Marian knew that indifference was not unusual in a new father and that many did not pay much attention to their children for the first few years. That did not make him a bad father, and she did not mind having the baby to herself.

Often Dale did not get home from the hospital until after eight. Patients were now coming to him from surrounding towns and counties; in McLeansboro he was the chief celebrity, lionized beyond the sheriff or the mayor or any minister. Aside from the attractions of his personality and general skills, he was the only doctor in the region who knew how to administer spinal, saddle-block and other procedures to women giving birth, acting as his own anesthetist. No other obstetrician could compete with him, and he could treat the whole family. If you had Dr. Cavaness, you had all you needed, the word got around.

Marian had stopped thinking about how long they would stay in McLeansboro. She figured it would be at least two or three more years before Dale wanted something more challenging and more remunerative: He would never get rich practicing in McLeansboro.

But one day out of the blue, just before Mark's first birthday, Dale announced that they would soon be moving to Eldorado. Dr. John Elder Choisser of Eldorado had decided to move to St. Louis and was selling both his practice and his house to Dale.

"You'll like the house," Dale said. "It's a big place on Fourth Street."

Fourth Street meant nothing to Marian. She knew Eldorado little better than when she had first gone there—Peck and Noma usually visited them, rather than the other way around—and she had no reason to think that any Eldorado house could be much more than adequate. The only homes she had seen in Little Egypt that she coveted were in Harrisburg, old ones with a touch of antebellum grandeur to them. She reserved judgment. Dale might have the right to say where he would work, but at least she could choose the house this time.

The Choisser place did please her. It was a big, two-story brick house with two bedrooms upstairs, another downstairs, a living room and a large, knotty-pine family room which the Choissers had built on to the back, with plate-glass windows all the way across, looking out on to a good-sized yard. Its only drawback was that it was next door to Smith-Reynolds Chevrolet, but in Eldorado a car dealership did not mean a high-volume operation with lots of traffic. Marian envisioned the move as progress.

She no longer minded the idea of having her in-laws close at hand. She had learned to handle Noma, and Peck had begun to take a welcome interest in Mark: He was already talking about hunting and fishing with him as soon as he could walk. Marian realized that Eldorado, poor as it was, would mean a jump in income for Dale. Dr. Choisser, who was a descendant of Eldorado's founders, already had a large practice that included several well-to-do Harrisburg families; Dale anticipated expanding it, and he expected to keep most of his McLeansboro patients as well.

He prospered from the start, opening an office on Locust Street next door to Lou Beck's pharmacy and joining the staff at Pearce Hospital. Lee and Irma Pearce had never blamed Dale for the divorce, and Dr. Pearce welcomed him, calling him "son" and indicating that Dale would soon become head of surgery. Everyone talked about how Dr. Pearce still loved and admired Dale.

With fifty-six beds, Pearce Hospital was busier and more up-to-date than Hamilton Memorial. It was not an attractive place, just a squat, functional building, less agreeable in appearance than the rival Ferrell Hospital; but Dale looked forward to upgrading the surgical facilities and making Pearce more profitable.

He settled in with the confidence of a man come home. It was as if he had cheated fate, carrying out his original plans for himself in spite of Helen Jean. He could now create his self-contained world of maximum efficiency, over which he had absolute control. From the house on Fourth Street, the hospital was a five-minute walk in one direction, his office the same distance in another. Around him were the streets and fields and hills he knew so well.

As his roster of patients lengthened, he gave the job of office receptionist and bookkeeper to Marilyn Leonard, whose husband, Chuck, taught mathematics at Eldorado High. Marilyn became Dale's confidante, observing every day the several facets of his success as a physician. She could see that the most important factor of all was probably his earthy charm. He had the knack of seeming to be one of the people and yet above them, a political sort of charisma akin to Huey Long's. He inspired simultaneous feelings of friendliness and admiration which, among the humble and the ignorant, approached worship. Marian had fallen in love with him when he was down and struggling; she knew his self-doubts, however vigorously he concealed them. To others he became a folksy sort of god.

He would listen to any complaint and shoot the breeze with patients about anything from personal problems to prospects for the deer-hunting season or soybean production. Eventually he had over fifteen hundred families on his rolls, more than any other local doctor, but his long hours owed as much to his garrulity as to his numbers of patients.

"How you been? What in hell's wrong with you? By God, you look okay to me. How about those Eagles? Think we got a chance against Harrisburg? I'll tell you one thing, it's not so bad it might not get worse. Open your shirt."

He would explain in detail each ailment and the reasons behind his choice of treatment, whether the patient had any idea what he was talking about or not. If an educated, brilliant man like Doc Cavaness would take the trouble to talk to them, a miner or a farmer's wife got a lift with every appointment. His style, positive and loud, had much in common with the kind of preaching people liked to hear from revivalists at camp meetings, long a fixture in Egypt:

"I'm putting you on azo gantanol. That's a fancy name for an antibiotic. Start off with four tablets just to kick it into gear. Then we'll go to sulfamethoxazole once the pain goes away. Don't worry if your urine looks a funny color, it's just the pill, you're not bleeding to death. You can bet the farm you'll be fine in a few days."

He was one of the few doctors in the region willing to take on workmen's compensation cases, and the high incidence of injuries to coal miners brought plenty of those. Each case required the doctor to go to court in Harrisburg to certify the nature and authenticity of the injury, and the state's payments to physicians were low, so most doctors did not care to bother. Nor did Dale ever turn away someone on public aid, which paid only three dollars for an office visit, a dollar for any prescription medicine, fifty dollars for delivering a baby, and nothing for prenatal care.

He could be tough with his patients, telling pregnant women, for instance, that if they wanted to "be a slob" and gain more than twenty pounds, they could get out and find another doctor. But he was attentive. Once when dysentery threatened the infants at Pearce, he canceled his office appointments and remained at the hospital for four days and nights until the outbreak subsided. Nothing seemed to distress him more than a baby in danger.

He never asked a patient for proof of credit or insurance. He told Marilyn not to bother him with bookkeeping matters, he did not want to know who had paid up or not, but once a year at her insistence they went through the outstanding accounts. Some of the bills he would simply throw in the wastebasket, when he knew that the person could not afford to pay. He instructed her never to remind someone about an outstanding bill when they came in for treatment: He was running a doctor's office, he said, not a collection agency. The only overdue bills that annoyed him were from people who delayed payment because they were too cheap to cough up the money.

People waited hours to get in to see him. He let friends in through the back door, but others might sit outside in their cars for two or three hours, wait another two in the reception room, and finally be examined at half past nine in the evening. They were as uncomplaining as pilgrims to Lourdes.

He could be sarcastic to anyone who doubted his diagnosis, as Marilyn had many opportunities to observe, no matter the social standing of the patient. A prominent Eldorado merchant, an elder in his church, scheduled a complete physical after his fiftieth birthday. When his blood tests came back, they indicated that he had syphilis. Just to be sure, Dale had his laboratory technician, Russell Anderson, double-check the results. They indicated positive again. Dale shared the news with Marilyn.

"That son of a bitch is going to wet his pants when he hears this," Dale said. "Have him come in early when nobody's around."

Marilyn could hear through the door as Dale broke the news.

"That's preposterous! I've never been unfaithful to my wife in my life. Never!"

"If you expect me to believe that bullshit, fine," Dale said. "I wouldn't want to accuse your wife of anything. However you got it, you've got it. You want it cured, or not? Weren't you in the army? You weren't in the chaplain corps, were you?"

The man stomped out, enraged. But within a couple of months he sold his business and moved with his family to Arizona, frightened that his secret might get out.

As much as she admired Dale and enjoyed working for him, certain things he did worried Marilyn, often to the point of making her want to quit. Most of the time she loved his sense of humor, but occasionally she thought he went too far. One morning he poked his head out of his examining room and told her that he had a patient inside he wanted her to take a look at. Since Marilyn was not a nurse, she wondered what Dale had in mind. She went in, and Dale told her to take a close look.

"Get right up to him. See if his eyes are dilated."

Marilyn noticed nothing except that the man's neck seemed to be swollen. When they were alone, Dale asked her if she had figured out what was wrong with the fellow.

"Of course not," she said. "I'm not a doctor. What are you driving at?"

"He's got the mumps!" Dale said, bursting into his loud laugh, a kind of rippling guffaw, haw-haw-haw-haw-haw. "He's got the goddamned mumps! Do you think you got close enough to him?" He doubled up with laughter.

Dale knew Marilyn's medical history—he must have checked it before launching his little scheme. She knew how serious and painful the disease could be for a woman who had just turned thirty and had not contracted it as a child. Dale had made sure that she had gotten close enough to the young man to catch the virus. She tried to laugh about it, but the more she thought about it, the more Dale's joke cast a pall. For the next couple of weeks she checked herself for symptoms. None appeared.

The incident made her think that some of Dale's other little ruses might be unfunny. One of his favorite tricks was to substitute the X ray of someone seriously injured or ill for that of a healthy patient. He would point out a break in a bone or an ominous spot on an organ, perhaps telling his patient that the odds were "at least fifty-fifty for recovery—you've got a better chance than the basketball team this year." He would let the misery sink in and then guffaw as he pulled out the actual, normal X ray.

Dale enjoyed letting a joke drag out for days. When Pann Beck, Lou the pharmacist's wife, was seven months pregnant, he suggested that he give her an X ray, assuring her that talk of harm to the fetus from radiation was groundless. He produced what he said was her fresh, still-wet X ray and pointed to the uterus, where a set of twin embryos was visible. Pann was delighted.

"Get Lou over here," Dale said. "He'll love this. He might be in shock."

Lou rushed over from the pharmacy and was thrilled. That evening he telephoned his brother long distance to break the news. When the Becks started buying double sets of booties and nightclothes and sent away for a perambulator built for two, Dale relented. He had not X-rayed Pann at all. There was no evidence whatever that she was carrying twins. The Becks took it good-naturedly. They shared a laugh with Dale and liked to tell the story afterward. But they were also shaken up. Dale said that it showed you could make people believe anything. He could have convinced Pann that she was going to have quintuplets if he had wanted to. That would have made the papers.

Marilyn appreciated that it was never boring working for Dale —most doctors were stodgy and self-important—but she thought that certain of his business practices went over the line. He saw nothing wrong with cheating the state or an insurance company to help out a patient, he said, and incidentally to secure another fee for himself. When he directed Marilyn to sign fraudulent forms, she balked. It was not only that she did not approve: She did not want to do something illegal herself and be held responsible, whatever chances Dale was willing to take.

The workmen's compensation laws provided plenty of leeway for fraud to the benefit of both the patient and the physician. A miner with a broken leg, for instance, could continue cashing disability checks so long as his doctor certified that the patient had been attending physical-therapy sessions. If the patient missed appointments, checks to both patient and physician were supposed to stop.

Dale would become furious with Marilyn when she refused to bend or break the rules, but she had not married a steady, contemplative high school teacher to live a high-risk sort of life. One day she threatened to quit rather than sign a form stating that a miner had attended diathermy sessions faithfully. Dale had set the man's broken arm, but the miner had not shown up since for treatment.

"If you want to say you saw the man come in here," Marilyn told Dale, "go ahead and sign the form yourself. They're not going to come after me. They put people in jail for that kind of thing."

Dale tried to convince her. It would be better if she signed the form, he said: That way, if anyone questioned it, it could be attributed to a clerical error. And what was she worried about, anyway? He would back her up. No government bureaucrat was going to doubt the word of a doctor.

Marilyn was adamant. Dale fired her. She had second thoughts. Chuck's teacher's salary was not enough for them to live on; she would never find another job as good as working for Dale; yet she did not budge.

Dale rehired her the next day, but not before she made him plead with her and give her a raise. She knew that he liked her feistiness, that he admired a battler and had contempt for softies. Probably he also did not care for the idea of her knowing so many of his business secrets and not working for him anymore. She had an arm on him now, enough to get him into a lot of hot water, although he knew she would never stoop to snitching on him. Their arguments got to be another kind of joke between them. She would quit or he would fire her, and she would be back at work within an hour or a day.

She quit again when Dale tried to get her to fill out an insurance form that covered not the patient but his brother. What difference did it make, Dale asked, when it was all in the family and the brother didn't care? Marilyn wondered whether Dale had seriously considered the consequences of getting caught. Was he prepared to try to face down an insurance investigator? Risk his physician's license? How could he be sure that the brother really approved of the scheme or wouldn't crack under pressure? She cleaned out her desk and walked.

The next day Dale found her on the golf course at the Carmi Country Club, where she was playing a round with Marian. He talked her into returning, with another raise.

Marian knew nothing of what lay behind Dale's disputes with Marilyn, figuring that they were just the usual sorts of office squabbles, a comical battle of wills between her husband and a strong-minded woman.

The Cavanesses and the Leonards became close social friends. Dale called Chuck by the nickname Pogo: He came from across the Ohio in Paducah, Kentucky, and was something of a down-home, ruminative philosopher, like the comic-strip possum. During the summers and on sabbaticals, Chuck sometimes went off to do graduate work in mathematics at various universities, and over the years he had accumulated master's degrees from Florida, Notre Dame, and the University of Chicago. He had all the credits needed for a doctorate except the dissertation, and although he was slower than Dale, he could match wits and trade nuggets of knowledge with him. The two of them liked to stay up all night over a bottle of B&B at the Cavanesses arguing over abstruse questions such as whether calico cats were always female. Chuck insisted that from empirical observation, he had concluded that the hypothesis was true, Dale that it was scientifically absurd. They made an attempt to locate a calico cat in the neighborhood and determine its gender, but at night all cats are gray and the disputation remained unresolved, ready to flare up again on any evening.

It was partly Chuck's intellectual inclinations that inspired Dale to order a complete set of the Great Books of the Western World from Field Enterprises in Chicago. The idea was for Pogo and Consuelo (Dale's name for Marilyn) and Maria and Lucky Pierre to read one Great Book a month and to devote an evening to discussing it. The tone of mental life in Eldorado might thereby be improved. They began with Plato's *Republic*, which Consuelo and Maria admitted bored them to tears. Plato gave way to Jane Austen; *Pride and Prejudice* killed off everyone's enthusiasm for the seminars.

They had more fun playing duplicate bridge and, with other couples, kept a tournament going from week to week at one another's houses, with Dale the most aggressive and skillful player, his powers of retention giving him an advantage and his will to win often causing brief explosions of temper at his partner, usually Marian. Chuck Leonard's deliberative style of play also exasperated Dale. One evening when Chuck was as usual staring at his hand, unable to make up his mind, Dale arose and walked out of the house, saying that he might as well go check on a patient at the hospital. When he returned, Chuck had just begun to select his cards. Dale announced that in the interval he had managed to deliver two healthy babies who would be walking and talking before Chuck played again.

With Chuck's help, Dale put together an elaborate high-fidelity system in the family room. They built it from the most advanced components of the time, the huge speakers alone costing five hundred dollars. Dale and Marian passed evenings with the Leonards and other guests listening to romantic albums: Jackie Gleason's *Velvet Brass*, Michel Legrand's *Holiday in Rome*, Morton Gould's *Starlight Serenade*, Julie London's *Julie Is Her Name*. After a few drinks the lush, movieish sounds transformed the house on Fourth Street into faraway places. People began to hum and sing and dance and laugh hilariously and tell each other they were gorgeous and plan extravagant holidays. A game of charades might develop. Dale was the cleverest mimic—by now his favorite actor was the chameleon Alec Guinness—and he courted laughter and applause by balancing a lampshade on his head and filling it with fruit (Carmen Miranda) or putting a golf ball around the room and falling down from a heart attack (Eisenhower). Whenever Dale played Edmundo Ros's *Whisky and Vanilla Gin*, a calypso record, and called for a limbo dancing contest, it signaled a long night.

With Pann and Lou Beck, Marian shared her love of classical music: Every member of the Beck family played an instrument, and the Becks hoped that their son, who took to the French horn the way other Eldorado boys did to their shotguns, would someday join a great orchestra in Chicago or the East. Now that Dale was drawing patients from all over Little Egypt and having them fill their prescriptions at Lou's pharmacy, the Becks prospered; but they chose to spend their money on lutes and mandolins and to save it for their children's education. From the outside their house on Glenwood Avenue looked like any other on the block; within, it was a musical and literary enclave, polished old instruments on the walls, shelves of books reflecting Pann's interests and her work on the local library committee. They inspired Marian to buy a baby grand piano for the living room and to begin practicing again, occasionally performing a Chopin nocturne for guests. The Becks, however, were strongly religious and did not drink. Socially they drifted apart from the Cavanesses, who developed a style of life some termed facetiously the Eldorado fast lane.

There were jaunts up to St. Louis for hi-fi shopping with the Leonards, dinner afterward at Schneithorst's steak house with a few rounds of brandy alexanders or brandies alexander, no one could decide which, for the road. Local excursions proved less exhilarating; there were so few options. A fried-catfish dinner in Old Shawneetown—by then nothing but ruins and a string of rough taverns under the levee—was fun until, just as Dale was paying the check, a fight broke out between two men in the doorway. The Leonards and the Cavanesses watched as one fellow knocked the other into the street and kicked his face in. Dale and Chuck professed to have enjoyed the show; the women swore not to return. A night out in Egypt was apt to end that way.

Dale broke the tedium of long drives with cocktails in the car. He favored a silver-plated martini pitcher for a while but had to toss it overboard one evening when he spotted a highway-patrol car in the rearview mirror. His red Chrysler—he bought a matching white one for Marian—ended up in ditches several times. Once he abandoned it near the Carmi Country Club after an intense evening and an attempt at a cross-country shortcut. Always in a hurry, Dale liked to pioneer his own roads. He traded the Chrysler in on a black Lincoln Continental convertible with what were known as suicide doors, ones that opened backward.

They took holidays with their more affluent friends in Florida and at the Broadmoor Hotel in Colorado Springs. Having resigned herself to an indefinite stay in southern Illinois, Marian relished these trips and, at home, tried to live as she would have elsewhere. She shopped for Dale's favorite Hart, Schaffner & Marx suits at Wolff's clothiers in St. Louis, for her own outfits at Stix, Baer &

Fuller, Garland's, or other fashionable St. Louis stores. Her parties, grand by Eldorado standards, were the most elegant in town. Giving a dinner or entertaining for the holidays, she might descend the stairs in pink chiffon, and she enjoyed putting out the mother-of-pearl plates and the silver. If some women resented her style, she had her own circle and was socially active, becoming president of the Women's Medical Auxillary and the Ladies Golf Association.

Her relations with Noma subsided into an unspoken nonaggression pact, not without the occasional border skirmish. Noma prowled around outside the house when Marian gave a party, counting the parked cars and showing up the next morning when everyone was hung over to emanate disapproval.

"I see you had quite a crowd. A lot of mouths to feed. I suppose there was plenty of liquor."

Noma dared enter the house one evening during a party to which she had not been invited. Dale escorted her out and told her not to try that again. Everyone could hear him screaming at his mother outside. "I can't stand that woman," he said when he returned. Marian reminded him that most mothers, particularly those of only children who were male, were meddlesome. "I hate her," Dale said.

Marian could not fathom Dale's feelings about his mother. He did not like her, but he loved her, was the way Marian formulated it. If he only hated her, would he have moved back to within a few blocks of her? It was as if he were still trying to prove his independence from her while permitting her to get his goat. When Noma told Marian about playing the death game with Dale when he was a little boy, Marian thought it was pretty peculiar; and Noma still liked to remind Dale of how she had almost died giving birth to him. But Noma was no monster, from what Marian could see, only possessive and old-fashioned, nothing extreme enough to explain the depth of Dale's resentment.

That resentment was not the only mystery about Dale. He never remembered an anniversary or a birthday—after two or three years Marian gave up expecting gifts or even cards—but he could be erratically, spontaneously generous, surprising her with a mink jacket or a string of pearls when there was no occasion. He seemed to insist on giving on his own terms and would permit no convention to dictate to him, acting as a man above or apart from what gave ordinary people pleasure and lent order and harmony to common lives. During their courtship he had been too poor to buy her an engagement ring; but in 1957, during a shopping trip to St. Louis, Marian noticed a little unwrapped box in the trunk of the car. When she asked what it was, he reached in and handed it to her without words or ceremony, there in the street. It was an emerald and diamond ring. It was the kind of gift, emblematic of their love, more appropriately given at an anniversary dinner—but there were none of those, and the ring was beautiful, and Marian accepted it and wore it gratefully.

All domestic rites irritated him. Marian loved the holidays and always made a fuss over them with parties, a big tree, wreaths, special tablecloths, strings of cards hung across the windows in the family room. Yet it was all she could do to get Dale to sit for the family photograph she liked to use as their Christmas card. When she could finally corner him to pose for the snapshot, he would run off immediately afterward, muttering that he had more important things to do, acting like some savage who had never seen a camera before and feared it would rob him of his soul.

Christmas brought out the peculiar side of his sense of humor. One year Marian hid the presents in the attic of what they called the summer house, a screened-in cottage in the backyard, against which Dale had built a big brick barbecue and in which he kept his tools and his equipment for casting his own ammunition for hunting—bullet molds, sizer-lubricators, a lead furnace. She wanted to show Dale what she had bought for the children, so he could react without surprise on Christmas morning, when he might be touchy. She took him out to the summer house and climbed the folding stairs to the attic, intending to hand the presents down to him. Before she knew what was happening, Dale lifted the stairs up behind her and bolted the ceiling trapdoor shut.

Marian panicked. She shouted and pounded on the attic floor. She could hear Dale's big laugh below. He kept her up there in the dark long enough for him to go inside and fix himself a drink. When he finally let her down, she was furious. If it were not for the holiday, she told him, she wouldn't be speaking to him. He laughed her off, saying she ought to learn to take a joke. How was he to have known she'd be so frightened? She had overreacted, he said.

That incident took place on the Christmas of 1964. Marian was glad that the children had not witnessed it. A second son, Kevin

Dale, had been born in 1956 on Dale's own birthday, and a third, Sean Dale, on May 20, 1962. The Irish names were Dale's idea because he considered himself Irish, and wearing green and having plenty to drink on St. Patrick's Day were exceptions to his indifference to holiday observances. He was unaware that his Scotch-Irish Cavaness ancestors would have worn orange.

Another exception to his scorn for holidays was the pleasure he took one Halloween in dressing up as a witch doctor and showing the boys how to wedge sticks into automobile horns to make the neighbors' cars honk, a rare show of interest in his sons' activities. Yet like Mark, Kevin and Sean had been planned, Marian and Dale agreeing that they wanted to have several children.

He did like to tease her in front of friends when she was pregnant, saying that she had made herself "great with child" to attract his attentions as an obsetrician. He delivered her babies himself without complications but, as with Mark, grew indifferent to them once they were no longer of professional interest. Marian continued to expect that his paternal instincts would emerge once the boys were in school and taking up sports. Surely Dale, who liked to play the teacher with others, would enjoy imparting his knowledge and skills to the boys. She tried to get him to come home at five-thirty or six for dinner with the children—he could go back to the hospital afterward, she said—but he rarely did. If he came home early, he said, he would linger and not feel like going back to work. He had all the responsibilities he could handle; Marian could hardly say that he was not being a good provider.

There was a story in the paper one day about a kidnapping up in Kansas City. The son of a wealthy couple had been abducted; a large ransom was being demanded, and the parents had decided to pay it. Dale was outraged, as much by the ransom demand as by the kidnapping itself. Paying blood money, as he called it, was a mistake, Dale said, pounding his fist on the breakfast table. If one of the boys were kidnapped, say Mark, he would not pay a cent. But if they killed Mark, he would hunt the bastards down and kill them himself in revenge. It was the only way to deal with this kind of thing.

Marian said nothing. She thought his attitude strange and spent most of the day puzzling over it before dismissing it as so much hot air. She would be prepared to do anything to get a child back and would count on the law to take care of the criminals. She figured that, faced with the actual situation, Dale would do the same. He had an odd way, sometimes, of expressing parental concern, ever anxious never to display what he regarded as personal weakness.

Apart from the bridge games and the trips, Dale preferred to pursue recreation away from his family, golf or poker with his male friends and especially hunting. He kept in shape by doing fifty push-ups and sit-ups every morning. He prided himself on winning at everying and on being able to outwalk and outshoot anybody in any kind of weather. He went hunting so frequently that Marian adopted a certain Mother Goose rhyme as her favorite song to sing Mark to sleep:

> *Bye baby bunting,*
> *Daddy's gone a-hunting.*
> *Gone to get a rabbit skin*
> *To wrap the baby bunting in.*

Dale gradually acquired a large gun collection, dozens of rifles and shotguns and pistols, many of them valuable. The family room reflected his primary interests: the hi-fi and record collection neatly stored away in a custom-built cabinet; a gun case to display the prizes of his arsenal, including a pair of Parker shotguns; a life-size metal hunting dog, pointing, painted white with brown spots; a brass caduceus, Mercury's winged staff entwined with twin serpents, on the mantel; and on the walls birds mounted in bubble-glass cases—quail, pheasant, grouse, a snowy owl.

Behind the snowy owl lay a story and a secret. Like most owls, this was a protected species. Dale told most people that he had shot it by mistake, going for pheasant on a hunting trip with Pat Sullivan. It was such an impressive bird and so unusual, Dale said, that it had seemed silly just to leave it there, so he had brought it back and had it stuffed and mounted as he had the other birds, by a master taxidermist in St. Louis.

Pat Sullivan remembered a different story, one that he kept to himself. The son of a coal miner, Sullivan had grown up experiencing the worst of the Depression in southern Illinois, moving from town to town as his father searched for work. But he had become big and jovial as he got rich in the contracting business, building everything from golf courses to Holiday Inns and dormitories for the new Southern Illinois University at Carbondale. He had known Dale since high school. Sullivan had been one of the Harrisburg Bulldogs who had called Dale "Toughie" after the epic Armistice Day game in 1942. The Sullivans lived in a large corner house on Walnut Street in Harrisburg, a light and airy place filled with treasures from their travels: Inside it looked more like Bar Harbor than Little Egypt. Marian and Betty Ray Sullivan, Pat's wife, became instant and close friends. The two couples visited Florida together and often spent weekends down at Kentucky Lake, where Pat owned the Holiday Inn and a boat.

Sullivan piloted his own plane, an F-model Bonanza. One autumn he flew Dale and another friend of theirs, Bob Davenport, up to South Dakota for a few days of pheasant hunting.

They hired a guide and bagged their limits each day. On their last afternoon Dale was gazing into the cold sky when he caught sight of an owl gliding, then circling. Snowy owl, the guide said, a large creature, maybe two feet long with a wingspan near six feet. It was one of the few kinds of owl that hunt during the day. Pat Sullivan let out a whistle of admiration. Dale alone raised his shotgun.

He fired, downing the owl with the first blast. It hit the earth with a thump heard across the silent fields.

The guide protested. What the hell was Dale doing? Didn't he know you weren't supposed to shoot owls? Every hunter knew that. Neither Sullivan nor Bob Davenport said anything: It was too late, and they knew Dale too well. They did not want an argument.

Dale started toward the fallen bird. Sullivan suggested that he just leave it. "Something'll eat it. Let's move on." It was a mistake. Better to forget it.

"Hell, no," Dale said, striding off. "By God, I want that thing on my wall."

The others followed Dale over to the owl. It lay, white and speckled with black, on some stubble of weeds, twitching. A few snowflakes swirled in the air, but the ground was bare, the owl very white against the brown. As the men approached, the creature struggled to rise, feathery legs scrambling, talons clawing the earth. Only one great wing moved. A spot of blood showed against the white where the other wing joined the body.

"Son of a bitch is still alive," Dale said. "I must've just winged him."

Dale bent down over the bird. With the quickness of a predator he grabbed it behind its head with his left hand and gripped the top of its head with his right, covering the yellow eyes. He commenced to twist the head around one way, then the other. He was trying to break its neck. But the head swiveled freely, and the strong curved beak kept opening and snapping shut. The owl made no sound, but it breathed.

"They can turn their heads two hundred and seventy degrees," the guide said. "You'll never kill it that way. Hit it on the head with your gun butt. Put it out of its misery."

"I don't want to bust his skull," Dale said. "I want this son of a bitch in one piece. Give me that bag."

Dale managed to get the owl into an empty game bag. Once it was covered, it stopped moving, inert as a heap of potatoes in the bottom of the bag.

"Cardiac arrest," Dale said with a laugh.

It was time to celebrate the end of the hunt. At the guide's house, they presented his wife with pheasant to clean and roast for dinner. What they did not eat they would store in the big freezer along with birds from the other days' shooting, already cleaned to take home. As agreed, Dale told the wife that he had shot an owl by mistake. The question was what to do with it now.

Dale peered into the game bag. He saw the owl's head move.

"I don't believe it," Dale said. "The damn thing is still alive! Can you beat it? By God," he nodded toward the freezer, "we'll freeze his ass in there. I got to hand it to him. I tried to wring his goddamned neck. Look at him. He's some fighter. So long, friend."

He opened the freezer chest, swung the bag in and dropped the lid.

The men went off to a bar. The guide's wife said that she would phone when dinner was on. They were ordering their second round when the waitress told the guide that his wife was on the phone.

"That was quick," Dale said. "She must've cooked 'em feathers and all. I'm going to finish this drink. I may have another."

When the guide came back to the table he said that he didn't know whether to believe what his wife had told him. She might be pulling his leg. She said that she had heard a noise in the freezer. She had opened it up, and there was that damn owl. It was not only alive, it was pecking at some steaks she had stored in there.

It had torn right through the wrapping and was pecking at the frozen meat.

The men rushed back to the house. The wife had not lied. There was the owl with its yellow-bright eyes. It had ignored the pheasant and gone for the steaks.

"It must've liked it in there," the guide said. "They live in the arctic. The cold must've revived it."

Pat Sullivan suggested that maybe the bird had earned a stay of execution, but Dale picked it up and carried it out the back door. They heard one screech as Dale gripped it by the feet and knocked its head against the concrete steps.

7

KEVIN CAVANESS WAS NEVER ABLE TO FORGET HIS EARLIEST memory of his father. The scene came back to him, if only for a second, nearly every time he found himself alone in the dark.

On a weekday morning, when Kevin was about four years old, he was at his father's knee at the breakfast table, envying his cup of coffee and trying to catch his eye from around the newspaper. Kevin was at the age when every little boy stumbles along in his father's wake, following him around the house and wanting to be like him.

He trailed his father upstairs to watch him shave. He stood entranced by the ritual, inhaling the soapy smell. He knew the routine by heart. After cleaning off the remaining specks of lather with the soapy cloth, his dad would turn and step into the bathroom closet for the shaving lotion and splash it on his face with quick slaps as he looked once more into the mirror.

This morning Kevin decided to play a game. As his father opened the closet door and stepped inside, Kevin rushed in beside him and pressed himself against the sheets and towels stacked at the back. He could not help giggling. He figured his dad would think that was pretty funny, too, finding Kevin in the closet like Jiminy Cricket.

But Dale backed out quickly, slammed the door and turned the lock.

In the dark Kevin sucked in his breath. He heard his father's footsteps clomping out of the bathroom and down the hall. He did not mean to leave me in here, Kevin thought. Did he mean to leave me in here? Did he see me?

"Dad? Dad? Here I am!"

But there was only silence. The dark. Kevin began to wail. He pounded on the door and rattled the handle. He sobbed and called out for his father again and again. It seemed a very long time before he heard footsteps.

Dale unlocked the closet door and opened it. Kevin ran into his father's arms, crying.

"Hey," his father said, picking him up and staring into his wet face, "what's the matter with you? What's wrong with you, Kev? You didn't have to be afraid. You shouldn't be afraid of the dark, see? What're you afraid of? You better learn that. You don't want to be a crybaby, do you? You some kind of scaredy-cat? You better learn sooner or later. You better stop that crying."

As Kevin grew up, he often thought of that dark closet, with the sound of the lock clicking and his father's footsteps fading down the hall. And then his father's voice: disappointed in him and full of warning.

In his earliest days Kevin had more trouble with Mark than with Dale. Like many older brothers, Mark made Kevin's life as miserable as he could, stealing his toys and tripping him up and sneaking in a punch or two to make him cry and irritate the grown-ups. Mark was also adept at escaping just in time to let Kevin take the blame, as when they threw oranges over the fence into the Chevrolet lot, or set fire to a bag of manure on somebody's porch, or tossed matches down the sewer to make the blue flames flare up until, finally, the sewer exploded with a tremendous boom and knocked an old lady off the toilet in a house across the street.

It was easy to get in Dutch in Eldorado, because there wasn't much to do. They could hang around Herpel's arcade or the black-smith's shop, where the man who everybody said was older than dirt would let them heat some iron and pound it on the anvil—that passed the time. They could run over and taunt old Cokey who sat on his front porch all day and would grab his shotgun from behind the door and shout, "I'm gonna getcha! I'm gonna getcha!" They could break into the city-hall basement through the coal chute or toss a baseball across the street trying to see how close they could come to the windshields of people driving past, until they'd hit one and the driver would light out after them.

If Mark wasn't letting Kevin take the heat for these pranks, he was finding ways to get at Kevin straight on. Kevin was playing with poster paints one day and Mark grabbed him, held him down and painted him green all over and left him bawling in the yard —and still managed to make it look as if Kevin had spilled the paint on himself.

But Kevin never questioned that Mark loved him—the rest was just the way a brother was, and nobody in Little Egypt minded roughhousing: It was what made boys grow up, as Peck had taught Dale. As often as they fought, Kevin and Mark could also play together, get away with schemes together, talk into the night with one another in their upstairs room. And Kevin looked up to Mark, who was such a handsome, outgoing kid, with a way of charming everyone. Kevin was sturdy, chunky and quiet, a listener who watched everything and everyone from behind his glasses. Kevin said little, but he remembered.

And most of the memories he gathered about his dad were dark ones. How unalike his parents were! Mom was always there, forgiving and loving, cheering everyone up. She had her breaking point, but you knew where it was, and any dispute with her ended up forgotten in her trills of laughter and her hugs. The only annoying thing about Mom was that she was always after you to do your homework and clean your room and mind your manners. Dad, when he was around, which was not very much, was the rule-giver, the one who doled out the serious punishment and the one who knew the answers to everything. That would have been all right, not so different from most of the other fathers Kevin knew, except that Dale was as unpredictable as winter. He could be kidding you one minute and whipping you the next; what you thought was a joke could turn sour in a second. When he got angry, his voice rose to a frightening, piercing pitch that could summon the dead and be heard for a mile, until Marian intervened, or tried to, and Dale stormed out of the house, and things were quiet again.

Kevin figured out that it was better to keep your distance from

Dad until you could gauge his mood; but he could not help himself from wanting to be around Dale, trying to attract his attention or just watching him. Kevin always found himself spontaneously happy on the rare evenings when Dale made it home for dinner—"Dad's home!"—and he liked to help his father prepare for hunting trips. He watched Dale heat the lead for bullets in the furnace in the summer house, mold them and oil the guns. Everyone would be up to see Dad off at dawn.

But just when Kevin thought he was being helpful, his dad might snap and bark at him and tell him to get lost. Marian said that Dale had a lot on his mind, so many sick people depended on him.

One evening Dale was reading the newspaper in the family room. Kevin was eleven years old, Mark thirteen, and Sean, who was out that evening with his mother visiting the Sullivans, was only four. As usual Sean had left some of his toys in the family room, hollow octagonal plastic blocks that snapped together to form multicolored strings. As Dale sat in his easy chair reading, Mark and Kevin passed the time tossing blocks back and forth to one another across the length of the room, making them whistle as they sailed. The game had gone on for about five minutes when Dale, not looking up, said:

"One more of those things, and you're gonna get it. My sack is getting full."

It was always a bad sign when Dale said that his sack was getting full. It meant that he had been storing up grievances, maybe for days. He would put one offense after another into his sack, until it was full. You had better watch out. That sack might have things in it you had forgotten about or had not even noticed; it could fill up at any moment.

Kevin was prepared to stop tossing the blocks, but Mark, the bold one, decided to chance one more. He whistled a red one over to Kevin.

Kevin waited. He did not wish to risk his father's wrath, but he did not want Mark to outdo him, either. Maybe the sack had room for one more. Dale continued reading. Kevin tossed the red block back. It whistled nicely that time.

"Okay, that's it," Dale said, throwing down the paper.

Kevin cursed himself for having miscalculated. He hoped that all his father would do would be to send them both to bed. There was no way of knowing.

Dale got up and went into the kitchen. He came back holding a metal spatula. He stood over Mark.

"Get those pants down." Dale always hit the boys bare butt. Kevin watched as his father went to work on Mark's bottom. He flailed away, grunting, three, four, five, six, harder and harder, until the head of the spatula bent and broke off.

Dale returned to the kitchen. He came back this time with a big wooden spoon. It made a solid smacking sound as Dale whacked it against Mark's reddening bottom. Mark began to cry.

"You want to bawl? You're going to high school and you want to cry? You some kind of pansy? You're a no-good little mama's boy, aren't you!" Whack. "Aren't you! Men don't cry. You want to be a baby? I'll give you something to cry about!"

Watching, Kevin prayed that his father would wear himself out on Mark. But energy was something Dale never lacked. It was Kevin's turn.

"Get them down. I warned you."

Kevin bent over with his jeans and underpants around his ankles. He heard the spoon swish and a hot burning stinging blow made him clench his teeth and dig his toes into the carpet and drove scalding tears into his eyes. With his head between his knees, the tears filled up under his eyes and burned. He knew that crying out loud would only make the beating worse. You got whipped again for crying, that was Dale's policy. You also got whipped for losing a fight at school, if Dale found out about it.

Mark was still whimpering in the corner.

"Why don't you learn to take it like your brother?" Dale said between whacks. He reared back and gave Kevin a really smart smack with the spoon. "See that? He doesn't cry. What's the matter with you? By God, you've got plenty to learn, my friend, let me tell you. You bet your sweet ass."

Finally Dale was winded. The boys crawled up to their room for the night. That had been a bad one, they agreed. A real downer. Just yelling at them would have been enough to get them to stop throwing the blocks. They should have stopped right away, but then you never knew, especially when you were alone with Dale: If Marian had been there he would never have whipped them so hard, might not have whipped them at all. The safest thing was to steer clear of Dad when he was on his own.

Dale had seemed to want to make an example of Mark that time, and he was usually tougher on Mark and angrier with him than with Kevin, but it could be the other way around. One Christmas Kevin asked for a special bicycle, a Stingray with fat tires, butterfly handlebars and a banana seat, just the thing for flying jumps from curbs and off-road tearing around, a bike that was supposed to be well-nigh indestructible and was the next best thing to a motor-cycle. Kevin went to sleep on Christmas Eve willing the bike to be there.

When Mark and Kevin went downstairs early the next morning, there was the bike under the tree. But the card dangling from the handlebars said "For Mark." That seemed peculiar; Mark had not even asked for a bike. Maybe the cards had been put on the wrong presents.

Dale was crouched beside the fireplace arranging logs, saying nothing. Mark, standing beside the bike, asked if it was really his. Dale nodded, yes.

"Where's mine?" Kevin said to his dad. "Mine's here some-where, isn't it?"

"Your what?" Dale said. "What makes you think you deserve anything? You think you get something just by whining about it? You think you earned it?"

Kevin rushed back upstairs and fell on his bed in tears. His father's words tore through him like shrapnel. What had he done? He had not even seen Dale for days. Mark had not asked for the bike, had not even wanted one. The unfairness of it weighed Kevin down until he did not have the strength to cry anymore.

He had been lying there for what seemed like half an hour when Marian came in and asked what was wrong. She had been out in the summer house wrapping a few last presents. Of course he had a bike, Marian said. Wasn't it under the tree with Mark's? She had bought one for Mark only so he would not be jealous of Kevin's. That was an afterthought. She had bought Kevin's first.

Marian went back downstairs. Through his door Kevin could hear his parents.

"Let him have it!" Marian shouted. "Let Kevin have that bike! What is the matter with you? Where is it?"

"Let it sink in!" Kevin heard Dale's piercing voice. "I don't want that kid thinking he can get something just for the asking. He's got to learn. Let it sink in!"

"Let him have it! He hasn't done anything!"

When Kevin finally got his bike, he could hardly bear to ride it. That his mother had bought it and had stood up for him did little to lift his spirit. His father had made him feel unworthy one minute, resentful the next—it was no use trying to enjoy the bike now. Why would his dad begrudge him?

Kevin failed to discover a way to please Dale. He liked school, especially science, but Dale refused to help him with his homework, dismissing him with some slogan or other: He should spend three hours per week per class, that was how his father had made a success of himself in school, that and brains, which he either had or did not have; you never learned anything except by getting it yourself; did Kevin believe for one minute that his father had succeeded by leaning on his parents?

It was the same with Mark: Kevin could take a cold kind of comfort that Dale paid no attention to Mark's studies or school activities either. If anything, Dale was more indifferent to Mark than to Kevin, avoiding even the presence of his eldest as if Mark were deformed or diseased. Mark made the high school football team, but Dale never attended the games. "Why should I waste my valuable time watching my kid sit on the bench?" Dale would dismiss Marian when she said it would mean a lot to Mark to have his father there. When Mark joined the Thespians and won the lead role—he was only a sophomore—in the school play, *Harvey*, he spent weeks memorizing his many lines. He was in almost every scene, but Dale did not show up to see a performance that everybody said would have given Jimmy Stewart a run for his money. Nor did Dale see Mark steal the show in the annual musical revue when he danced and sang "Eleanor Rigby."

"Did you know your son can really *sing*?" Marian said afterward, but Dale changed the subject.

Marian tried. She nagged. She cajoled until the boys were embarrassed by her pleading with Dale to do something with them, take them somewhere on his own, they needed him. One Saturday he gave in. He told the boys to get in the car, they were going off to work on a project together. Marian packed a lunch.

Dale drove them to Galatia, to some property he had bought there near Lake Harrisburg. He marched them into the woods and told them to start hacking down branches with machetes he had brought along.

"What're we doing?" Mark wanted to know.

91

"You're building a lean-to," Dale said. "We can use a lean-to out here."

The boys worked through part of the afternoon. They were not sure what a lean-to was or what its purpose would be, but they were having fun; it was an adventure with Dad. Dale showed them how to secure stakes in the ground and bind them with twine. The lean-to looked almost half finished when Dale said that was enough, they would come back and complete the job tomorrow. They never did. The half-built lean-to collapsed with the first snow.

Grandpa Peck made up for some of Dale's indifference. Grandpa was always taking Mark and Kevin hunting and fishing. He would show up in his old car with his two dogs, saying "Let's go get us some squirrels!" To haunt the creeks with Grandpa, learning how to hold your breath and lean against a handy tree trunk, rock-steady for a shot, hearing the soft pop of the .22 as you squeezed one off and watched the fat little thing tumble out of a tree and hit the ground with a smack—that was Kevin's idea of a perfect day. His most treasured possession was the rifle Peck had given him. Always so quiet and calm, Grandpa showed him how to clean the squirrels right away so they wouldn't get rank and gamey when Noma fried and served them with her fluffy dumplings: Marian prepared quail but drew the line at squirrel.

Kevin relished too the regular Sunday dinners at his grandparents' house, the rattle of the pressure cooker, comforting smells, the heaps of meat and potatoes, biscuits and rolls, and always the peach cobbler or some other special dessert. Marian was usually there for the Sunday get-togethers, Dale rarely. Kevin would not have traded these times with his grandparents for anything, except maybe for a few outings with his dad. Once in a while Dale let Mark and Kevin trail along hunting, but he went out with Pat Sullivan and Pat's son Greg far more often than with his own sons. He was always giving Greg Sullivan, who was Mark's age, expensive gifts—a hunting vest, even a beautiful Browning shotgun one year, brand-new. Mark and Kevin got the castoffs.

Nearly every time Dale was with his own, he blew up about something or did something to unnerve everybody. One summer afternoon at Shawneetown the boys were swinging themselves Tarzan-like into the river from a stout, long rope hung from a tree that bent over the bank. No other adults were doing it but Dale decided to show that he could swing out higher and farther than anyone else. As he climbed the ladder, rough boards nailed to the tree trunk, he ripped open the sole of his foot on a nail. Kevin, watching from below, could see the blood start, but Dale hardly paused, reached the top and grabbed at the rope. Kevin gasped as he saw that his father had taken hold of the rope too far down, leaving slack above. When he jumped it was a free-fall for the first eight to ten feet, and then the rope snapped taut and Dale lost his grip, splashing with a dull thud into the muddy shallows about three feet from shore.

He gathered himself and swam out to the small houseboat, decorated with potted trees, that acted as a floating dock. He scrambled aboard. Blood poured from under a nasty flap of torn flesh on his sole. He called for scissors; someone produced a rusty pair from a tackle box and, as everyone watched in wincing awe of his machismo, Dale snipped away the skin and dived back in.

In the car later the foot oozed blood. Kevin thought he could see a bit of tendon protruding and expressed concern, but Dale told him to quit acting like a sissy.

The next morning Dale could not get his foot into a shoe; he was off to the hospital wearing a bedroom slipper, the foot wrapped in gauze but otherwise untreated. That day, as nurses told Marian, he fed himself antibiotics and nearly fainted while delivering a baby. But he had made his point: He was tougher than his sons could ever hope to be. If he did get injured or sick, he could take care of himself. It was just like the time two of Mark's friends, teenaged sisters, wanted their ears pierced. Dale offered to do the job, but when the girls flinched, he took the needle and shoved it right through his upper lip. He laughed and grinned with the needle sticking out. The girls postponed their operation.

With the income from his practice growing, Dale began buying up property all over Little Egypt, including two farms, one the Galatia property, the other a five-hundred-and-sixty-acre place called Hickory Handle, near the village of Herod in the hills south of Harrisburg. He started a cattle-breeding operation, specializing in exotic breeds noted for their immense size, and announced that one day he would produce a unique beast, a perfect black Limousin bull. He would cull the herd to that end, he said, gradually darkening the animals from their normal oxblood or deep-tan color. He understood genetics, he said, and someday his cattle would be worth a fortune. Ordinary dumb-ass farmers were too ignorant of science to understand what they were doing. They'd be stuck with their little bitty Herefords when he'd be laughing all the way to the bank with his Simmental and Charolais and Limousin.

He had Mark and Kevin working on the farms on weekends and during the summers, although they were never sure what they were supposed to do besides digging postholes and mending barbed wire. When they inquired about their chores, he would turn away or bark something engimatic: "A man doesn't ask somebody what to do, he gets it done"; or "By God, what are you, some kind of a jackass, you have to be told what to do on a farm?" "I want results, not excuses" was one of his favorites. "That's your inheritance out there, eating grass," he proclaimed, pointing to a cow. "Just what do you intend to do about it? Suck around?"

Kevin and Mark tried to look busy. Kevin did not enjoy working on the farms. He did not know what to do, and the hired hands resented him, he could tell, and preferred bullshitting and drinking with Dale to supervising kids. Dale ran wilder out there than in town and could lose his temper in a flash, with no Marian around to object. Something would strike him wrong and he would reach for the nearest object to give the boys a whipping. He picked up a good stout board near the barn one day and broke it across Mark's rear end: As usual in the country, Dale was drunk. He always had a bottle with him out there.

One afternoon after a few snorts Dale ran his new Ford pickup into a mudhole and got stuck. He floored the thing, rocked it back and forth, cussed it, but the wheels spun and sank deeper. Dale would not give up. He kept gunning it till the radiator blew. He climbed down from the truck and slogged through the mud over to a bulldozer and drove the bulldozer up behind the truck and bashed into the rear. The truck still would not move. So Dale backed up the bulldozer and made a run at it, crashing into the rear and collapsing it halfway up the truck bed, gasoline pouring out from the ruptured tank. At length he managed to shove the truck's remains onto high ground. It was a total loss.

The hired hands laughed at this outburst, urging Dale on, but Kevin, even with his kid's love of noise and destruction, found it frightening. He watched his father tip up a vodka bottle afterward.

Drink must have had something to do, Kevin figured, with another expensive show of temper one July afternoon at Hickory

Handle. Kevin watched as Dale and a couple of the men attempted to load a Limousin bull onto a trailer. This particular bull, enormous and nearly black, was the pride of the herd and had just won first prize at the Saline County Fair. He weighed over two thousand pounds and was said to be worth a good ten thousand dollars.

And he was stubborn. Dale and the two hands were having a hell of a time getting the bull to walk up the chute to the trailer. They pulled and shoved; they used the electric prods on him. Nothing worked. The air was hot and close. Everyone was in a sweat.

Dale began to scream at the beast and whack him with his fists. The bull still would not budge. He strained against the ropes and looked ready to charge right through the trailer if they ever got him into it.

"Son of a bitch!" Dale yelled with a fierceness that made Kevin retreat to a safe distance—discreetly, so that his father would not notice his fear. He watched Dale turn and rush to his car and pull from it the .357 magnum revolver that he always kept loaded in the glove compartment. Everyone fell back as Dale strode toward the bull with the nickel-plated pistol flashing in his hand.

He came within a couple of feet of the animal, drew back the pin, and pointed the gun at an eye, holding it with both hands, combat-style.

"Okay! You're hamburger!" Dale said.

He fired. Even out there in the open the magnum exploded with an ear-ringing crack.

Kevin looked away. He heard the bull bellow and fall dead on the chute. It sounded like a building collapsing.

When his fright subsided, Kevin felt sorry for the bull. He had been proud and beautiful in his big, ugly way. Now, it was true, he was just hamburger.

It took the rest of the afternoon for Dale and the men to haul the dead bull up the chute into the trailer so he could be taken away and sold for meat. Everyone was drinking beer and Dale had his bottle. By the time he was ready to go home, Dale was staggering. He told Kevin, who was still shy of his twelfth birthday, to drive.

"I can't," Kevin said. "I don't know how."

"What do you mean, you can't? Don't ever say you can't. Just do."

Kevin protested that he was afraid to drive his father's new Olds 98, so Dale said they would take one of the hands' cars.

They got into a battered Pontiac Silver Streak. Dale leaned over to turn the key, showed which was the accelerator and which the brake, dropped the gearshift into drive, and said steering would be just like riding a bike. Kevin lurched ahead. At least the old Pontiac was an automatic.

It was dusk, and Dale told him how to turn on the lights. The farm road was not so difficult, but out on Route 34 Kevin was scared. He pointed his toes to reach the pedals and peered through the steering wheel. He kept touching the brakes to make sure he could stop. Because he could barely see over the hood, he tried to cling to the side of the road when he saw oncoming headlights. At the end of the hood was a plastic Indian-head ornament that lit up with the headlights, a tiny beacon that led the way, or so Kevin imagined. He hoped that the Indian could see better than he could. He jerked the wheel from side to side, to line up the side of the road with that glowing, red-orange head; but he kept running onto the shoulder and swerving back.

"Step on it," his father said. "You're driving like an old woman." Then Dale passed out.

The lights on the dash were dead except for another Indian head, a little red one that glowed in the center of the speedometer to mark the sixty-miles-an-hour point. Kevin kept glancing down at that little red Indian head: When the needle crept up to it, blotting it out, he slowed, then sped up until the head disappeared again. He was watching the red Indian when he drifted over the lip at the edge of the concrete road. The car rocked as he lurched it back over the lip, banging his father's head against the window. Dale woke up, mumbled something, and passed out again.

Kevin prayed all the way to Eldorado that he would not end up like the bull.

Kevin accepted his father's ways. He had never known Dale to be different, could not imagine him acting anything but strong and loud and cold. He wished that Dale would be more like other dads, able to spend much more time with their sons, without being so critical of them. After Sean was born, Dale was around even less and exploded even more. Marian was no longer able to calm him or make him go away when he worked himself into a lather, although he still more or less behaved himself when outsiders were present. Jewel Kinnear, the lady who did housekeeping and baby-sitting for the Cavanesses, had the knack of cooling Dale off. Kevin felt safer when Jewel was near. She talked back to Dale, held him in check, and could even get him to break into a grin instead of the sneer he adopted when he was riled. When all else failed, Jewel could convince him to leave the house when he started to lose his temper. She was a widow and one of her sons had been shot to death at Cahokia Downs race track by three punks who robbed him of fifteen dollars. Nothing fazed Jewel. She chain-smoked Camels, drank her coffee black, and could handle the boys with her mixture of toughness and affection. They loved her.

She had been baby-sitting one evening and was making sure the boys were in bed when everyone heard noises down in the kitchen. Marian and Dale were home earlier than expected. Dale's voice filled the house. There was no mistaking that tone.

Jewel went downstairs to see what was the matter, telling the boys to stay in bed; but they followed behind.

Through the kitchen door Kevin and Mark could see their father leaning against the sink, breathing hard. Marian stood with her back to him, coughing and clearing her throat. Her pearl necklace lay scattered on the floor. When Jewel spotted the boys, she said:

"Now, Dale, you're not doing much of a job trying to fix that necklace. Look at that, you've let all them pearls fall down. You better pick them up. Now, Dale, you'll never find them all if you don't pick them up now. See, boys? It broke when he was trying to fix it."

Kevin was not fooled, but he loved Jewel for calming things down as no one else could. Dale sank onto his hands and knees to search for the pearls he must have torn from Marian's throat.

When Jewel was not there, anything could happen. One night Kevin was alone, asleep in his room. Mark was spending the night at a friend's; Sean was with Peck and Noma, who enjoyed taking care of the baby once in a while. Marian and Dale had gone out to dinner, but Marian was coming home early to be with Kevin.

Kevin woke up suddenly to the sound of his father's voice, a roar from his parents' room. He was puzzled to see that his bedside lamp was on, the shade askew and dented. His desk chair was turned over, covers had been dragged from Mark's bed, the room was a mess. Down the hall his father and mother were yelling at each other, worse than usual.

Kevin got up and crept along the hall toward the noise. He heard something being thrown against a wall, his mother's voice begging Dale to stop.

The first thing Kevin saw was his mother lying on the floor in a black dress, one arm over her eyes, her lower lip bleeding.

Dale stood against the dresser in his dark suit, one hand on his hip, tie pulled down, chest heaving, sweating. Kevin's thought was that his father looked as if he had just had a good workout. But Dale's eyes were wild and a vein in his neck throbbed.

Kevin hesitated in the doorway, blinking, a small figure holding up his pajamas with one hand.

"He tried to kill me!" Marian blurted out and then covered her bleeding mouth with her arm.

Kevin looked up at Dale.

"Yeah. That's right," Dale said. He was breathing hard. "I tried to kill her."

Kevin felt helpless. He had no idea what to think or do. He turned and walked back to his room, switched off the light and pulled the covers over his head.

Everything was quiet now. Kevin stuck his head out of the covers and stared at the ceiling.

Dale came into the room and bent over and hugged Kevin long and hard. It was the biggest hug Kevin could ever remember getting from his dad.

He watched Dale leave the room and heard him go down the stairs. Then he heard the sound of the glass door that opened into the garage.

Kevin got out of bed and went to the top of the stairs as Marian emerged from her room holding a cloth to her face. They stood together looking down the stairway, listening as the electric garage door opened and the car started.

At the upstairs window they watched as Dale's car headed off down the street into the dark.

Marian put Kevin back to bed and told him that everything was all right now. She was holding her right arm with her other hand.

As he lay there, he tried to reconstruct what must have happened. Why had his room been all messed up? He figured that

Marian must have come in to wake him, so that Dale would stop hammering her. Dale had dragged her out again somehow. I must have been in some deep sleep to have missed all that, Kevin thought. Something was telling me not to wake up.

What had they been fighting about? Kevin had often heard them quarrel about money. Would that have been enough for his father to get that angry? Kevin could not imagine getting that angry about anything.

The next morning Kevin got himself dressed and diffidently went downstairs. Marian had her right arm in a scarf she had made into a sling. Her lip was swollen and she had the beginnings of a black eye. Kevin wished she would tell him what had happened and where his father had gone and whether the fighting would ever stop. It seemed to get worse and worse.

But his mother brought him his cereal and chatted about what she had made him for lunch.

"What's the deal with you and Dad?" Kevin asked.

"Everything's all right. He did get mad and push me, and I fell. It was an accident, dear, it's really nothing and I don't want you to think another thing about it, okay? Have you got your books? Don't be late for the bus."

She did not look at him as she spoke. Kevin thought that she was ashamed, and he did not want her to feel that way.

"Dad didn't really try to kill you, did he?"

"Of course not! That was just talk. You know what foolish things people say when they get angry. It's all over now. Hurry up."

There were other bad nights before Kevin and Mark began to understand that there was something else wrong between their parents besides money and arguments over how to treat the boys. One Saturday afternoon Marian agreed to drive Mark, Kevin and a friend of Kevin's named Philip over to Harrisburg Lake to do some fishing. She would drop the boys off and pick them up before dark.

The route to the lake was through Dale's Galatia property. As Marian turned down the gravel road, everyone noticed Dale's car parked beside a trailer he had put out there, about a hundred yards ahead.

"I didn't know Dad was here," Mark said.

"I didn't know either," Marian said. "You know your dad. You never know where he might be."

As they approached the trailer, Dale suddenly popped out of it, bounding down the steps and into the road, peering at them. He seemed to be wearing a white surgical smock and nothing else.

"That son of a bitch," Marian said under her breath. Showing his bare backside, Dale made a dash for the trailer door.

Marian slid to a stop, rushed out and up the steps and started screaming:

"That bitch! What's she doing in there?"

Marian tried to force her way into the trailer. Dale stood in the doorway, hands outstretched as if barring an intruder. Behind Dale, Kevin caught sight of a blond head appearing as if for the view and quickly withdrawing.

"Martha!" Marian shouted. "Why is Martha here? Let me at her!" Marian struggled with Dale.

The woman in question was well known to the boys, although they had not been aware of her new role in the family's life until now.

The rest was chaos: Marian screaming, Dale trying to force her back down the steps. Mark, who always went wild when his parents fought, shouted, "Leave her alone!" and began heaving dirt clods and sticks against the side of the trailer.

Kevin, embarrassed in front of his friend, took Philip over to the edge of the woods and sat him down on a log. From there they watched Mark beating on the trailer and the adults shrieking and struggling. Mark grew hysterical, crying, pounding his fists.

"This is terrible," Philip said, and he started crying, too. "I feel so sorry for you. What are we going to do? I want to go home. I feel so sorry for you. Oh, awful."

"I'm sorry," Kevin said. He was the only calm one—outwardly calm. "I'm really sorry about all this. There's not much I can do, I guess. We better just sit here and let the storm blow by."

Marian gave up and got the boys back into the car. She apologized to Philip, who asked to be taken home right away.

Kevin did not see his father for weeks after that. Almost every morning Dale would come into the house before anyone was up, take a shower, and leave. Sometimes Kevin and Mark could hear their mother ask Dale where he was staying.

"Leave me alone" was all that Dale said.

8

DISCOVERING DALE WITH ANOTHER WOMAN WAS DISTRESSING enough for Marian, but she was also pregnant again. Until his affair surfaced, she and Dale still made love amid their quarrels. After a heated argument, even after one of his outbursts of violence, Marian was so relieved, even grateful when things returned to what she had come to accept as normal—so anxious to banish hatreds—that she welcomed him back into her arms, trying to salve the wounds in the time-honored way.

That was how, she guessed, on some night near Christmas of 1965, the season when their fighting was always at its worst, that she had become pregnant again. She and Dale had never formally decided to stop having children, but she had stopped taking birth-control pills because they gave her headaches and depressed her. Dale seemed neither elated nor disappointed at the news.

And early in 1966 he surprised her by announcing her pregnancy at a dinner party. Everyone applauded. Dale came over to where she was sitting, bent down and kissed her. Marian thought that they had agreed not to break the news so soon, but she was pleased at his apparent pride.

Within another month, everything went to hell when she discovered Dale with Martha, a woman Marian knew well, out at the Galatia farm. Her fury ignited against the woman, the threat, not against Dale. She wanted to get at Martha and scratch her eyes out—only Dale had thwarted her charge into the trailer, and Martha had retreated. Then Marian heard Mark's shouting and got the hell out.

Martha Culley was recently divorced from her husband, Duke Culley, whom Dale had professed to like so much that the two couples had spent much time together since their first meeting at a party a few years before. Dale took up with Duke as a golfing and drinking buddy and spoke of him as if he were the greatest Rudie in the world. Duke fit his name: six feet four, Mount Rushmore handsome, a college football player, a Washington University law-school graduate. Marian liked him. As for Martha, Marian had considered her amusing, warm, rather more flamboyant than was usual with southern Illinois ladies, a blonde who would appear to have been more at home wowing them belting out ballads at the Grand Ole Opry in Nashville than trapped behind the prosceniums of Little Egypt—something of a Harrisburg Mae West, with her throaty contralto and head-swiveling wardrobe.

Had Dale not been so gone on Duke, Marian believed that she would never have been more than a casual acquaintance of Martha's. Dale invited the Culleys everywhere, even loaned Duke money, or so Marian understood, so that the Culleys could go along on a golfing holiday to the Greenbriar Hotel in West Virginia. We need another couple, Dale had insisted, although Marian would have preferred to be alone with Dale. Had Dale really been after Martha all along, using his friendship with Duke as a cover? How long had Dale been carrying on with Martha, and could their affair have precipitated the Culleys' divorce? Marian had no idea. Dale had taken Martha's side, vehemently, when Duke walked out on her and their four children; but in Marian's opinion Martha's indifferent housekeeping and irregular cooking were nearly sufficient cause for the split. It did not seem likely that Dale would turn against a male friend without some ulterior motive.

Marian could recall only once having had anything like a personal conversation with Martha. Martha had dropped by for drinks one afternoon and had started bitching about Duke's supposedly inadequate income and what she regarded as his laziness, in contrast to Dale's work habits. To make her feel better, Marian confided that Dale was not exactly an ideal husband and father, no matter how much money he made. He was never home till late. Half the time she had no idea where he was.

What a mistake that moment of confidence had been! It was after Duke had left Martha, Marian now realized, that makeup and lipstick started showing up on Dale's shirts. "Grateful patient" was all he had said when Marian questioned him, and she had wanted to believe him.

Marian tried to confront Dale, but he avoided her. He stayed away from the house, appearing only early in the morning to shower and change clothes, as Mark and Kevin had noticed. Marian kept doing his laundry. She knew he was with Martha because friends had spotted his car at her house in Harrisburg, but Marian was not ready to give him up. She still loved him, and what choice did she have? Where would she go? She had no mother to run to, no income of her own, three children and another on the way. Surely he would get over Martha like a virus. Maybe he had been temporarily deranged by the thought of having a fourth child.

Marian stayed home. Her pregnancy was making her queasy anyway, and as usual she had stopped drinking and smoking, was watching her weight, following doctor's orders. She had no wish, reason, or excuse to go out, and she was embarrassed. Fending off the boys' questions about their father's whereabouts was bad enough—she assumed that they had figured everything out; but she could not bring herself to discuss it with them, and she made her excuses for Dale, the usual line about how hard he worked.

One evening she was alone, feeling sorry for herself and thinking how good a big drink of Scotch would taste, when a friend called and talked her into driving up to the Carmi Country Club to play bridge.

She had been playing with the three other ladies for an hour or so at the club when Dale walked in with Martha on his arm. Nobody said anything. Dale and Martha sat down across the room and began a game with another couple. Marian asked to be taken home.

When Dale showed up again for his laundry, Marian broke down. She had planned to let him have it, give him an ultimatum, but all she could do was ask him how he could be so cruel. Did he have to show up in public with that woman?

"You don't understand," Dale said. "Martha and I are just friends. She's been going through a rough time since her divorce."

The lie was so big: Here is a man, Marian thought, who doesn't give a damn what his wife or anyone else thinks and who believes that he can do as he pleases and get away with anything. It was this bravado that had attracted her years before; now it was turned against her. Other women, Marian knew, had children to hold their husbands, make it impossible for them to leave. But you could count on Dale to do the opposite of the conventional. He prided himself on marching to a different drummer, one of his favorite clichés.

On another morning she asked him how he could stand living with a slob who never did the dishes, whose house was a pigsty, and whose four children survived on breakfast cereal and peanut butter.

"Oh, I've already told her," Dale said matter-of-factly, "there isn't going to be any of that lying around in bed all day and letting the garbage pile up."

Still Marian did not lose faith. Dale was temporarily off his rocker, that was all. He had done something he already regretted and was being defensive about it. He will wake up one morning next to her and wish he were with me, Marian told herself; he'll come back and we'll be stronger than ever. Men were always saying that when you weld a piece of broken metal back together, it is sounder than it had been before. A marriage needs a break sometimes, a shock, a rough patch to shake everyone up. Surely when he realizes that his child is about to be born . . .

It was May. One afternoon Dale telephoned Marian from the hospital. He had to make a run near Harrisburg, he said. Would she care to come with him? He had to look in on a patient out near Rudement.

Marian fixed her hair and makeup. It was finally happening. She was ready to forgive him. She already had. It was just like the McLeansboro days, going with him on a house call. Why else would he be asking her to take a drive with him?

Dale picked her up. They talked of nothing on the way over, a distance of about twelve miles. It was a bright spring day. New grass brightened the fields. Beyond Harrisburg in the foothills dogwood and redbud trees bloomed—a day to exult and to banish miseries. Marian waited in the car as Dale went inside the small house to see his patient. She felt not quite happy, but hopeful.

On the way back Dale avoided Route 45. He is giving himself time, Marian thought, taking the side roads to make the trip longer. Or had he not decided what to say? Had he simply wished to see her, to try what it was like to be with her after these weeks? He might be unsure of himself. She felt sorry for him. She was so relieved to be with him and wanted the trip to last, whether he said anything to her now or not.

They were driving along the Billman Road when Dale broke the silence.

"I have to tell you something," he began.

"Yes, tell me anything you want. Here I am."

"I hate to tell you this when you're six months pregnant. I don't love you anymore, and I don't need you, and I don't want you."

9

AUGUST ARRIVED. DALE REMAINED AWAY. HE WAS THERE IN Marian's hospital room, however, when she started having her contractions, nattering on about cattle farming to an old man who was just being released and was soaking in the latest information on heifers. Marian told Dale that the baby was coming. He ignored her and kept on with his lecture. Finally he ordered her wheeled into the delivery room.

"It's another boy" was all Dale said when Marian came out of the anesthetic.

Jewel and Noma helped her at home for the first few weeks. She named him Patrick after Pat Sullivan, who agreed to be the godfather, and as usual she added Dale as the middle name. She still believed Dale would come home. She had to.

Once Patrick was on a regular schedule, Marian had plenty of time to meditate on her marriage. Some of her wishful thinking evaporated. She could see how things had deteriorated gradually, right under her nose, without her noticing or wanting to notice. Behavior she had dismissed as eccentric had become regular. She had ignored or had disbelieved many of the stories Mark and Kevin had told her about Dale's behavior when she was not around. She had minimized what she had seen with her own eyes, especially during the holidays.

Dale's violence had increased along with his drinking. There was the incident Kevin had witnessed, when Dale had bent her arm back until she thought it would break and had socked her on the mouth and eye. On another occasion they had been lying in bed and she had said something Dale didn't like: She had always spoken her mind to him, had prided herself on that, on not being like so many of the women she knew in southern Illinois, silent and obedient. But Dale had reacted like a typical down-home son of a bitch, grabbing her thumb and bending it back until she could hear the bones cracking.

"We better get that X-rayed" was all he had said the next morning, without an apology. At least when he had hit her on their first anniversary he had apologized.

One night they were home from a party, standing in the kitchen, when Dale opened the refrigerator to see what there was to eat. A bowl of gravy fell out and broke on the floor.

"Damn," Marian said. "I'll clean it up. Leave it alone."

"Is this all there is to eat?" Dale asked, and he bent down, scooped up a handful of gravy and threw it in her face.

When she shouted and cursed him he punched her in the eye, knocking her to the floor. There were no apologies.

Marian rationalized all of these outbursts by attributing them to drink. Some people get mean when they drink, she told herself, deciding that there was such a thing as a drunk Dale and a sober Dale and that the two had little to do with one another. She isolated the incidents, separated them from one another as well as from the sober Dale, to avoid seeing patterns and connections. Since they occurred over a period of three or four years, she had time to recover from each and file it away. None seemed serious enough to weaken her faith in the future or to threaten her happiness with her home and her boys. As for his harshness with the boys, a lot of southern Illinois fathers were rough on their kids. It was the old-fashioned way. Marian did not approve, but she did not consider such behavior abnormal, and she never hesitated to criticize Dale for his sarcasm or to tell him when she thought he had punished the boys enough or too much.

Since childhood Marian had learned to make the best of things. Compared to the difficulties her mother had faced and surmounted, hers seemed trivial, the ups and downs that any woman lucky enough to have a husband and a home could expect. She had long ago acquiesced to living in southern Illinois; her city dreams had faded. She believed in Dale, loved him as ever, and was not a quitter. The violence was not something she wished to discuss with a friend or an outsider; her brother lived in California now, happy and successful with his own family, and it did not occur to her to telephone him or write him about what were surely passing troubles. The violence was humiliating but better forgotten. Dale had not meant to break her thumb: He had been drinking and had forgotten how strong he was. She had been drinking some herself: Maybe she had said something truly awful, that was possible. It was more of an accident than an assault.

But now, with the new baby and with her husband off with another woman, Marian had plenty of time to think, and she began to wonder how well she knew Dale. He had his life thoroughly compartmentalized; there was so much of it about which she knew nothing. The children had been her realm; everything else besides their social life was his. She had her own checking account, into which Dale deposited money when it was needed. He paid her charge accounts at the grocery and liquor stores; even the utility bills at the house went to his office. She had no idea how much money he was making or what he was doing with it. Occasionally he would bring her papers to sign, but she never examined them. She knew nothing about business or property; it never occurred to her to question a successful man who she believed was far brighter than she and who, after all, was the one making the money.

She did worry from time to time about the vast amount he must have been sinking into the farms for cattle and equipment, eventually for the elaborate catfish-breeding operation he installed: terraced, aerated pools; hatcheries; a processing plant. When she did dare ask him whether he was confident that the farms would turn a profit, or were they more of a hobby of his, Dale responded curtly that since their sons were probably not going to amount to anything anyway, they had better have something to fall back on when they were grown-up and broke. She knew the boys well enough to see that they had no interest whatever in agriculture. They had many years ahead of them still to find themselves. Wasn't Dale being

109

rather premature in dismissing their prospects? Not everyone could be a genius like him! He could spend more time with them, if he wanted to inspire them. But if Dale had in mind becoming some sort of gentleman farmer as well as a doctor, she could hardly object.

Marian now saw that just as Dale had excluded her from his business and professional life, he excluded himself from family life. Every Christmas Eldorado offered a prize for the prettiest decorations. When Marian won it with her wreaths and colored lights and spotlit photos of the children on the lawn, Dale reacted as if she were celebrating someone else's children. The boys kidded her about the photos, which made perfect snowball targets and provoked razzing at school, but Marian knew that her children appreciated her efforts to show family pride. She continued with the decorations in 1966, even with Dale gone, adding Patrick's photograph. There was no use in trying to get Dale to pose for the Christmas card, so she designed a five-pointed star of individual photos, with Patrick's in the center and a shot of Dale from another year at the lower left point.

She tried to figure out how and why Dale had changed: His personality had not fundamentally altered, but it had grown extreme, like his drinking. He had always been the life of the party; now he got drunk quickly, launched into nonstop monologues, challenged people. Theirs was a drinking crowd; no one seemed to mind; but Dale made Marian nervous with the vehemence of his arguments about the state of the world or the genetics of cattle or whatever. He would grow red in the face, grab people by the lapels, raise that piercing voice.

His practical jokes had gotten out of hand. One night they were driving home with Pat and Betty Ray Sullivan along the Marion-Harrisburg Road. Marian always liked being with the Sullivans. She was close to Betty Ray; Pat, perhaps because he was such a successful businessman, perhaps because he was big and burly and conveyed with nonchalance an air of authority, was able to hold Dale in check, more or less, with a word or a gesture. Near Shady Rest that night, Dale hit a deer, knocking it into a ditch and killing it. After surveying the damage to his fender, Dale drove on, and they dropped the Sullivans at home.

On the road to Eldorado, Dale suddenly stopped, burst out laughing, turned around, and headed back toward Marion on Route 13.

"What are you doing?" Marian asked.

"You'll see," Dale said. "We're going back and get that deer. We're going to make Pat a present of it."

Marian knew better than to argue.

She went along with the gag. She helped Dale hoist the big buck into the trunk of the car.

"It's all bloody," Marian complained.

"Never mind. This'll be worth it."

At the Sullivans', Marian was sorry to see that the lights were out. Dale dragged the deer out of the trunk, through the front yard and onto the porch, propping it up on a wrought-iron bench against the white brick.

"I don't think they're going to appreciate this," Marian said as Dale sped off. The Sullivans' house was immaculate, freshly painted, a Harrisburg showplace. Marian could not imagine that Pat and Betty Ray would be amused. Dale asked her whether she had lost her sense of humor.

The next morning, as he told them later with some vehemence, Pat went out in his robe and pajamas to fetch the Sunday paper and noticed the blood that had seeped over the porch. The sight of that deer sitting on the bench was grotesque; nor did he and Betty Ray relish the idea of the neighbors' gawking at it as they walked to church. They dragged it several blocks away into an alley and spent hours cleaning up the porch. Pat was incensed, but a headline in the Harrisburg *Register* three days later broke the ice between the Sullivans and the Cavanesses:

DEER FOUND WITHIN CITY LIMITS

Another of Dale's pranks turned out to be less easily resolved. The Cavanesses were spending the Fourth of July with three other couples at the Sullivans' Holiday Inn at Kentucky Lake, a resort and recreation area south of Paducah across the Ohio River. It had been an uneventful holiday, with the kids enjoying speeding around on the Sullivans' boat. The Sullivans had gone home a day early; on the night of the Fourth, Dale was up late drinking with the other men after the women and children had gone to bed.

Duke Culley was not as drunk as Dale but was well-enough oiled to come up with a silly idea.

"Wouldn't it be funny," Duke said, pointing to a cabin cruiser parked on a trailer near the swimming pool, "to wake up in the morning and find that boat in the pool?"

That was all Dale needed. Duke protested that he had only been kidding, but Dale hurried over to the boat. He was unable to roll the trailer by himself at first and called for help, but everyone refused, telling him to stop before he did something he'd regret. This spurred Dale on and he found the strength to back the boat up to the edge of the pool. A good-sized Chris-Craft, it was about twenty-five feet long.

The boat was not locked onto the trailer. Dale was able to launch it into the pool, which it nearly filled, gallons of water slopping over the sides.

The men could not help sending up a cheer, but a subdued one: They did not want to wake the other guests. Their appreciation of Dale's bold move turned quickly to alarm. The boat's owner had opened its seacocks. It started sinking. Dale wanted to jump aboard to save it, but the others held him back. It was too late.

Within a couple of minutes the boat had sunk to the bottom of the pool, sending oil and gasoline to the surface. The men hurried to their rooms, woke up their families, and headed home in the middle of the night.

Pat Sullivan's mother was the manager of the inn. She telephoned her son early the next morning to report the disaster. It would take a special crew to raise the boat from the pool. The owner was livid and demanding compensation. The pool's filtration system was ruined. With no swimming pool for the rest of their holiday, most of the rest of the guests had checked out.

Dale never confessed to what he had done, and the other men never exposed him. Somehow Bob Davenport got blamed, but Pat Sullivan knew that the incident had Dale Cavaness written all over it. Sullivan went through a few days of apoplexy trying to figure out how he could prove Dale's responsibility and stick him with several thousand dollars' worth of damages; but Pat tried to see the humor in the situation. He would write off the losses. He guessed that it was the price you paid for having such a brilliant, eccentric friend. And after all, Dale never sent the Sullivans a bill for any medical services. They felt lucky to have him around, a first-class physician in a depressed and poverty-stricken area.

In an obscure way that neither could fully articulate, both Marian and Pat Sullivan felt sorry for Dale, the feisty little guy who had always been tough to tackle and who still had the need to prove himself. Pat was out hunting with Dale one November afternoon when Dale fell in a creek bed and broke his arm. The break, on or near the elbow, was obvious, you could see the splintered bone. Pat wondered how Dale could keep from fainting from the pain.

"I'll get you to the hospital," Pat said. Dale insisted on driving himself.

"What's the matter with you?" Pat protested. "I'll drive. You might pass out."

"The hell I will."

When Dale reached town, pale and sweating, he did not head for the hospital, pulling up instead in front of his father's house.

"Got to let the dogs off," Dale said. "And they're hungry. Better feed them before we go over and get this damn arm fixed."

Pat telephoned Marian and told her that it looked as if Dale was out of his mind with the pain. Here he was with a broken elbow and he was feeding the dogs. Marian said that she would get things ready at the hospital, but that if the break was as bad as Pat said it was, she ought to drive Dale to St. Louis to see an orthosurgeon.

"I'll bet Dale won't hear of that," Pat said. "He'll try to fix it himself."

At the hospital Dale gave orders, refused a preparatory anesthetic, and passed out. When he came to after the operation, he went into convulsions. Both the surgery and the anesthetic had been botched. Marian thought he was going to die. The elbow never healed properly; and he was never again able to extend his left arm fully.

In retrospect Marian wondered whether Dale's brain had been permanently affected by the convulsions, but there were so many other incidents involving his bullheadedness and pride in enduring pain that any one of them seemed enough to have deranged an ordinary man. And there was no talking to him. He would never admit that he was carrying the idea of bravery and guts to absurdity.

Marian remembered waking up one morning to find Dale next to her with his throat bandaged from ear to ear. He had been out playing poker the night before. She had not heard him come in. The doorbell rang. It was one of Dale's buddies, asking if he was all right. Hadn't Marian heard? Dale had almost been killed. Was he doing okay?

There were conflicting versions of what had happened the previous night, but none differed on the essentials. Dale had gone to play poker with some of his cronies at Kemo Golish's Amusement Company. The Golish brothers for years had supplied and maintained all the pinball machines in Saline County, and their warehouse outside of Harrisburg on Route 13, formerly the building where Charlie Birger had processed and stored some of his liquor, was a kind of speakeasy, most of Saline County being dry in those days.

One of the poker players was a barber named Huck Gee, a big, ornery fellow who had a reputation as a troublemaker. The game had been going along for several hours when Huck Gee finally went bust. He accused Dale of cheating, or Dale accused Huck Gee of shorting the pot: Either way, Huck Gee left the game vowing that he was going to get Dale Cavaness.

When the game finally ended, Dale stepped outside to find the big barber waiting for him, holding a broken bottle. Huck Gee lunged for Dale's throat and got him, twisting the bottle, slashing him from one side to the other. Dale went down, blood pouring from his neck. Huck Gee ran off down the highway.

Dale was not through. He was up like a jumping jack and after the barber. He caught him fifty yards down the road, knocked him to the ground with a football tackle, rolled on top of him and grabbed him around the throat. It was quite a sight, everyone said, Dale's old speed coming to the fore, blood pouring from his throat, catching his man and downing him, squeezing and strangling him and pounding his big bald head against the pavement. Somebody called the police; the other poker players pried Dale off Huck Gee just as the cops arrived. The barber went to jail, the doctor to the hospital.

The doctor who sewed up Dale's throat at the Harrisburg hospital said that Huck Gee had come within one millimeter of severing Dale's jugular vein.

What Marian remembered more than anything, other than her terror and revulsion at the entire incident, was Dale's attitude as he sat in his chair in the family room that morning receiving well-wishers, friends, nurses and employees from the hospital and the office. He could not talk, but he was grinning like a kid. He was David who had whipped Goliath. He was the scrapper who would never quit. He was indomitable, the man who could take anything and give worse than he got, a winner. When he was asked in the next week whether he wanted to press attempted-murder charges against Huck Gee, he refused. Huck Gee had learned his lesson, Dale said. He would never mess with Dale Cavaness again.

The story became a local legend and was written up in the papers. Marian wondered whether she was the only one who thought the whole business disgusting and frightening. Everybody else seemed to consider Dale a hero. She was glad her husband could defend himself, but she wondered whether he was courting death.

Even as Marian ruminated about Dale's behavior over the years, she still tried to convince herself that his affair with Martha was just a fling. Late one evening in 1967 she was lying alone in her bed, staring at the ceiling, when she heard the garage door open and a car drive in. Dale came upstairs, stripped to his shorts and crawled into bed with her. He had not been there beside her for more than a year.

They lay side by side, not touching, silent. He smelled of whiskey. Marian turned her back and hugged the side of the bed. She wondered what on earth his presence meant. She was torn between asking him to get out and waiting to see what he had to say.

A car started honking in the street, short beeps and then a continuous blare. Dale did not move. Marian went to the window.

"It's Martha," Marian said. "What in hell does she think she's doing?"

"Let her honk," Dale said. "Let her get picked up by the cops. She's drunk. Let her go to hell."

Martha gave up and drove off. Marian permitted herself to hope that the two had finally broken up. She did not appreciate Dale's coming back like this, with no explanations, no apologies, but there he was.

Dale left for work the next morning as if everything were back to normal, saying good-bye to the boys, even asking them a few perfunctory questions about school. Sean, who had just started kindergarten and was the most openly affectionate of the children, clung to his father, not wanting to let him go. Dale had to shake Sean loose.

But Dale did not return that night. He and Martha had merely had a tiff, Marian realized bitterly, a lovely little boozed-up lovers' quarrel.

Dale's coming home like that, never intending to stay, using the house and her bed as an escape from that woman—it was worse than violence, insulting and cruel and beyond Marian's comprehension. What had she done to deserve this? What would she tell the boys?

By the summer of the next year Marian's checks had begun to bounce. She still had credit at the grocery store and elsewhere, but she was sickened at the prospect of losing face with local merchants, people with whom she had enjoyed trading for years. Her bank statement showed an overdraft.

She telephoned Dale at the hospital and at his office; he did not return her calls. In desperation she made an appointment to see him.

Dale admitted her to his private office and closed the door. Marian was struck by his seedy appearance. He had gained at least twenty pounds, he was sweaty with hair unbrushed and greasy. And he was not wearing one of his fine suits but a pair of cheap green polyester pants. Instead of asking him about money, she found herself telling him that he looked terrible. What was he doing to himself? Why wouldn't he admit that he had made a mistake and come back? What about the children?

"What are you here for?" was all Dale said. "You know I don't like to be interrupted during office hours." He was icy.

Marian explained that she had to have some money. She did not know what his finances were, but surely he understood that he had a family to support. There was no money in her account. He would have to start giving her regular payments of some kind.

"I don't have any money," he said. "There isn't any money. I'm broke. What are you doing, sitting in the house? You better get off your butt and get yourself some kind of a job. With your clothes and your tastes. It isn't going to come so easy anymore, I can tell you. Now leave me alone. I'm busy."

Marian began looking for work.

10

MARIAN HAD NO WAY OF KNOWING WHETHER OR TO WHAT extent Dale was lying when he told her that he was broke. She gathered from the Sullivans and others that his cattle operations were not doing well and that other investments were going sour. But unless she went to a lawyer, filed for divorce, and got the court to require an accounting, she would be in the dark about his finances. She hesitated to take those steps for several reasons. Dale had all the advantages in any legal battle in Saline County. She doubted that she could find any lawyer who would be willing or able to stand up to him, or for that matter any judge. She knew Dale well enough to believe that he would stop at nothing to win, especially with Martha urging him on, and would probably be able to hide whatever assets he had. Nor did she like the idea of dragging her children into open warfare with their father: It might come to that, but Marian did not wish to make the first move. On top of these considerations, in spite of the mounting evidence of Dale's intransigence and disaffection, she still harbored hopes that he would return to her. Seeing how rotten he looked at his office encouraged her to believe that eventually he would tire of living that way and come to his senses. Her hopes were by now less than bright, but they persisted; she still could not see how she could possibly go it alone with the four boys.

Pat Sullivan had tried to warn Dale for years about some of his business errors. Pat had let Dale in as an investor in a company formed to construct dormitories at Southern Illinois University and had lived to regret it. Dale was constantly demanding unnecessary meetings and coming up with absurd ideas to cut costs and improve profits. He was so vehement about his crackbrained construction theories, and he was taking up so much time with his meetings, that Pat was finally able to trade him a horse farm in Hamilton County for his interest. Pat watched with amusement as Dale suddenly began wearing cowboy boots and talking as if he were about to establish another King Ranch.

As Pat Sullivan understood them, Dale's problems were similar to those of many physicians who were inept with their investments. They had all this cash on hand, and they mistook their competence in earning money as doctors for business sense. Instead of putting their money into conservative stocks or government securities, they got involved in hands-on businesses, the kind—like cattle breeding—that require constant personal attention to make them profitable. Doctors often got bored with the routines of their practices and sought the excitement of business risks, without understanding that they were in over their heads.

But if Dale's business mistakes were common to doctors, he seemed compelled to commit them in the biggest possible way; and his apparently limitless bravado led him into one disaster after another. His choice of exotic European cattle breeds, for instance, was based on scientific knowledge but ignored practical experience. By the mid-sixties breeders all over the country were beginning to discover that bigger was not necessarily better. These huge breeds had a disproportionate ratio of bone to meat, making them less valuable per pound on the market; and their enormous, increasing birth weights meant a higher death rate for both calves and mothers.

But Dale was determined to prove himself a master of business as of medicine. He was the same about everything, from bridge to golf to shooting. He would not try something unless he could be the best. Everyone who knew him well called him Napoleon, though not to his face. He was Napoleon in Little Egypt.

Pat Sullivan was especially pessimistic about the future of Dale's investments in catfish farming at both the Galatia and Hickory Handle properties. It was not only the expense of the ponds and hatcheries; it was another example of Dale's obsession with the scientific side of production and his ignoring of basic business sense. When Dale began construction of the processing plant at the Handle, Pat asked him whether he had taken marketing into consideration:

"Who's going to buy these fish, Dale? Have you contracted to sell them? There sure aren't enough people around here to eat them. They can get all they need from the river. I mean, have you contacted the Bird's-Eye people or some frozen-food outfit?"

"I'm not worried about that," Dale brushed him off. "It's a gold mine. All over the country."

"Well, I'm telling you," Pat said, marveling at the extent of the operation, "you're going to be up to your ass in catfish."

Even Pat Sullivan with all his common sense and friendly concern could not know every dark corner of Dale's business follies. Marian's uncle Eddie Bell, who had had some success investing in the stock market, got a telephone call from Dale one day asking for advice. He had some cash on hand, Dale said, and needed a promising stock. Eddie Bell recommended Curtiss-Wright, which at the time was selling at about forty dollars a share. Dale said that he would take the advice.

Six months later Dale called again. What in hell was the matter with Curtiss-Wright? he wanted to know. It had not moved at all. It was down half a point. Eddie Bell told Dale to be patient. The stock would show some sort of gain in due time, and in the meanwhile it was paying a nice dividend and Dale's money was safe.

"I'm looking for a profit," Dale said. "I don't care about any penny-ante dividend."

"How many shares did you buy?"

"Six thousand," Dale said.

"Six *thousand*! You bought six thousand shares of one stock just on my recommendation? Jesus H. Christ."

Dale hung up. Eddie was horrified that Dale had sunk something like a quarter of a million dollars into a single stock. He doubted that Dale had that kind of cash: He must have bought the stock on margin; he might have lost it all by now. Eddie wondered whether Dale was as bright as everyone, including Dale himself, believed.

Another Eddie, an unlikely figure named Eddie Miller, knew more about Dale's business dealings and financial situation than anyone else. Eddie Miller took over for Marilyn Leonard as Dale's office manager and bookkeeper after she quit for good in 1958. For the decade that followed, Eddie became, more than Marilyn ever was, the doctor's confidant in everything having to do with the income and outflow of money from his medical practice and from all the other enterprises that gradually took up more and more of Dale's time and energy.

Marilyn and Chuck decided to leave Eldorado for more lucrative and promising positions in a wealthy suburb of Chicago. To the end Marilyn's relations with Dale were friendly but stormy; he continued to try to get her involved in practices of which she did not approve, and by the time she finally left she had come to know a vindictive side to him that she found unattractive. He ran for election to the school board, as he told her gleefully, only to get back at the history teacher who had given him B's and prevented him from becoming class valedictorian back in 1943. That teacher was now the principal at Eldorado High, a man whom Chuck enjoyed working for and whom everyone liked and respected. But Dale had it in for him.

It was one of the principal's minor duties to collect the money from the sale of hot dogs and soft drinks after Friday night or Saturday football or basketball games. A big game could bring in two or three hundred dollars. The principal took the money home in a shoebox and delivered it to the athletic department promptly Monday morning.

Once on the school board, Dale started a private investigation. He arranged for the students who were selling food and drink to count up the receipts and give him the results before turning the money over to the principal, swearing them to secrecy. He discovered, he told Marilyn, that the principal was skimming. The amount he was turning in to the athletic department was a few dollars short of the students' totals. He confronted the principal and threatened to expose him. It would be his word against Dr. Cavaness's.

The man protested his innocence, Dale said, but resigned, moved away, and took a job selling insurance. Dale had routed his old enemy. To Marilyn and Chuck the episode was unpleasant. Even if the man had been guilty, which they doubted, it was not a crime warranting his resignation. He was underpaid anyway, and it would hardly have been a blot against his character if he had taken a couple of dollars for beer money.

Marilyn spent her last three weeks at the office training her replacement. Edward E. Miller, C.P.H.M. (Certificate of Public Health Management), had been a patient of Dale's for two years. He was in his mid-twenties then, a shy, sensitive young man with a weight problem, a Harrisburg native who lived with his sick mother and played the organ at the Presbyterian church. He was fascinated by Dale—his dynamic manner, his warmth, his worldly air, his beautiful suits. He told his mother that he had never seen suits like the ones Dr. Cavaness wore. He leaped at the chance to work for Dale.

Eddie Miller's roots in Little Egypt were deep—his grandmother had been present at Charlie Birger's hanging and had always insisted that Charlie's last words had been "Good-bye, beautiful world," not the accepted version—and like most of Dale's patients he was but dimly conscious of the wider world. To him Dale Cavaness seemed an emissary from sophisticated places beyond the understanding of ordinary folk, a man of medical genius who out of love for his home and a desire to serve had returned, an inspiration to all, yet still a man of the people. He had put Eddie on a diet—morbidly obese was the term for his condition—and was compassionate about his compulsive eating. Eddie's mother loved Dr. Cavaness, too. She had numerous ailments; she said that no other doctor treated her so well. Mrs. Miller depended on her son. She was delighted when he quit his job over in Evansville, Indiana, to go to work for the doctor in Eldorado. It was a step up for him, and now he would be close by at all hours of the day.

During his training period with Marilyn, Eddie found himself shocked by her tumultuous relationship with the doctor. There was an antagonism between them that, as a patient, Eddie had never noticed. He could not imagine talking back to the doctor the way Marilyn Leonard did. She did not even call him doctor. She acted as his equal, which to Eddie seemed indecorous and inappropriate.

"Dale," Marilyn might say, "I'll teach Eddie how to keep the books, goddamnit, and you go find a cure for cancer. If you tell him how to do it, you'll go broke in six months."

121

And Dr. Cavaness would leave the room, slamming the door, saying that it was a good thing that Marilyn was quitting, so that he'd be spared the trouble of firing her.

There were by then five other people besides Eddie Miller working in the office: a file clerk, an insurance clerk, a receptionist and appointments secretary, and a couple of nurses, all of them women. No one talked to the doctor the way Marilyn had. Even after Eddie figured out that Dr. Cavaness actually respected Marilyn for standing up to him, and that it was to Marilyn that he had delegated extraordinary authority for writing checks for every kind of business and personal expense, Eddie knew that his relationship with the doctor would have to be different. Eddie abhorred conflict, for one thing, and he believed in good manners and respect for authority. He resolved to win the doctor over not by confrontation but by making himself indispensable.

Eddie loved figures and records the way he loved church music, as a refuge of order and symmetry. He delighted in making a business letter into a perfect work of art, beautifully spaced, impeccably grammatical, phrased just so. Inside his misshapen, grossly overweight form he had the soul of an accountant or a monk devoted to intricate manuscripts. And he had no distractions. He lived for his organ music, his mother, and now for Dr. Cavaness.

For the first three or four years, everything went as Eddie had hoped and intended. He put Dr. Cavaness's business affairs into glorious order; he came to know far better than the doctor the condition of every account, the whereabouts of every sum. He paid all the bills, including those for the Cavaness home, and he deposited five hundred dollars at a time into Marian's checking account as she needed it, which was whenever the bank called to say that she was overdrawn. His correspondence was a marvel of neatness and precision. In appreciation Dale had built for him a special cubicle, so that he could labor undisturbed. He was the first to arrive in the mornings and the last to depart, often figuring and fussing until late in the evenings.

Apart from the joy he took in imposing order itself, Eddie's greatest satisfaction came from serving this man whom he admired so fervently. His work, Eddie told himself, freed Dr. Cavaness from petty concerns. It gave Eddie a kind of vicarious satisfaction to be near and helpful to someone of such triumphant will and energy and intelligence, a man who drove himself beyond the limits of ordinary men and women, whose learning and brains set him above others. Eddie felt better about himself just having the privilege of aiding this man of decision, this paragon of iron determination. Eddie's was the kind of devotion found usually only in a good soldier or the loyal citizen under a dicatorship.

A few things did bother him. There was never enough money. From the start Eddie found himself juggling accounts and fending off creditors. It was remarkable the way the doctor could spend money as if it did not matter to him or was merely the means to a higher goal—thousands on cattle and farm equipment and numerous other investments, a golf course, a public skeet range, lots here and there, interests in a fluorspar mine in Hardin County, a coal mine in Kentucky. From what Eddie could tell, none of these was bringing in any money as yet, but he assumed that the doctor knew what he was doing for the long term. The income from his practice was nearing two hundred thousand dollars annually and growing, but he was always short.

Eddie got an idea of the scope of Dr. Cavaness's financial plans one morning when the doctor presented him with boxes of new stationery bearing in red and blue ink the letterhead NEW RUHR ENTERPRISES, along with the office address and telephone number.

"This is it," the doctor said. "We're going to use this stationery for all the business correspondence. Keep the medical stuff separate. All the other business is now New Ruhr. I'm consolidating everything."

Eddie said that was fine. He sat at his desk contemplating the letterhead. It sounded remotely familiar, but Eddie could not place it nor understand exactly what the doctor meant by consolidation. Should he change the checks, all the accounts? He went in to see Dr. Cavaness. What was Ruhr? Was it some kind of an acronym?

"You don't know what the Ruhr is?" Dr. Cavaness said. "You ought to know. Everybody ought to know. That's what's wrong around here. Ignorance. Don't you know about Ludwig Erhard, father of the German economic miracle? He was on the cover of *Time*, for Christ's sake. He was Man of the Year. The Ruhr is the economic heart of Germany. Hitler knew that. He had to get the Ruhr back from France to get things moving again. Erhard has made everything happen there. It's an industrial promised land, don't you see?

"What I'm going to do, by God, is turn southern Illinois into another Ruhr. The stationery is just the start. We're going to have economic expansion here like you never dreamed. I'll be head of a consortium. We'll bring in heavy industry, automobile manufacturing, everything. We've got the coal. That's the base. We start with coal and go on from there. It can't miss. Everything is now New Ruhr Enterprises. The interstate at Marion will be just like the Autobahn!"

Dr. Cavaness kept talking about Ludwig Erhard and the Ruhr off and on for the better part of a year. Eddie was reluctant to use the stationery. He tried it a couple of times, writing to a cattle dealer in Oklahoma City and to the Purina feed corporation, manufacturers of catfish pellets. He received puzzled replies stating that the companies had no records of a New Ruhr Enterprises among their customers. Eventually he gathered that the doctor had forgotten about Erhard and the Ruhr. As much as he revered Dr. Cavaness's medical expertise, Eddie found it difficult to imagine southern Illinois as an industrial miracle. An awful lot would have to change.

The doctor, short of cash, borrowed from banks, from friends, even from Dr. Pearce. The relationship with Dr. Pearce was peculiar, Eddie thought. The two men treated each other like father and son, affectionate one minute, screaming at one another the next. Dr. Pearce, to judge from the telephone conversations and the gossip, was nearly as short-tempered as Dr. Cavaness, whose explosions Eddie had had to tolerate from the start. Eddie heard that Dr. Pearce drank heavily, was in trouble with the state for neglecting his welfare patients, and had once in a rage thrown a nurse through a plate-glass door at the hospital. Eddie believed all of this, given the way Dr. Pearce sounded over the phone when Dr. Cavaness asked for money. He would borrow as much as twenty-five thousand at a time from his former father-in-law, sometimes for medical equipment, sometimes for his personal account. He did always try to pay Dr. Pearce back: Eddie had instructions to reimburse Dr. Pearce before anyone else. Most of the others were on hold.

The financial situation seemed to get worse year after year, along with Dr. Cavaness's temper. He would arrive in the mornings looking as if he had not slept and suddenly blow up about some trivial thing, turning on one employee or another, pounding his fists on a desk and screaming that by God, if this or that wasn't taken care of, there would be hell to pay and heads rolling. Eddie endured his share of these outbursts, more as the years passed. His policy was to lower his eyes, grip the sides of his desk, wait for the tantrum to pass, and try not to speak to the doctor for the next two or three days, a silent kind of protest he hoped but doubted would register.

But at other times the doctor could be so sweet and understanding, so personal, that Eddie felt that he could forgive him anything. One day Dr. Cavaness told him that he had just seen his first wife, Helen Jean, for the first time since their divorce. He might never see her again. Her father was ill. She was in town to visit him and to check on things at the hospital, where she had run into Dale. The meeting had been uneventful, Dr. Cavaness said. They had greeted each other politely and that was that.

Eddie and Dr. Cavaness were alone together in the office when he talked about seeing Helen Jean. The doctor reached into his desk and brought out a bottle and poured himself a stiff one into a coffee cup. He offered Eddie a drink.

"No, thank you, Doctor. I don't drink."

Dr. Cavaness wanted to talk about Helen Jean. He had worshiped that woman, he said. He had thought that they were going to have a perfect life together. Did Eddie know that Dr. Pearce had originally called the hospital Pearce-Cavaness? Eddie said that he had heard that. Could Eddie possibly realize how much Helen Jean had meant to him? Had he ever loved anyone like that? Eddie was silent. He thought the conversation was getting more personal than was proper for an employer-employee relationship. But Dr. Cavaness was getting worked up.

"I put that woman on a pedestal! I did everything for her! I scrubbed floors for her! She betrayed me!" Eddie did not know whether the doctor was going to cry or start pounding on his desk or both; he calmed himself, draining his cup. "I can never feel that close to anyone again. Never."

Eddie thought that this was certainly sad for the doctor but also for Marian and the children. Dr. Cavaness hardly ever mentioned them, except to complain that Marian was spending too much money. Of the doctor's family only his father and mother were frequent visitors to the office. He always saw Peck Cavaness immediately, admitting him to the examining room before any of the other patients. Noma Cavaness he let wait and dealt with summarily. Eddie could not understand a man who treated his mother that way. When he spotted her sitting in the waiting room, sometimes for hours, Eddie would come out to chat with Noma, bring her a cup of coffee. It pained him to see her staring at the wall, unattended as a nobody.

Everyone in the office professed to adore Dr. Cavaness's sense of humor; Eddie was not so sure about it. Sometimes his wisecracks brightened the day; at other times the doctor carried things too far and made Eddie nervous. Many of Dr. Cavaness's jokes took advantage of the ignorance of patients, simple people who believed everything the doctor told them as readily and as literally as they believed the Bible.

A widower in his late sixties complained that every time he walked in front of his television set, it changed channels. The man wondered whether he was electrically charged, a human remote-control unit, and asked the doctor to check him out.

Dr. Cavaness obliged, running all sorts of expensive tests, electrocardiograms and so on, and pronounced the patient nonmagnetic and nonelectroconductive. Eddie was as amused at this as the rest of the staff, although he considered the administering of the tests unethical. But the old fellow persisted. His set still changed channels, he said, every time he walked past it. He had to sit dead still to get through an entire program.

"I'll cure him this time," the doctor said. "Set up another appointment. If what this guy wants is a diagnosis, he'll sure as hell get one."

Dr. Cavaness ushered the man into the examining room and told him to take off his clothes:

"I want you buck naked." He called for a light bulb. "Make it a hundred watt. We want to be able to pick up any current."

Dr. Cavaness told the man to bend over. He stuck the end of the light bulb in the man's rectum, twisting it around.

"It lights up all right," the doctor said. "I'll tell you what. You're a regular electrical conduit."

"What do I do now?"

"There's only one thing you can do. Every time you watch TV, you've got to wrap your feet in aluminum foil. That's the only way you'll be nonconductive."

The man did as he was told but was soon calling again saying his set was still changing channels. When Dr. Cavaness refused to see him, he finally caught on. He complained around town that Dr. Cavaness had made a fool of him, but people either did not believe it or thought it was funny, another good Dr. Dale story.

If Eddie Miller considered that episode distasteful and cruel, the doctor thought it was so funny that he told everybody about it, even Kevin and Marian, repeating it over and over at parties. He did not brag about the time he reduced his sixteen-year-old file clerk to tears and near-hysteria when he called the police on her. She had driven the doctor's new Olds 98 on an errand but by mistake returned with a car of the same year, model and color which was parked in the same lot but happened to be owned by another man. By a chance remote but familiar to policemen and thieves, the same keys fit both cars.

Dr. Cavaness realized the girl's mistake when he noticed his black bag missing from the trunk. He knew who the owner of the identical car was, clued him in, and talked a couple of Eldorado policemen into bursting into the office, handcuffing the girl, and telling her that she faced twenty years in prison.

The joke was all right for a minute or two, but Dr. Cavaness pressed it. He shouted at the girl that she was a no-good liar and urged the cops to throw the book at her. He relented when she began sobbing as the police led her out the door.

The girl quit her job. Dr. Cavaness said he had no use for anybody who couldn't take a joke.

The incident altered Eddie's perspective. He was friends with the girl and her family. He tried making excuses for Dr. Cavaness, but he saw that the doctor's misdirected sense of humor had wounded a defenseless creature, a naïve, unworldly young woman who had placed her trust in authority and had been betrayed. He wondered whether Dr. Cavaness understood the pain he had caused.

At some point around 1965 or '66, Eddie began to feel anxious about his job. I know too much, he thought. The doctor began revealing things and showing sides of himself that Eddie would have preferred not to know about. Just after seven one morning Dr. Cavaness arrived at the office looking as if he had slept in his clothes, smelling of drink, carrying a thermos cup. He sat down with Eddie and said that he could not resist telling how he had spent the evening.

He named a certain businessman who had been hounding him about an unpaid bill. The man had threatened to file suit. Eddie had already answered a hostile letter from an out-of-town lawyer.

"I fixed that son of a bitch," Dr. Cavaness said. "He won't be bothering us from now on."

Dr. Cavaness had been sitting around last night, he said, having a few drinks and thinking about this bastard and how he thought he was so high-and-mighty.

"I decided to make a house call."

He drove over to the man's house. It was late, after midnight. He took out the pistol he always kept loaded in his glove compartment and walked right up and rang the bell. The wife opened the door in her nightgown. He told her to get her husband out of bed. He showed her the gun.

The man came down in his robe. The doctor directed them into his car. He drove them out into the country and ordered them out. He told them that he hoped they enjoyed the stroll home. If they ever said one word about suing him again, they could figure out what the next step would be.

Eddie wanted to quit right then, but he held his tongue. Maybe the doctor was still drunk and hallucinating or bragging about something he had imagined in his dreams or in a drunken fantasy.

What Eddie learned about Dr. Cavaness and women also made him anxious. From his earliest days at the office, Eddie had observed the doctor's power over women. Most of the nurses and other female employees seemed to be in love with him. The spectacle had its amusing aspects, as when the doctor bought hundreds of dollars' worth of tickets to get a young woman elected Miss Boat Queen in an Ohio River beauty contest and then hired her briefly as a nurse. That young woman was none the worse for her acquaintance with Dr. Cavaness, but over the years Eddie became aware of another, more typical pattern with the doctor and his girlfriends: Eddie could count at least twenty.

The doctor would ingratiate himself one way or another, win the woman over, and then brutally drop her. Eddie could document these affairs: He was the one who wrote the checks to the women, arranged for gifts to be sent to them. One specially favored woman was deeded a few acres of the doctor's Hickory Handle farm.

The women's reaction on being dropped was usually unpleasant to witness and, having acted as the doctor's official dispenser of largesse, Eddie felt like an accomplice, at least an accessory to what seemed to him crimes against the human heart. One married nurse became a Demerol addict after Dr. Cavaness rejected her. Her moods rocketed from euphoria to depression until she lost muscle coordination and collapsed in fits of vomiting. Dr. Cavaness fired her.

He was adept at finding a weakness and exploiting it. He won over a married patient whose child had died, inching his way in, commiserating with her, until she divorced her husband in anticipation, it seemed obvious, of the doctor's divorcing his wife and marrying her. Her husband took her back after the doctor dumped her. One time after another, the story repeated itself. He would flatter the women, send them gifts of cash or, sometimes, cheap jewelry or perfume, seduce them, and then cut them off.

Most of them continued as patients or as nurses, hanging around, hoping. He paid decent wages. All seemed to remain loyal to him, as if he had cast a spell.

It was the same with the doctor's drinking as with his womanizing: Everybody knew about it; nobody questioned it. The drinking, by 1966 and after, became legendary, part of the Dr. Cavaness mystique. Eddie recognized the extent of it when he found four thermoses full of liquor on the front seat of the doctor's car. His curiosity piqued, Eddie made a habit of glancing into the car; the thermoses were always there, ready for the road. At the office the doctor had one bottle in his desk, others stashed in a cabinet. It became usual for him to show up at the office cup in hand, jittery from a hangover. He would drop his pants in front of the employees and have one of the nurses give him a shot. What was in the syringe, Eddie did not know, maybe vitamin B_{12}, maybe something else.

He performed most of his operations in the mornings. The nurses told Eddie that they kept a special oxygen bottle in the operating room so that Dr. Cavaness could clear his head before cutting someone. It was no secret, they said. Everybody knew about it— except of course the patients.

Dr. Cavaness distributed amphetamines among the staff like candy. There were always plenty of samples from the salesmen lying around, packets of Fastin and Obestat and other appetite suppressants. He put Eddie on a regular dosage of Obestat to control his weight, until Eddie noticed that the pills were making it impossible for him to concentrate or sleep and turning him into a nervous wreck.

"Eddie, you'll just eat yourself into oblivion," Dr. Cavaness said when Eddie asked him to help him get off the Obestat. "You want to kill yourself? Go ahead." Eddie managed to break the habit on his own, deciding that he would rather be fat than deranged. He wondered why his own doctor would give him such bad advice.

By 1967 Eddie was trying to get up the nerve to quit. Working for Dr. Cavaness had become like having a secret life that nobody would believe if you tried to tell them about it. He still admired the doctor's brilliant mind; he continued to believe that Dale Cavaness had at least started out with humanitarian impulses. But he could no longer ignore the signs that the doctor was going to pieces, cared more about money than medicine, was out to destroy himself and did not mind if he took down other people with him. Eddie did not know a great deal about the doctor's family life, but he gathered that it had become a shambles; the word was that he was not living at home. At times Eddie felt sorry for Dr. Cavaness, who for all his success seemed to set himself up for failure. Even when he made a sound investment, he pulled out before it had time to mature. He put money into a development at Lake Barkley over in Kentucky, for instance, which would have made him rich had he not sold out to cover his losses in a coal mine.

By 1967 the financial situation was so chaotic that Eddie began concealing deposits from Dr. Cavaness, hoping that if he did not know the money was in the bank, he could not spend it. The doctor ordered Eddie to cut off Marian's credit at the grocery and liquor stores. She was spending too much and becoming an alcoholic, the doctor said, neither of which Eddie believed, although he imagined that anyone would need to drink to stay married to the man. He also told Eddie to stop putting money into Marian's checking account.

Eddie could not bring himself to follow these orders, although disobeying them frightened him. He did not cancel Marian's credit, and he surreptitiously transferred money from other accounts into hers, hoping that the doctor would not notice or would forget and shift his anger onto another woman or a creditor. Eddie believed that Marian must have badly misjudged her husband—not that she was alone in that. Certainly she had underestimated his hostility and capacity for treachery. He guessed that she knew little of the extent to which her husband had betrayed her, nothing of the way he had mortgaged his family's future.

A new tale of Dr. Cavaness's womanizing was making the rounds. Supposedly he had at least one other affair going besides the one with Martha Culley, which by then everyone knew about. This other woman lived in an apartment in Harrisburg. Dr. Cavaness arrived to visit her one night and encountered a friend of his there: The other man had been seeing the woman earlier in the evenings and departing before the doctor customarily arrived. The two men fought in the street, in view of the neighbors. The other fellow was taller and looked far stronger, but the doctor had won, nearly biting off his rival's little finger and sending him howling away. What the doctor then did to the woman, no one could say. There had been a lot of shouting coming from her apartment.

Given the traditions of Little Egypt, as Eddie Miller knew, a story such as this one would do little to shake the faith of most of Dr. Cavaness's patients; it would only add to his aura as a man beyond ordinary mortals. The doctor was a monarch who ranged about his kingdom with impunity. And what could his wife do about it? Where could she go? She was trapped. She could only hang on, serving out what was probably a life sentence.

Dr. Cavaness was now directing his rages more frequently against Eddie, berating him, ridiculing him, telling him that he was lucky to have his job. Eddie told his mother that he was going to have to quit, but she urged him to stick it out, afraid that he would end up unemployed, unable to support her; and he could not bring himself to tell her how bad things really were at the office, how he was having to do things that might put him in danger if the doctor found out about them, how he was taking abuse that was wiping out whatever self-confidence he had left.

Eddie's only solace, his only way of getting free from the demands of Dr. Cavaness and of his mother, was playing the organ at church on Sunday over in Evansville. He would leave on Saturday afternoons, have dinner in Evansville, sleep in a motel, escape into music on Sunday morning, and return to fix his mother's supper, dreading Monday.

Dr. Cavaness knew about these excursions. He kidded Eddie about them, saying that if it weren't for his weekends, Eddie might crack up, what with all the pressure he had from his mother and his responsibilities at the office. There was something nasty, something taunting about the way Dr. Cavaness talked about the weekends, that frightened Eddie. Did Dr. Cavaness want to control the weekends also? Was it not enough that Eddie slaved for him all week, was endangering his sanity for him?

One Saturday evening Eddie was eating alone in an Evansville café when a strange man walked in and said hello, calling him by name, looking him in the eye, then sitting down at another table. The man was rough in appearance, almost an itinerant, dirty, unshaven. He ordered coffee.

The only people Eddie knew in Evansville were members of the Presbyterian church. He panicked. He paid his check and drove straight home to Harrisburg. He felt certain that Dr. Cavaness had had him followed—but why? To intimidate him? To try to get something on him? To see if he was up to something on the weekends?

Only the previous Wednesday Eddie had finally got up the nerve to tell Dr. Cavaness that he wanted to give notice. The doctor had gone into a rage. There was the usual fist-pounding and screaming. The doctor threw a lamp against a wall.

"I won't stay here!" Eddie found himself shouting back. He was surprised by his courage. It was the first time he had defied Dr. Cavaness.

"You won't leave, either!" the doctor yelled. "You can bet your sweet ass on that!" He leaned over the desk spraying spittle. "If you think you're leaving, you're crazy. What makes you think you can get another job, anyway? I'll ruin you. I'll wreck your life. Your mother will be in the street. You have no idea what I can do to you. You're a nobody. You work here and take what you can get, is that it? Well, let me tell you something, mister. You stay put or you'll regret it, you can count on that. I guess you haven't thought about what I can do to you. And I've got more than one option."

Eddie was terrified. He thought of the people the doctor had taken out into the night at gunpoint. He thought of the school principal, of the women the doctor had ruined, of Marian and the children.

And after encountering the stranger in Evansville, Eddie was paralyzed. He saw that he had succeeded in making himself indispensable—but to the doctor's ego, not only to his business. And he knew too much.

Eddie thought about himself and everyone who worked for Dr. Cavaness. The doctor could not tolerate independence or insubordination of any kind. We are all his slaves, Eddie said to himself.

Understanding the dominance Dr. Cavaness had achieved over him drove Eddie deeper into self-disgust. At home at night, his mother positioned in front of the television set, he shut himself into his room. He came to believe that if he did not quit his job he would end up in an institution. Every few weeks he forced himself to start clearing out his desk at the office, but the doctor always threatened him, jeered at him, and weakened him again. It was like a fatal marriage, Eddie thought. His position was the same as Marian's. If she ever tried to leave, the doctor would find some way to ruin her, directly or indirectly. She was a prisoner.

Eddie tried to envision himself in another job. He saw himself going to pieces, getting fired, failing his mother. On many days he resigned himself to working for Dr. Cavaness or to going insane, or both. He lived constantly with a sharp pain shooting upward from his chest to his throat. He ate more compulsively than ever and ballooned. His music no longer soothed him: The gloom of the hymns weighed him down. He was like a man with a cancer who can think of nothing else.

11

EDDIE MILLER FINALLY GOT UP THE COURAGE TO QUIT ONE DAY late in 1968. Dr. Cavaness tossed an arts and crafts catalog onto Eddie's desk and told him to order four hundred dollars' worth of macramé materials for a certain married woman.

"She needs a hobby," the doctor said.

Eddie thought over this latest demand. He was dizzy with indignation. He knew the woman, understood her fragile nervous state. The doctor was setting her up and asking Eddie to participate in the scheme, to act as his pander again. If I do this, Eddie thought, I am no better than he is. Before giving himself a chance to change his mind, he took the catalog in to Dr. Cavaness and placed it on his desk.

"I won't do it," Eddie said.

There was the expected reaction. But Eddie walked back to his cubicle and began clearing out his desk. He was frightened, but he felt clean and proud. The doctor rushed in ranting, waving his arms. Eddie continued packing up in his careful, methodical way. He wanted to leave everything in perfect order. His last act, before walking out the door with Dr. Cavaness screaming at him, was to straighten the rows of ledgers on his shelves.

Two days later a note scrawled in the doctor's hand was delivered to Eddie's house: "You'll regret this" was all it said. His mother was frantic, but Eddie found another job with a doctor in Harrisburg. Dr. Cavaness telephoned the other doctor and accused him of trying to sabotage his practice, demanding that he fire Eddie.

Eddie held on to his new job. Memories and nightmares about Dr. Cavaness haunted him. At home he was afraid to answer the telephone. But he prayed, immersed himself in music, pleased his new employer with meticulous work. He was encouraged when two other office workers left Dr. Cavaness and visited Eddie to tell him how much they admired him and had been inspired by his bravery. They too had felt trapped and feared reprisals. They all agreed to keep one another posted about notes or telephone calls.

Eddie's departure meant that Marian's checks started to bounce, although she had no way of understanding the cause and effect, no idea of the role he had played in keeping her solvent. She took a teaching job at the Harrisburg nurses' training school that brought home eight hundred dollars a month. The size of her paycheck showed her what it would be like to try to support her children by herself. Thank goodness the house was clear and Dale still paid the grocery bill. With baby-sitting expenses five days a week, she was no longer living the life of the carefree socialite, she kidded herself, no longer part of the Eldorado fast lane, the southern Illinois jet set! One month she found herself with an extra hundred dollars and bought Mark, Kevin and Sean monogrammed shirts to wear to school. They made fun of her and refused to put them on, but she wanted them to know, somehow, that she thought her boys were special.

She wondered how much Dale was giving Martha. She tried not to let her sons know what a bastard their father was being: She despised women who did that; it only tortured the children and screwed them up. They were Dale's sons, and someday he would pay for their college educations and learn to be proud of them. Dale came by in the mornings for his laundry; she felt foolish doing it, but, she reasoned, apart from the hopes she still harbored, it was an excuse for Dale to see the boys.

Sean was particularly attached to Dale, hugging him and clinging to him whenever he saw him, sometimes getting up early so as to be sure not to miss him, in contrast to Mark and Kevin, who kept their distance. Kevin especially was reserved around his father: But that was Kevin, watchful and self-contained; of them all, Marian worried least about him. In Dale's absence, Sean followed Mark around and imitated him until people began to say that the two brothers were alike, although to Marian they were not.

Sean had none of Mark's casual airs and outward self-confidence: Marian knew that in his heart Mark must have been suffering from his father's coldness to him, but he had many friends, was a great favorite with the girls, seemed to be managing to find his own world. Sean clung to adults and was uneasy at school. He froze when faced with a test, no matter how many hours Marian spent coaching him in reading and arithmetic. Sean was always in search of a grown-up audience and became a kind of local character in his quest for approval. He liked to walk into town wearing his cowboy hat, his little boots and his toy six-gun, buttonholing adults in mimicry of the Westerns he saw on television. He strolled into Lou Beck's pharmacy one afternoon, settled onto a stool at the soda fountain and called out in his version of a John Wayne voice:

"Why, Lou Beck! I haven't seen you in well nigh thirty years!"

Raising four boys on her own became a challenge Marian sometimes despaired of meeting. There were continuous crises, some that would have been minimized by having a sensible man around who could exert discipline without losing control, others that required her to contact Dale in spite of everything, as reluctant as she was to rely on him. Grandpa Peck did his best to fill in for his errant son and made no secret to Marian of his disgust with Dale's irresponsibility. But Peck was pushing seventy. Things happened that were beyond his help.

On an autumn Sunday afternoon in 1969, when Mark was fifteen, Kevin thirteen, and Sean seven, Peck piled the boys into his old Plymouth Fury and took them hunting at the Galatia farm. They were not after anything in particular, squirrels or rabbits maybe, out just to enjoy the Indian summer day in the open. Mark carried a pump-action .22, Kevin the single-shot .22 rifle that Peck had given him and that Kevin was sure was the best gun in the world. Sean trailed along, too young to hunt but anxious to be a part of the adventure.

They walked down the graveled road, tire tracks with weeds sprouting in the center hump, Mark in the lead, Kevin a few yards behind him, Sean and Peck bringing up the rear. Mark and Kevin were shooting as they walked, picking out tree trunks, rocks, tin cans.

Mark stopped to shoot at the surface of a pond. Kevin kept on, wondering whether Mark had found a turtle, drew up next to his brother on the left and, as Mark paused in his firing, walked past him. Mark fired again.

Kevin fell to his knees. He was still holding his rifle. He saw blood on the rifle. He felt pain on the right side of his face and was conscious of a terrific ringing in his right ear.

Kevin heard Grandpa call his name, felt him grab from behind and pull him to his feet. He swayed in Grandpa's arms and figured he was about to pass out. His face throbbed, blood ran down his T-shirt. He bent his right arm and the blood was warm in the crook. He brought his hand up to his face, fingered a wound in the wet, loose flesh at the bottom of his ear and below.

Maybe Mark only shot a hunk out of my ear, Kevin thought, maybe I'm lucky. He took deep breaths and was surprised that he was standing, with all this blood.

Then he heard Mark's voice:

"I killed him! I killed him!"

"Do I look dead?" Kevin wanted to say, but the words would not come out. Grandpa's face was horror-struck. I guess he thinks I'm dead, too, Kevin thought. Maybe I am, but why am I standing?

Mark threw his gun into the woods, shouting, "I killed him, I killed him."

"Get the gun and help me get Kevin into the car," Grandpa said. "Hurry up."

"He hates me! He hates me!" Mark cried.

It was about two hundred yards to the car. Sean ran about speechless, frantic.

They helped Kevin into the backseat, still holding tight to his face with his right hand. He could make out two wounds now, one with his thumb, just below the ear, the other with his little finger, up beside his nose. He pressed his fingers into the holes to try to stop the blood. I survived a gunshot, he thought, but I might bleed to death.

Mark was crying. I'm the one who's hurt, Kevin thought, but

I'm not crying. On the main highway Grandpa pushed the Plymouth up to ninety, fishtailing around curves. Kevin wondered whether they would fly off the road and die that way, all of them together.

"Are you all right back there?" Grandpa shouted.

"It hurts," Kevin said. His head felt like someone was hammering it with a sledge. Sean, squeezed in beside Mark in the front, started crying.

"What are *you* crying for?" Kevin said.

"It hurts!" Sean said.

It was eleven miles to Eldorado. They had to find Dale. The Fourth Street house was on the way to Pearce Hospital and Grandpa stopped there first: Marian might know where Dale was. On a Sunday he might be anywhere.

But Dale happened to be at the house picking up some clothes; they spotted him in the garage. Mark leaped out of the car shouting "I killed Kevin! I killed Kevin!" and Marian ran down the steps, took one look at Kevin and started jumping up and down.

"Get him to the hospital," Dale said.

The bullet had tunneled through the side of Kevin's face, entering near the jawline below the ear and exiting beside the nose. It had been such a close shot that stipplings of gunpowder dotted the face and dirtied the entrance wound. For some reason the hospital's stock of proper cleansing agents was depleted, and it was a Sunday; so Dale contacted a local gun merchant, had him open up his shop, and swabbed the wound with gun solvent. He ran a wire up the entrance wound and out the exit to remove bullet fragments.

Friends gathered with Marian at the hospital during the two-hour operation. Everyone crowded forward as Dale emerged from surgery.

"He's going to make it," Dale said to no one in particular as he walked down the corridor, striding past Marian without looking at her.

Marian waited at Kevin's bedside for him to wake up. When Dale strode in with a nurse to check on his patient, he spoke to Marian for the first time since the accident.

"Don't think this is going to make any difference in our relationship," he said.

Standing holding the still-unconscious Kevin's hand, feeling as if she had just been knifed, Marian thought that if Dale felt compelled to be that cold and cruel he might have had the decency to wait until the nurse was out of the room.

Kevin recovered. The facial nerve had been hit but not severed; the right side of his mouth drooped for several weeks, as if he had had a stroke, then returned to normal. Kevin held no grudge against his brother. He knew he ought not to have walked in front of Mark, who had been aiming with his right eye, his left eye shut. Kevin had come up on Mark's blind side.

"You were real lucky," Dale told him. "If your head had been turned a quarter inch either way, you'd be blind or dead. It's amazing the way that bullet went through. You couldn't hold a man down on the ground and shoot him and expect a bullet to pass through that way."

There were other close calls. Knowing Sean's enthusiasm for cowboys, Grandpa Peck took him riding one day at a friend's farm. Sean brushed too close to the rear of a horse and got kicked in the side of the head.

By the time Peck brought him home, Sean's face was swelling, blood and fluid were dripping from his ear and, trying to clean his wounds, Marian noticed that the top of the ear had been torn loose. She rushed him to Pearce.

At the hospital Dale cleaned and stitched up the ear without an anesthetic, to Marian's irritation and alarm. Afterward he poked at Sean's face and gave him a rude slap that set him crying anew and made Marian protest. Wasn't he being rather rough on the boy?

"He'll be all right," Dale said. "You don't need to call me about this again. I don't have time to play baby-sitter. Let the kid grow up."

Dale's behavior upset Marian more than the injury had done. She was always hearing what a kind and considerate doctor Dale was, but he had treated Sean no better than a wounded calf.

Yet she resigned herself to hanging on, living this way indefinitely, concentrating on her children, letting Dale do as he pleased, calling on him in a crisis, as she believed she must. Eventually, she supposed, she and Dale would divorce; but she would stay on in the house until the boys were old enough to fend for themselves. She often considered moving away, but uprooting the children and relying on Dale to send money seemed too risky.

She made it through Christmas, 1969. Dale had now been gone nearly four years. He had slept in her bed only once in all that time, on the ghastly night when Martha honked in the street. For the past several months, Marian realized, apart from the period of Kevin's injury, she no longer lay awake all night. Nothing Dale did surprised her now. If he wanted somebody like Martha for his old age, or one of the other women he appeared to get involved with, so be it. His actions were beyond reasonable explanation.

Patrick's baby-sitter was Marian's only paid help: The era of housekeepers and gardeners, not to speak of shopping expeditions to St. Louis and Colorado and Florida holidays, was over. Every once in a while Marian caught herself drinking too much. There were nights when, exhausted after a full day's work and making dinner and tidying up the house, she wanted to lock herself in her room with a glass and forget the world. A drink or two brought memories of Dale and herself wishing that they could grow old together, die on the same day and have their ashes scattered on Candlewood Lake. What a man he had been then, alive with energy and fun and promise! What a son of a bitch he had become!

Was there a chance that he could change back into the man she had loved—loved still, if only he would be himself again? But then she would scold herself for being so foolish, idiotic, immature—all the other things that you were not supposed to be. And she would pour her drink down the sink and count blessings: her sons, her decent job, the house that was her security. At her age, her mother had been keeping house for a Latin teacher. All around her in Eldorado, people were living on relief.

On the afternoon of February 17, 1970, Marian was at work, teaching young women how to take a patient's blood pressure, when she was called to the telephone. It was a member of the Eldorado Volunteer Fire Department, auxiliary branch, telling her that she had better get home. Her house was on fire.

Marian's first thought was for Patrick, there with the baby-sitter. Patrick was fine, the man said. He had escaped with his dog. The baby-sitter was all right, too, but Marian had better get home right away.

By the time she arrived, the fire was out. She embraced Patrick, who was standing in the street with the baby-sitter and neighbors.

The house was gutted, a ruin of ashes and water. The fire had started in the family room, where the fiberglass drapes went up quickly, the flames spreading upward through the paneling to the upstairs bedrooms and the roof. Had the main crew of the volunteer fighters not been busy putting out a grass fire in the countryside, they might have been able to save the house. The auxiliaries had done the best they could, but they were inexperienced and had arrived too late. More time had been lost when they had run over the hoses with their truck.

Everything was gone. In the living room the big breakfront holding Marian's grandmother's mother-of-pearl dishes and cut-glass bowls and vases had been smashed with an ax. Her heirlooms lay in pieces in the inches of water on the floor. At least her piano had not been damaged, Marian thought bitterly. She had sold it to pay bills a year before.

The upstairs was hopeless: all her clothes, Dale's suits, everything belonging to the boys. And everywhere the powerful, sickening smell of ashes and water. Nothing was left of the family room, the hi-fi and record collection, the stuffed birds, Dale's best guns. The firemen counted eighty-eight rifles, pistols, and shotguns taken from various parts of the house, most of them beyond saving. Piled on the front lawn, they looked like the end of a war.

In the downstairs hallway Marian managed to save some albums of family photographs and Dale's love letters from their courtship, which she had stored in a cupboard beneath the Great Books of the Western World.

Dale arrived. They could not speak to each other. Kevin rushed up, holding Sean by the hand. Kevin, who was in the eighth grade, had been attending a special class at the high school and was riding in a bus when he passed within a block of the house and saw the smoke and flames. He could not convince the driver to stop. Back at the elementary school, he told the principal that his house was burning down, fetched Sean out of class and ran home with him.

"What are we going to do?" Kevin asked his mother as they stood staring at the wreckage.

"I don't know," Marian said. Patrick held on to her skirt and she pressed his head to her.

Patrick, then three and a half, had started the fire. He had been playing with his toys in the family room. The baby-sitter—an old woman, not Jewel Kinnear—was in the kitchen. Patrick had taken some of his toys out of their box and placed them in a paper sack. Somehow he had got hold of a book of matches and managed to strike one and set fire to the sack. The drapes caught. The baby-sitter panicked and ran into the street. Patrick's dog led him out.

Marian had warned the baby-sitter about Patrick's fascination with fire and had instructed her to make sure that he never got near any matches. It was bad enough that she had not been watching him closely, but to run away, leaving him in the burning house! It was a miracle that the dog had barked and Patrick had followed him out: That was what the firemen said must have happened. As for the baby-sitter, she disappeared once the firemen got there.

But Marian blamed Dale more than the baby-sitter. Marian would never have left the child at home had Dale not forced her to go to work. This was exactly the sort of thing that happened to mothers who did not stay home with their young children. She would never have had a fourth child had she known that she would be unable to care for him properly.

Everything was going to hell. She had no home, no money. She could not go to work and leave Patrick again: It would take months—years!—to reassure him that the fire was not his fault but the fault of irresponsible adults. What on earth was she going to do?

Marian and the boys stayed with Peck and Noma for the first few days. Then Kevin and Mark went to friends' houses. Shirley Oshel, a friend who had helped Marian get the nurse's training job, kindly offered her house while she and her husband were away in Springfield for several weeks. Marian and the boys remained at the Oshels' for as long as they could, but Dale did nothing to have the old house torn down and a new one started. By May, Marian was stuck at the Harrisburg Motel with Patrick, the other boys living with friends once again.

Marian was beside herself. She knew that the house on Fourth Street was insured for a hundred thousand dollars: She asked Dale how long he expected her to wait to have the debris cleared and a new house built. He said he had no idea. She told him that it was a disgrace. Had he forgotten that he had a family? What was she supposed to do, go live in a boxcar? If he didn't do something quickly, she would go out and buy a new house herself. She was desperate, depending on friends, wearing borrowed clothes; the boys looked like orphans. Dale told her that she had better not go and do something stupid. He would have to sign the papers for a new house. She would only make a fool of herself.

Dale bought a used forty-foot trailer and a new one and placed them in a lot on Scott Street, at the edge of town. Marian and Pat would have to live in one, the three older boys in the other. For the time being, Dale said.

12

BY THE END OF THE SUMMER MARIAN AND THE BOYS WERE STILL living in the trailers, and the shell of the house on Fourth Street remained standing. Marian believed that work on the new house ought to have been started by now, but nothing was happening. She had been unable to force Dale to talk to her about the plans. She did manage to wheedle him into paying Kevin's tuition at a private school in St. Louis. He was such a good student that she wanted to give him the advantage of a better education than he could receive in Eldorado, and she hoped that being in a different atmosphere would encourage him. She was pleased when Dale agreed to come up with the money—she took it as a sign that he might be mellowing; maybe the fire had shocked him into paying more attention to his children.

But the experiment did not work out. The school, Chaminade, was too radical a change for Kevin. He lasted only three weeks before telling his mother that if she did not come to take him home, he was going to hitchhike to Florida. The Catholic brothers beat the students with coat hangers, Kevin said, and the other boys made fun of him because of his country accent and would have nothing to do with him. He returned and entered Eldorado High School.

The Cavanesses celebrated Thanksgiving in the trailers that year. Dale dropped in for an hour or so. Grandpa Peck took Marian outside and for the first time confided to her that he was worried that something was seriously the matter with Dale. He did not know what it was. Dale had returned Peck's dogs to him one day after hunting, and Peck dared to challenge him.

"Where are you going now?" Peck asked as Dale got back into his car. "I suppose you're going off to see that damn girlfriend of yours. Why don't you see your own family? You've got a son four years old. Do you ever see him? When are you going to build them a new house? You expect them to go on living like vagabonds? I never treated your mother and you that way. Everything I had was yours."

Peck told Marian that he had been working himself up to confront Dale. It had felt good to let it out. But Dale turned on him:

"It's no business of yours! You take care of your own business, old man!"

Peck stepped in front of Dale's car. He pleaded with him to calm down and get hold of himself. He was ruining his life and his children's.

"And then do you know what he did? He just revved up that car and threw her into gear and headed right at me. I had to jump out of the way. I had to roll in the dirt to get away from him. I think he would've run me down. I know he would have."

Peck looked bewildered as he told the story, and very sad. He did not know what was happening to his son, but was inclined to blame everything on Martha. If only Dale could get rid of her, everything might be all right again.

Marian believed otherwise. Whatever was eating away at Dale lay inside him, and as much as she resented Martha, Marian could not imagine that any woman could endure Dale's behavior indefinitely. She would have to be awfully peculiar herself to countenance a man who would try to run over his own father. Sean was present one day when one of Dale's jokes backfired against Martha—the story was confirmed by one of the hired hands at the Galatia farm, who repeated it to Mark. Standing around one afternoon near the lake with Martha, Sean and a couple of the hands, Dale had opened the trunk of his car and forced her into it—just picked Martha up by the seat of her jeans and dropped her into the trunk, slamming the lid while she screamed.

He jumped behind the wheel and backed the car up to the edge of the lake, yelling, "I'm gonna drown you now! I'm gonna drown you!" He kept on backing until the waterline reached the rear bumper and nearly covered the rear wheels. Martha was screaming. Then he threw the car into gear and gunned it, but the wheels started spinning and sinking deeper into the mud. Dale had to rush around behind and open the lid to rescue Martha from drowning. Mad as a wet hen, was how the hired hand described her. Sean said that he had been frightened, although everyone had laughed afterward.

If the tale had involved anyone else, Marian would not have believed it; but it sounded just like Dale. It reminded her of the boat in the swimming pool and of the time when Dale had made fun of another doctor's preppy clothes and had pushed him out of a houseboat into Lake Harrisburg, ending an afternoon's fishing.

With the chaos in their lives, Marian worried that she was losing control of her boys. Half the time she had no idea where Mark was or what he was up to; even little Patrick had taken to running off by himself every time Marian turned her back. He drew a crowd one day when somehow he managed to climb halfway up a television tower. The blackened brick of the house on Fourth Street still stood, a year after the fire. Dale must have blown the insurance money on something else. Marian was desperate.

She wrote her brother in California about her plight but tore the letter up. She was too ashamed to admit the failure of her marriage, and she was reluctant to burden Bill with her troubles. She confided in trusted old friends such as the Sullivans and the Davenports, spending hours confessing her despair, crying, trying to figure out what had gone wrong with Dale. Opening up to anyone was a last resort for Marian; she prided herself on being able to solve her own problems, but she could no longer hold back. Friends consoled her, but they could offer no solutions.

She telephoned Uncle Eddie Bell in St. Louis and told him that her marriage was in trouble. She might have to move to St. Louis, but she was not yet sure how to manage it or whether she could convince the boys that it was necessary. She did not tell Uncle Eddie any details—how she had just about been thrown out into the street with her kids, how cold and peculiar Dale was acting—

only that she was afraid that she and Dale might have to get a divorce. Uncle Eddie promised to do everything that he could to help. He wished her luck and offered his love. He hoped that things would work out.

At around nine-forty-five on the evening of Thursday, April 8, 1971, four days before Easter, Dale was driving out of Harrisburg on Route 34, heading for his Galatia farm. He drew up behind a Plymouth station wagon. He was alone in a borrowed Chevy El Camino pickup, an open bottle of Scotch whisky beside him on the seat. He swerved into the left lane to pass the station wagon and nearly hit an oncoming pickup, forcing it onto the shoulder to avoid a collision. He dropped back behind the Plymouth and, seconds later, started to pass it again. A coroner's jury, working from police testimony and eyewitness accounts, pieced together what happened next:

> We find that Donald Ray McLaskey (29) and Deidrea Loraine McLaskey (10 months) came to their deaths by reckless homicide in which Dr. Dale Cavaness, going north, approximately three miles north of Harrisburg, first struck the left rear fender of a Plymouth driving north; then the Cavaness truck traveled to the left into the south lane and struck the McLaskey car coming south, hitting it with a strong impact, demolishing the truck and McLaskey's car, killing McLaskey and Deidrea Loraine McLaskey. The evidence showed that Dr. Cavaness was driving while intoxicated.

Deputy Sheriff Jim Mings, on his way home from Harrisburg to Raleigh, came upon the scene immediately afterward and radioed for help. He saw the crumpled wreck of the McLaskeys' car sitting in the road with a baby, obviously dead, impaled on the outside mirror. A man lay dead on the pavement. Inside the car a woman, unconscious or dead, was rolled up in a ball on the floor, her head covered in blood.

The deputy ran down the road toward a man, a woman and two children who were huddled together near the remains of their station wagon at the bottom of an embankment. A hundred feet farther along, lodged in some trees beside the road, was an El Camino. The front end and windshield were smashed; the driver still sat behind the wheel. He was talking loudly, nonstop, apparently uninjured but delirious. The deputy approached, smelled liquor.

"Are you hurt?"

"It doesn't matter," the man in the El Camino said. "I've got plenty of insurance." He continued babbling.

At Doctors' Hospital in Harrisburg, Dale was too drunk to sign his name but coherent enough to refuse to take a blood test. His leg was banged up; otherwise he was unscathed, and he kept saying that there was nothing to worry about because he had plenty of insurance. Investigators at the scene had already found the bottle of Cutty Sark Scotch, about one-quarter full. They also recovered a loaded .357 magnum pistol and a shotgun, cased and loaded with the safety off.

Detective Jack T. Nolen of the Illinois Department of Criminal Investigation and State's Attorney Archie Bob Henderson entered Dale's hospital room at about fifteen minutes past midnight, two and a half hours after the moment of the accident. Dale was being attended by a doctor and a nurse. Nolen and Henderson demanded that Dale submit to a blood test. They did not tell him that the other two drivers, dead and alive, had been tested.

"What is this?" Dale complained, slurring his speech. "Aren't we all friends here? Aren't we supposed to be friends?" He stared at the other doctor.

"Not when death is involved," the doctor said, inserting the needle. This was the first Dale had been told of the deaths. "Don't you understand that two people are dead? A father and his baby? The mother is critical. She's in a coma."

"Everybody's got to die sometime," Dale said.

The doctor and the others withdrew from the room in silence, not looking at one another.

Dale's blood registered 0.24 alcoholic content, 0.10 being sufficient proof under Illinois law to show that a person was intoxicated, 0.30 considered potentially lethal. Dale had had nearly two and a half hours to sober up before the blood sample was taken. At the time of the accident, he must have had enough Scotch in him to make almost anyone else pass out. He was cited for drunk driving, illegal transportation of liquor, improper overtaking on the left, and unlawful use of weapons.

Two weeks later the Saline County coroner's jury brought in its double verdict of reckless homicide against Dale. Dorothy Mc-

Laskey, the mother of the dead baby girl, emerged from her coma on the Saturday after the accident, but lapsed into unconsciousness again when a nurse told her that her husband and daughter were dead. She was conscious again on Monday, the day after Easter, and she slowly recovered physically.

To the surprise of most of the citizens of Saline County, the grand jury indicted Dr. John Dale Cavaness on two counts of reckless homicide. He faced a prison term, but few people thought he would ever serve a day. He knew too many important folks; and his lawyer, J. C. Mitchell of Marion, was well-connected and clever. No one was surprised when Dale entered a not-guilty plea.

Marian learned of the accident late on the night of the event when Dale's chief nurse at Pearce Hospital, Emma Lou Mitchell, telephoned her at the trailer.

"Have you heard about Dale? It's terrible. He's been in an accident. Two people were killed, maybe three. He's all right. He's over at Doctors' Hospital."

Marian called the hospital and managed to get through to a doctor she knew there, who told her that Dale was drunk out of his mind. It was a disaster. He seemed to have no idea what he had done.

Emma Lou Mitchell had said nothing about Dale's being drunk, nothing about his being possibly responsible for the deaths. She had spoken of Dale as if he had been the victim. To Marian, Emma Lou's attitude was predictable. Marian had once in a moment of desperation asked Emma Lou whether she thought Dale was going off his rocker, and Emma Lou had looked at Marian as if she had blasphemed.

A detailed account of the accident, including a photograph of the McLaskeys' car and statements by state troopers that Dale had been drunk, carrying liquor in his car and transporting loaded weapons, appeared the next day in the Harrisburg *Daily Register*. The article strongly implied Dale's culpability. But immediately Dale's patients began telephoning Marian with their sympathies —not for Marian and the family but for Dale. We all know what a wonderful man he is, they said. Tell him that we stand by him in this. Please tell Dr. Cavaness that he is our doctor and that he will always be our doctor and that we don't hold this against him.

Marian wondered what it would take to get Dale's patients to hold anything against him. He was God to them. But surely some patients would defect now? Surely some would have second thoughts once they had time to think?

When Dale showed up at the trailer a few days later, Marian searched for signs of contrition, worry, shock—but he nattered on as usual about cattle and catfish.

"Dale," Marian said, "do you have any idea what you've done?"

"Yeah, I know, sure," he said. "What about it?"

"But Dale. Those poor people. And what about yourself? Do you know what you're doing to yourself? Do you know what this could mean?"

"As long as I have my little black bag, I'll be just fine."

His little black bag. Marian was conscious of standing there with her mouth open. She managed to mumble something about his patients' losing confidence in him.

"My patients? Are you kidding? You couldn't drive them away with a stick!"

13

WHAT VIOLENCE, ADULTERY AND NEGLECT HAD FAILED TO accomplish, being forced to live in trailers and having Dale indicted for reckless homicide finally did. Marian had become so beaten down, paralyzed by losing her husband and then her house, that she had begun to wonder whether she would have to live like an unemployed miner's wife forever, with no decent clothes, her children at loose ends, ashamed to face her friends, waiting for nightfall so she could sit alone in the dark and pray for sleep. Finally she was shocked into action. She made plans to get out of Eldorado as quickly as she could.

She accepted that Dale had no intention of building her and his sons another house. He behaved as if he cared no more for her and his children than for the victims of the accident, and she was frightened. The lack of public reaction against him, the loyalty of his patients, of Pearce Hospital, of the whole town seemed to have added to his sense of omnipotence as the untouchable doctor. He was bound to crash, and Marian did not want herself or her children around to suffer the aftereffects. It occurred to her that Dale might do almost anything, especially when he was drunk. The man was not normal: She did not pretend to know what normal was, but he was not it.

Marian's anxiety climbed. Alone at night in the trailer with Patrick, she bolted the door and began letters to her brother: "Dear Bill . . . Things have reached a crisis . . . I am worried about Dale . . . I am frightened of him . . . he drives around with loaded guns, drunk all the time . . . I should have known all this years ago . . . if anything should happen to me, please . . ." but she tore the letters up. There was no other way out but to make a complete break. Why alarm her brother, when it was up to her to act?

St. Louis was the natural refuge. She made several trips to the city to scout around for a job and a house. With Eddie Bell's help she found a beautiful old farmhouse on Conway Road in Chesterfield, a suburb with a reputation for excellent public schools; and she landed a job at Barnes Hospital in the Education Department, training new nurses in hospital procedure. The farmhouse was partially furnished, the rent four hundred a month. Her job, which the hospital agreed to hold open for her until September, when the boys would start the new school year, would pay nine dollars an hour. Dale would be forced to fork over some child support, especially if she filed for divorce in St. Louis. She and the boys would survive. They would start a new life.

Marian told the boys that they were leaving in August. They were miserable. Mark would be starting his senior year in high school, Kevin his sophomore year; they did not want to leave their friends, and Kevin's brief, unpleasant experience at Chaminade had given him a jaundiced view of St. Louis. Sean especially was upset at leaving his father. And what about Grandpa Peck? Who would take them hunting and fishing, and where would they go in the city? Only Patrick was able to see the move as an adventure: He would be starting fresh in kindergarten. Marian's pep talks about the cultural advantages of St. Louis met with indifference or worse. She tried selling them on St. Louis Cardinals baseball. They grew sullen. She worried that they would blame her for uprooting them, forgetting that it was Dale who had broken up the marriage. Marian chose not to reveal all her reasons for fearing and mistrusting Dale, hoping that the boys would eventually understand.

Dale did nothing to discourage her from leaving, but on the last

154

day he showed up to say good-bye as she was packing their few belongings into the car.

"You're taking my boys from me," he said, and he started to cry. Marian could hardly believe it.

"Dale, what are *you* crying for? You're the one who left. I never wanted this. Stop crying. I don't want the boys to see you."

She felt herself wavering, feeling sorry for him; but she was determined not to fall for this show. It was too late. Dale stopped the tears, wiping his eyes.

"Why don't you leave me two of the boys?" he said. "You take Mark and Kevin. I'll keep Sean and Pat."

"What? Are you out of your mind? For God's sake, Dale, if you want to see Mark through his senior year, that's one thing. Mark's the one who probably needs to stay more than any of them. Mark would stay if he could, I think."

"Oh, no," Dale said. "Not Mark. You know I've never gotten along with Mark. I can't have Mark stay here. I'd kill him."

And Dale got into his car and left without saying good-bye to the boys.

You can count on Dale to make things as difficult as possible, Marian thought. But at least he had shown some feeling, mixed-up though it was. He had no idea what he wanted, that was his trouble. He achieved everything and then threw it away. She did feel sorry for him. He had made such a mess of his life. But he would still see the boys, she would make sure of that, on vacations and holidays. Raising boys without a father always led to disaster. Apart from his children, he would appreciate them more. People always did.

Just as they were piling into the car, Peck drove up. The boys rushed toward their grandpa and threw themselves at him. Marian thought it strange but not altogether surprising that Noma had not deigned to see them off. True to form, Marian thought. She probably blames me for everything.

Grandpa Peck broke down. He was too old to endure such a parting, too full of love for his boys, for whom he had tried to do so much. He cried uncontrollably, propped against his old Plymouth, his boys around him, hugging him, tugging at him. Marian had to turn away.

"I'll never see you again," Grandpa was saying. "Oh, oh, this is terrible. I'll never see you again before I die."

"No, Grandpa, no," Kevin pleaded. "We'll see you soon. We'll come back, Grandpa, honest we will."

Marian filed for divorce in December of 1971. After a hearing later that winter, Dale agreed to pay three hundred dollars a month per child until each was eighteen. Marian did not ask for alimony. She did not wish to be more dependent on Dale than she had to be, and she figured that, with her take-home pay of about twelve hundred a month, she would be able to make it.

And she did, except when Dale's checks were late or bounced, as often happened, and she would have to write him or try to get him on the phone and borrow money from Eddie Bell or others to see her through the month. He never paid for extras like clothing or books. Four boys ate a lot.

Her new routine was up at five to fix the boys' breakfast and lunches, off to work by six-thirty. She worked from seven to three-thirty and was home by four-thirty or five to fix dinner, asleep before nine. She found a young girl in the neighborhood to stay with Patrick when he arrived home from kindergarten and to keep the peace until Mom appeared. Her schedule exhausted her, but Marian was so relieved to be out of Eldorado, so pleased to be able to manage on her own, that she did not mind; and she loved the old farmhouse on Conway Road with its garden and cedar trees and the pond that froze for skating in the winter. It was only thirty minutes from the heart of the city, but Chesterfield had a semi-rural quality, roadside stands selling vegetables and preserves, several large nurseries. Marian felt that she had come home—to her city, to a sense of self-confidence and hope that, she now understood, she had almost lost in Little Egypt.

Unfortunately the boys, especially during that first year, did not share in Marian's enthusiasm. They were homesick. They found, as Kevin had experienced at Chaminade, that their southern Illinois accents branded them as hicks, easy marks for ridicule by their schoolmates, who shunned them and called them hillbillies and clodhoppers. Marian knew that in the long run they would adjust, but the boys regarded themselves as outcasts; and they were confused, not understanding why they were there. Mark was particularly disoriented and lost all interest in school. Marian worried that he was hanging around with an unsavory crowd and smoking marijuana; she prayed that he was not taking LSD. It was not that there were any more drugs in St. Louis than in southern Illinois: Pot and acid had spread down there by 1968 and '69. Smoking dope, Marian knew, was common among kids Mark's age. Mark had changed from a good student to a dreadful one. When she talked about getting into college, he looked blank. At home he shut himself into his room with his music.

Kevin's grades also fell; and Sean, always on the roly-poly side, started putting on weight and clung to Marian as if he feared losing her, always waiting for her at the garage door when she came home from work. As for Patrick, he was withdrawn. Marian hoped that he was young enough for her to lead in new directions, but when she took him to a performance of *Peter and the Wolf* by the St. Louis Symphony—just the thing, she thought, to appeal to an unformed kid—he fell asleep. She was unable to talk any of the other boys into accompanying her to cultural events.

Mark failed to graduate from high school that year, although he was permitted to participate in the commencement exercises. Dale came up for the event and behaved badly, drinking and making sarcastic remarks about Mark's failure; but Mark and Kevin spent the summer working for him on the farms and living in the trailers. Mark acted lost and aimless, and Dale said that he would teach him to discipline himself, which he did by yelling at him and telling him that he had become an embarrassment. He waited up for Mark one night, hiding in his bed and prepared to let him have it when he stumbled in late and drunk. When Mark came home early and sober, Dale raged at him anyway, hurling an iron skillet against the wall and sticking a butcher knife into the floor at his feet. He forced Mark to telephone his mother in St. Louis to tell her that his father was making him toe the line.

"Tell her that I'm not beating on you," Dale said, picking up the skillet again. "Go on! Tell her you're lazy and no good but that I'm not going to hurt you, I'm not going to beat hell out of you, but I'm not putting up with your crap either."

Mark pretended to dial the phone and managed to fake talking to his mother. He told Kevin what had happened, but they agreed not to upset Marian by informing her of Dale's latest tirade. Mark said that he would never work for his father again. When the summer was over, he was going to get a job somewhere away from everyone and start a new life. He would get his high school diploma somehow. He didn't know about college: His senior grades were

157

so bad, where could he get in? And what was the point? He was no student. He wasn't some kind of damned genius like his father. He didn't want to be like his father anyway. Working on the farms was a joke. They were never told what to do except stare at the cattle and the catfish and watch Dale get drunk. The whole thing was a farce. The dikes at Hickory Handle gave way one day and the place was covered in dead fish. At night people snuck in and stole the fish. What was he supposed to do, keep watch all night? He was getting out.

Kevin agreed with Mark but kept quiet. In spite of everything, he and Sean still felt more at home in southern Illinois than in St. Louis. There was something about the land between the rivers that drew them back.

On November 20, 1972, Dale stood with his lawyer before presiding Judge Dorothy Spooner at the Saline County Courthouse and changed his plea to guilty on two charges of reckless homicide and one charge of driving while intoxicated. He was fined five hundred dollars on each count and placed on probation for three years. The sentence was the result of a plea-bargain agreement between Dale's attorney and the state's attorney of Saline County, Deneen Watson.

When Dorothy McLaskey learned that Dr. Cavaness had been given no more than a slap on the wrist for killing her husband and daughter, she was outraged, but she was not surprised. From what she knew of the doctor's power and influence, she had not even expected the grand jury to indict him. Hanging would have been too good for him as far as she was concerned. Since the accident she had survived and partially recovered with the help of her mother and her sister, a psychologist who lived in Connecticut. Her memory was impaired, and every afternoon at five o'clock, no matter what she was doing, she was overcome by a compulsion to weep. Her sister deduced that Dorothy cried because five was the hour when her husband had always come home from work at the telephone company. She kept a snapshot of her husband and her baby with her and looked at it every day.

Dorothy McLaskey sued Dr. Cavaness. She hoped that the guilty plea, however minimal the punishment, would help her to collect a large amount of money, but she had trouble standing up under the questioning of the insurance-company lawyers during her deposition. They accused her of having been drunk on the night of the accident, even of having been driving when it happened. She knew that the blood tests and other evidence proved her innocence, but her mental state precluded a protracted fight. She settled for a hundred thousand dollars. It did not seem much for the lives of her baby and her husband.

She moved to St. Louis and took a job as a nurse in a school for retarded children. She hoped to marry again someday, but the doctors told her that she would never be able to have another child of her own.

About the time of Dale's conviction, the owners of the Chesterfield farmhouse decided to sell it. Marian begged Dale to give or to loan her enough for a down payment: The place was perfect for her and the three remaining boys; Mark was now on his own, working at various jobs in St. Louis and the upper Midwest. But Dale refused. He was broke, he said; it was all he could do to make the child-support payments. Marian moved into the Forum West apartments for the next year, glad at least to be able to stay in the same area so the boys would not have to change schools again. A year later Dale relented and sent her five thousand dollars for the down payment on a house in the Shenandoah development in Chesterfield, a modern, two-story place with four bedrooms. Marian looked forward to a few years of stability.

And they were relatively stable and peaceful years, except when Dale came up for one holiday or another, drunk and argumentative, or when the boys visited southern Illinois. In 1974 Sean pleaded to be allowed to spend part of the school year with his father, and Marian reluctantly permitted it, partly because Sean was doing so poorly at school. She was willing to try anything, and the longer she was away from Dale, the more she tended to forget how impossible he could be.

Sean craved being near his father, but he was lonely stuck out in a trailer at the Galatia farm, fixing his own meals, having trouble getting rides to and from school. He began telephoning home and crying: His father was either never around or angry when he was; maybe it had been a mistake to stay so long. Marian told him to come home whenever he liked, although it did not seem a good idea to switch schools again in the middle of the year.

When Patrick went down to visit him, Sean showed his brother a hole in the trailer's wall. The hole had been made by his head when Dale had picked Sean up and thrown him—but Patrick was not to tell Mom about it; she might worry and make him come home. He was not ready to return to St. Louis yet; he liked the freedom of the outdoors, even if Dad was tough on him.

There was too much freedom around Eldorado, Marian knew, but the boys always wanted to head down there, and she was not about to try to forbid them to see their father. Kevin fell into trouble near the end of the Christmas holidays in 1974. He had done nothing himself, but he was arrested with a friend who had thrown a brick through the window of an Eldorado auto-parts store and stolen twelve dollars from the cash register. Kevin was charged with theft, but the case was transferred to St. Louis and dropped.

Also in 1974, while still on probation for the reckless-homicide convictions, Dale was indicted on charges of "deceptive practice" for falsifying claims to the State Division of Vocational Rehabilitation. The sort of phony billing with which he had fattened his income and endeared himself to his patients for years was finally discovered. He had concealed giving women obstetrical care, which was not covered by state insurance, by claiming to have performed such procedures as a laparotomy or a cholecystectomy, terms for abdominal exploration and gallbladder removal. He was only trying to help people, he said.

His lawyer demanded a jury trial—the perfect strategy given Dale's local popularity and renown—and launched a series of motions for continuance. A year passed, and another, and a third without a trial or a judgment.

But few people believed that Dr. Cavaness had much to fear from Saline County justice; he had already got away with paying a fifteen hundred-dollar fine for two homicides; it took a lot of wishful thinking to imagine that a little larceny from the state would cramp the doc's style.

Two teenaged boys found out what it was like to try to bring Dr. Cavaness to justice when they complained to the sheriff that the doctor had terrorized them and nearly drowned them when he had caught them hunting frogs on his Galatia property. The boys and their parents wanted the doctor thrown in jail or at least fined and reprimanded.

But Dale readily admitted to the truth of the boys' account of what had happened. He had indeed caught them gigging frogs (hunting frogs with a forked stick), had run them down, wrapped them in tire chains, and dragged one of them through the waters of Harrisburg Lake until the boy begged for mercy.

Dale said that he had taught the boys a good old-fashioned lesson. They had been trespassing.

The authorities filed no charges.

14

BY THE FALL OF 1976 KEVIN WAS ENROLLED AS AN INDUSTRIAL-technology student at Southeastern State College in Cape Girardeau, Missouri. Sean and Patrick were getting on better at school, and Marian was beginning to glimpse a brighter future. Only Mark remained a worry. After wandering as far as Nebraska, he had been laid off from his most recent job as a telephone lineman in Lexington, Kentucky, and had drifted back to southern Illinois. Once again he was working for his father on the farms.

Dale complained that his eldest son was amounting to nothing and was a pot smoker. When Marian spoke to Mark on the phone, she urged him to come back to St. Louis and live at home until he could find a better job there. She hated the idea of his being under Dale's thumb again and subject to his father's baiting and sarcasm. She could tell from Mark's tone of voice that he was down on himself but, after all, he was not the first young man to spend a few years roaming before latching on to something. He was only twenty-two years old.

As Easter, 1977, approached, Mark asked Marian to come to

Eldorado to celebrate the holiday with him. She dreaded the idea of going down there. She had been back a few times to visit friends and for Noma's and then for Peck's funeral. Noma had died in 1973, Peck two years later. The services at the First Presbyterian Church had been hard to take, especially Peck's, with Dale and the boys awash with weeping; the processions to the family graveyard in McLeansboro made Marian feel too acutely the pain of old associations. Merely visiting southern Illinois plunged her into gloom and anxiety. Dale had let the ruins of the house on Fourth Street stand until 1974: Eldorado was so small that she could not avoid catching sight of that ghostly emblem of disaster. Now the lot next door to the Chevrolet dealer was empty, making it easier to remember good times; she could see the bridge parties and the children playing in the yard. She had no idea whether Dale still owned the property or where the insurance money had gone.

He had hung on to Grandpa's house on Maple. Supposedly he was also looking after other properties which Peck, after inheriting them from the Dales, had left in trust for the boys. Marian suspected that Dale was using the trust to pay child support and Kevin's college tuition, but she did not have the resources to hire a lawyer to find out.

Reluctantly Marian agreed to go down to Egypt for Easter. Mark sounded lonely; too many speeding tickets had temporarily cost him his driver's license, so it would be difficult for him to get to St. Louis. And the other boys were as usual eager to visit the place they still considered home. They could stay at Grandpa's house, which Dale was renting out to nurses who would clear out for the weekend.

Marian drove down on Thursday, April 7; Kevin got a ride over from his college, which was across the Mississippi, a hundred miles west of Eldorado. They were surprised that Mark was not there to greet them. When he did not show up the next day, Good Friday, they wondered what he might be up to. He had sounded so eager to see them.

On Saturday morning Patrick ran off to play with a friend. At about eleven, Dale showed up at Grandpa's house. Everyone sat around in the kitchen drinking coffee. Marian tried to keep the conversation going—the clear early spring weather, Kevin's college life—but her stomach was in knots. As she always did on holidays—in St. Louis, for instance, when Dale made his entrance drunk and sour—she told herself that she was doing this for her boys. She would try anything to make Dale behave like a civilized human being. One Christmas Eve in St. Louis, when Dale was pouring himself a tumblerful of vodka and berating Sean for his low grades, Marian, trying to be funny, invoked Noma's ghost to try to derail him, saying that his mother would not approve of how he was behaving and was gazing down at him and shaking her finger. No, Noma was not doing any such thing, Dale said. She was not gazing down at him, because she was not up there. She was down *there*, he shouted, pointing at the floor.

Now Marian sat in Grandpa's kitchen hoping that they might get through this holiday without incident, smoking one cigarette after another and saying to herself that it would all be over by Monday and she could go back to work and her new life. It was not that she hated Dale after all these years, it was just that he made her so nervous. The one blessing was that he never stuck around for very long. Sure enough, he drank one cup of coffee and was ready to depart.

"I've got to get going," he said, fidgety as always. "I've got things to do."

"I wonder where Mark is," Marian said. "I can't imagine where he'd be. I was sure he'd come around last night. He asks us to come down and then doesn't show up. That's not like Mark. It's almost noon."

"I can't sit around here all day," Dale said. He was wearing baggy jeans tucked into work boots and a torn plaid shirt, looking like someone called in to fix the roof.

"Did you talk to Mark yesterday?" Marian asked. "Didn't he say he was coming over here?"

"I haven't seen that damn Mark since Monday night," Dale said. "You never know what the hell he's up to. I told him he couldn't go on working for me the rest of his life. Said he should see about getting a job in the coal mines."

"That's a ridiculous idea," Marian said. "Mark in the coal mines?"

"What's wrong with the mines? You want him on state aid? By God, do you think I'm going to support him for the rest of his life?"

"Mark isn't going on state aid," Kevin said. "Him and me—"

"He and I," Marian interrupted. "My goodness, Kev, you're in college now. I'm getting a little worried about Mark. I'm afraid he's hurt somewhere."

"That's a mother," Kevin said. "If a kid doesn't show up, he's lying bleeding to death in a ditch."

Kevin leaned over and put his arm around his mother and spoke to her softly.

"Mom, calm down. He's not driving. His license is suspended, you know that. I bet he's just been out partying with some of his buddies."

"Bunch of aardvarks," Dale said.

"He's probably at their house passed out in Carbondale or Harrisburg or somewhere."

They sat in silence for half a minute or so. Kevin poured himself more coffee and brought his mother a fresh cup.

"I don't know," Dale said. "I got a funny feeling about him." He did not elaborate. He stared into his cup.

"Well," Kevin said. "What do you mean?"

"I think he's dead."

Marian looked out the window and sighed, as though Dale had just said something designed specifically to irritate her and that she chose to ignore. Kevin stared at his father, who did not return the glance. Kevin stood up.

"That tears it," Kevin said. "I'm going looking. I'm getting some wheels and starting to hit people's houses that know him. Where's the Jeep?"

"It's—I don't know," Dale said. "It's out at the Shea house."

"Where're the keys?"

"Think the keys—they must be in it. Yes. I got to go to Herod to do some things. I have to see after some things at the Handle. I'll get with you later."

And Dale took off.

Kevin said that Marian would have to drive him out to the Shea house, so-named because of its last occupants, now an empty cottage on the Galatia farm. Sean decided to tag along.

They climbed into Marian's tan Dodge and headed for Galatia. Driving the familiar road brought back many memories for Marian, many of them unpleasant. Everyone seemed to be having trouble with their kids these days. At least Mark had been too young for Vietnam, although going into the army now might do him some good. Marian decided that she would try to talk him into finally earning his high school equivalency diploma and attending some junior college. He was not dumb. It was time for him to buckle down. Once he got onto the right track, he could be happy. He had been at a terrible age to go through a divorce and a change of schools, and he had fallen into bad habits.

Marian turned onto the dirt road that led to the farm and the Shea house and the trailer where Mark was living. Sean grew excited in the backseat:

"Is Mark here? He could be here." A peeling shack came into view. "There's the Shea house! There it is!"

"Those keys had better be in the Jeep," Kevin said.

Marian swung around the rear of the house. Parked parallel to it, in a kind of unfenced yard, were the ten-by-forty-foot trailer and the white Jeep pickup truck, separated by a lone hickory tree that was just coming into bud. No sign of Mark. The new grass had grown up half a foot or more.

"Okay, Mom," Kevin said, "you wait while I see if this ignorant thing starts. Don't go running off. I don't want to get abandoned out here."

Marian watched from the car as Kevin and Sean started walking through the tall grass toward the truck, Kevin in the lead, Sean trotting along behind. As they passed the pickup's tailgate on their right, Marian noticed something in the grass to their left. Trash? A dog lying there?

Kevin reached the driver's side of the truck. The door was ajar. Kevin started to look inside. Sean, lingering and looking around, suddenly shouted, "There's Mark!" and pointed at something in the grass, what Marian thought was a dog.

Sean started to run; Kevin grabbed him. The boys stared down at whatever was in the grass.

Marian pushed open the door of her car. She had to see what had frightened Sean. "What is it?" she called.

"Stay in the car!" Kevin shouted. He was holding on to Sean. "Stay in the car! Don't come over here!"

But Marian was out of the car, moving forward. She started screaming.

"Is it Mark? Is it Mark?"

"Get back in the car!" Kevin shouted.

"It's his belt buckle," Sean said. Kevin tried to cover his brother's eyes.

"His boots," Kevin said. "What is this? What's happened to him?"

"What're we gonna do!" Sean wailed.

"Take it easy," Kevin said, "just take it easy. Oh, Lord!"

Marian was screaming.

"Get back!" Kevin shouted.

Kevin held on to Sean and started walking slowly toward Marian, picking his way between the tailgate of the pickup and Mark's remains, trying not to look down at his dead brother.

"What'll we tell Mom?" Sean whimpered.

"Take it easy. Keep walking. Mom! Don't go over there! No!"

Marian reeled toward the Shea house and stumbled onto the porch, her legs and arms flying in all directions. She beat her fists on the sides of the house, choking and sobbing. She knew that Mark was dead.

Kevin and Sean reached their mother. The three of them clung to one another, moaning and sobbing, murmuring Mark's name.

Minutes passed before anyone could think of what to do next. Kevin said that he had better try to call the cops. There was a phone inside the house. Maybe it still worked.

He was able to telephone. They waited on the porch, huddling together for what seemed like hours. Kevin grew angry. What could be holding up the cops? Twice he telephoned again to see what could be keeping the sheriff's deputies.

"They're probably giving somebody a speeding ticket," Kevin said.

Finally along the road came a black-and-white with two officers in it, but it rolled slowly past, the driver lifting his hand casually in greeting. Kevin sprang from the porch, waving. He recognized the driver, a young deputy.

"Hey, you idiot!"

The car slid to a stop.

"What's the problem, buddy?"

"What's the problem! This is it! *This is it!*"

"Okay. Calm down."

"He's over behind the trailer," Kevin said, pointing. He did not want to go over there again.

"I better get my camera."

"Sure. Get your camera."

Marian, leaning against her car now with her head cradled in her arms, began to sob again. It was as if the appearance of the police confirmed in her mind what she had still been trying to disbelieve. The deputy whom Kevin had recognized approached.

"Look, lady. You're just gonna have to calm down."

Kevin wanted to clobber him but restrainted himself, afraid he might pull his gun.

"That's my son over there!" Marian cried.

"You're gonna have to calm down."

"It's my son!"

Kevin led his mother and Sean back to the porch. The trailer blocked their view of the truck and the body, but Kevin could hear the officers open the truck and the whirr of a Polaroid camera. Now an officer from the Eldorado police department drove up and joined the others. Kevin had to see what the officers were doing. He walked over to his mother's car to get a view.

The officer taking Polaroids of the scene was dropping the used pieces of paper on the ground. Two of the cops flicked cigarette butts into the grass. Another had his head poked into the truck. To Kevin these officers were not conducting what seemed like an orderly, professional investigation. How would they be able to distinguish their own trash from evidence? Were they capable of reconstructing Mark's suicide—or was it murder?

Kevin had a clear recollection of what he had glimpsed inside the truck in that instant before Sean had blurted, "There's Mark." He had been thinking about what he had seen there, during those long moments when he had been waiting for the police, trying to comfort his mother and brother. His instinct was to try to figure out what had happened: What else could he do? He knew that if he started becoming hysterical, Marian and Sean would crack, too.

He remembered distinctly that on the passenger side of the seat a shotgun was lying with the barrel pointing toward the driver's side. The gun, which Kevin recognized as one of Dale's, was inside its case, but the barrel-end stuck out several inches, as if the end of the case had been blown off when the gun had been fired. And he believed that he had noticed blood on the driver's side door.

The gun looked as if it had been booby-trapped. The hook end of a wire coat hanger was wedged into the trigger guard through another hole in the gun case. On the coat hanger was a camouflage hunting vest with its lower part caught in the closed passenger-side door.

Watching the officers, Kevin wondered what they were thinking. Was this a booby-trap murder, or had it been an accident? He imagined Mark standing outside the truck on the driver's side, reaching in, grabbing the gun by the barrel. The coat hanger, hooked on to the trigger at one end and caught in the passenger-side door by the vest, had pulled the trigger, shooting Mark and sending him staggering and sprawling the ten or twelve feet back onto the grass where he lay.

But this sequence quickly seemed absurd to Kevin. No experienced hunter, which Mark certainly was, would reach across a seat and pull a gun toward himself by the barrel; nor could Kevin believe that the coat hanger had managed to end up in that lethal configuration by itself. And if Mark had wanted to commit suicide, he would not have left the gun in its case.

Kevin was sure that someone had rigged the scene to make it look like an accident. Mark had been murdered. But by whom?

Sheriff Arnold Stafford drove up in one car, Coroner Wendell Lambert in another, and Special Agent Jack T. Nolen of the Illinois D.C.I. in his unmarked state car.

Detective Nolen walked over to Kevin and Marian, who were standing beside the Dodge. Sean had taken refuge in the backseat. It was nearly two-thirty in the afternoon.

Marian managed to tell Detective Nolen that they had arrived just after one o'clock to pick up the Jeep. The boys had noticed something lying on the ground. They recognized Mark's belt buckle and—she broke down. Nolen tried to comfort her. There was not much he could do.

Nolen asked the other officers to stop throwing their cigarette butts and Polaroid papers on the ground. How was he supposed to be able to distinguish their trash from what was already at the scene? He saw that Sheriff Stafford already had a shotgun in his hands and was aiming it at the sky.

"Hell of a gun," the sheriff said.

It was a big .12-gauge, three-inch magnum; a goose gun, Browning automatic. Nolen was irritated. He would have to rely on the sheriff and his deputies to describe the interior of the truck as they had found it. Nor would he be able to take fingerprints from the gun. He told everyone not to disturb the scene further.

Kevin watched, barely able to keep his emotions in check. He could see that the investigation was being screwed up. He chewed on his tongue and swallowed blood.

Nolen walked over to take a look at the body. He had to suppress a gasp.

There was very little left of it. It lay on its back, mostly raw bones, shreds of red meat clinging to fresh skeletal remains. The flesh from mid-thigh up was gone, baring thick thigh bones, the balls and sockets of hips, the pelvis, arm bones, the delicate bones of wrists and hands and fingers. An anatomy lesson. The empty rib cage arched upward, a hollow cavity to the spine, all internal organs gone. Only the lower legs, still encased in jeans, and the feet in lace-up work boots remained intact.

Nolen saw a dozen or so dead bodies every year; he was a veteran of autopsies; he had never seen anything like this. What must it have been like for the mother and brothers to see it, to recognize it as their own? Nolen could feel their eyes on him.

Nolen knew the woods. Animals had gotten to this body—varmints, wild dogs. Then the turkey vultures. The possums usually attacked a carcass first, nibbling their way in through the anus to the innards. A human being was only another meal to them.

There was no flesh on the face, just a skull in the grass, with perfect young man's teeth exposed and gleaming. Only the left eyeball still lay in its socket, and the brown, thick, swept-back hair was untouched.

Without a liver with which to test the body's temperature, the coroner would be unable to determine the time of death accurately; the flesh remaining inside the boots and jeans would tell something. Nolen estimated that it had lain there no more than twenty-four hours, maybe less, it looked so fresh. The boy had been killed on Good Friday.

Sheriff Stafford found a black leather wallet in the grass near the body: The identification was that of Mark Dale Cavaness.

Detective Nolen told Marian and Kevin that they could leave. Kevin asked Nolen to please try to get hold of his dad, who was probably over at his Hickory Handle farm near Herod.

"We'll send someone," Nolen said. "Can you take care of your mother and your brother?"

Kevin said he could. He helped Marian to the car and headed for Grandpa's house. The Harrisburg Ambulance Service passed them on the highway.

Coroner Lambert placed Mark's remains in the ambulance to be driven to an Eldorado funeral home. Detective Nolen, poring over the body site, found four buckshots on the ground where the rib cage had rested. He examined a plaid shirt deputies had picked up near the truck. Between the left breast pocket and the snap buttons was a hole, surrounded by dried blood, that measured about two and a half by four inches. A pack of Vantage cigarettes and a book of matches remained untouched in the pocket. Mark Cavaness had been shot through the heart. With a shotgun, such a relatively small and neat hole could only have been made by a very close shot. Blood on the driver's seat, floorboard, inside door panel, and outside, just behind the door opening, indicated that he had been shot at point-blank range either while he was sitting behind the wheel (turned toward the passenger side), getting in or out of the truck, or standing beside it.

Nolen found more buckshot on the floorboard. According to the sheriff, the gun had rested exactly as Kevin remembered it, except that it had also been positioned across an ax handle, as if to raise the shooting angle: the coat hanger hooked into the trigger, the vest on the hanger caught in the passenger-side door. The safety had been off; there was one round left in the chamber and one in the magazine.

Whether the end of the case had been blown off or worn out, it was hard to say at this point. The stock end of the case did show wear, and some of the case beneath the barrel had worn away. But if the gun had been fired inside the case, why was there no spent cartridge inside the case?

Instead, Nolen found one spent .12-gauge cartridge on the driver's side floorboard. If the gun had been fired inside the case, either from the action of the coat hanger or by someone pulling the trigger, that cartridge could not have ended up on the floorboard. Nolen reasoned that someone had fired the gun with the case off from inside the truck, killing Mark, and had then replaced the gun in the case and rigged it to make the death look like an accident or a booby-trap.

Nolen kept his conclusions to himself, but he felt certain that this had been a murder covered up in haste. The killer had constructed a phony scene and had fled, leaving Mark to be ravaged.

Where exactly Mark had been sitting or standing when killed—that was impossible to say since the animals might have dragged the body. The buckshot found underneath the body had probably fallen through the rib cage to the ground as the outer flesh and inner organs were devoured. There might have been more buckshot in the body, eaten by the animals.

It was nearly four by the time Dr. Cavaness drove up. Detective Nolen remembered the doctor well from the night of the McLaskey accident, which as Nolen recalled offhand had occurred at about the same time of year five or six years ago. Nolen was not about to forget the scene, how drunk Dr. Cavaness had been, how uncooperative and unremorseful. Nor had Nolen forgotten how the doctor had gotten off with a small fine and probation. Certain officials in Egypt, as Nolen was fond of saying, had balls the size of mustard seeds. That was why Nolen was glad that he worked for the Illinois D.C.I. and could handle cases on his own. He could be sure that his end of a job would be done right, whatever happened in the courts afterward.

But today Dr. Cavaness was not drunk and appeared to be as distraught as any father who had just found out that his son was dead. He offered to help in any way that he could and asked what had happened.

Nolen gave a minimal description of the scene, offering no hypotheses or conclusions.

"It could have been an accident?" the doctor asked.

"It could have been, yes, that's certainly a possibility. When was the last time you saw Mark?"

Dale said that he had last seen and talked to Mark on Monday, April 4, at Mark's grandfather's house. He had not seen him since then, but that was not unusual. He had talked to Mark about assisting him in getting a job in the coal mines. Mark had been working for him on the farm.

"You give him a wage? How much do you pay him?"

"Two dollars an hour," Dale said.

"So you weren't worried about him, not seeing him?"

"Well, yes, I was worried Thursday and Friday, because his mother and brothers, they were coming down for the holiday, and

173

we couldn't locate him. But you see, he doesn't have a driver's license and he depends on somebody to haul him around. So he can get stuck someplace."

Nolen showed Dale the shotgun. Dale identified it as belonging to the Cavaness family. Nolen wanted to know where the gun was usually kept. At his own trailer, Dale said, southwest of the Shea place, down by the lake. Mark had been living in this trailer, here, and he had the use of the gun when he wanted it.

Dale Cavaness, 1943

Dale (right), Marian, and a friend, New York, 1951

Marian, St. Louis, 1951

Marian and Dale, 1964

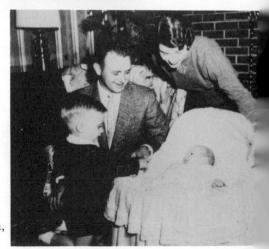

Mark, Dale, Marian, and Kevin,
1956

Mark (left) and Kevin (standing);
Sean (left) and Patrick (seated), 1969

Mark, 1972

Mark, 1969

Kevin, Mark, Marian, Dale, Sean, 1965, in the family room

Mark, Sean, Kevin, 1964

Mark, Dale, Kevin, Marian, 1960

Dale, Kevin, Marian, college graduation, 1980

Sean Cavaness, circa 1981

Dale with lab assistants, Pearce Hospital, 1957
(*Courtesy Marilyn and Chuck Leonard*)

Dale and Marian after a ball, St. Louis, 1965

Dale with Mark,
McLeansboro, 1955

Dale and Marian; Peck and Noma Cavaness, circa 1960

1966 Christmas card. On a whim, Marian altered the spelling of her name for a brief period.

Dale at his office, 1957
(Courtesy Marilyn and Chuck Leonard)

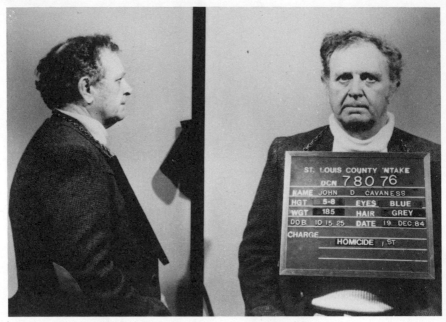

Mug shot *(Courtesy St. Louis County Police Department)*

Kevin and Charli Ann Cavaness, St. Louis, 1988

15

DALE DID NOT SHOW UP AT GRANDPA'S HOUSE UNTIL ABOUT EIGHT that evening. It was a quiet scene, friends moving in and out, Marian sitting at the kitchen table with Patrick, Kevin close to Sean in the living room. The Sullivans, the Davenports, the Becks and others came up to him murmuring condolences. Kevin had started phoning people as soon as he and his mother and Sean had returned to Grandpa's, found Patrick and broken the news to him. Kevin would have preferred to be alone but thought familiar faces might help his mother through.

Sean rushed up to his father and hugged him; Kevin stood back, torn by conflicting emotions, sorrow, anger at the nameless killer or killers and at what seemed to him the sloppiness of the investigation. He was unmoved by the offerings of help and endless cups of coffee. From time to time he went off into one of the bedrooms or to the bathroom to cry by himself or to try to comfort Sean. He did not want to cry in front of other people or his father. He wondered why it had taken his father so long to get to Grandpa's—surely he hadn't gone to see Martha?—but he was not about to ask.

Dale made his way into the kitchen. Marian cradled a Coke in her hands, staring into it.

"This is going to be a tough one," Dale said to Marian and to the friends standing around. "The cops say there wasn't much left. I didn't see the body myself. It was gone when I got there."

"Don't talk about that, Dale," Marian said.

"What they say is, it was all dismembered. The way I get it, there was an arm over here and a leg over there—"

"Dale!"

"—like, I don't know, it might be real tough to piece this thing together, I mean to find out how it happened, with the body all torn apart like that. I—"

"Dale! Stop. I can't take that kind of talk. You're talking about Mark!"

"Just dealing with the facts," Dale said, and he left the kitchen.

Pat Sullivan took Dale aside and out into the backyard. The night was crisp and quiet.

"Dale, this is the most awful thing," and Pat threw an arm around his old friend, towering over him, like a father comforting a son.

Dale wept. He buried his head in Pat's shoulder.

"Dale, you know we all love you. We love you and Marian and the boys. We'll do all we can. We'll help you through this. My God, losing a child, like this. If our Greg—"

"Do you think it was an accident? Who would've wanted to kill him?"

"I don't have any idea."

"Do you think it was drugs? I always worried about Mark and drugs."

"I know you did."

"It could have been an accident. This D.C.I. guy gave me the lowdown. It could have been an accident."

"Sure, it could have been an accident. Who would've killed Mark? One of those things."

"I was worried about Mark."

"Yes. You'll get through this, Dale. Thank God you have the other boys. We'll help. We all love you."

The funeral was set for Monday. For Marian and the boys, Easter Sunday was like another long Good Friday. Grandpa's house filled again with people bringing hams and turkeys and pies, but no one

184

ate. In the afternoon some of Kevin's old buddies arrived to take him out, to try to distract him. Marian was alone in the house when Dale walked in. He said that they needed to discuss the funeral arrangements.

"Everything's taken care of," Marian said.

Her moods had careened from numbness to grief to rage and bitterness. She had been brooding through the night and morning about everything—Mark, Dale, the endless troubles they had had, the way her life had been in the depths, then seemed to rise again. Now this. She had been right about the mistake Mark had made in coming back here. Everything Dale touched seemed to turn rotten—except his patients. The patients! They were phoning and dropping by. She could not blame them but . . .

"I want to tell you something," Marian said to Dale now that they were alone. "If you have any ideas about inviting Martha to the funeral, just forget it. Forget it, is that clear?"

"No. I'm not inviting her."

"Were you planning to invite her, before I said something? Because if you do, I don't know what I'll do."

Marian's eyes had been dulled from weeping, but now they shone black.

"Martha's not coming," Dale said.

"Don't get any last-minute ideas about inviting her. I never know what you're going to pull anymore. I couldn't take that."

"She's not coming."

Marian's anger suddenly gave way to weeping again. She wished Dale would comfort her. It was their son. They should be able to share something. She threw herself into a chair in the living room and looked up at him. He did seem grief-stricken, red-eyed, disheveled. But she could tell that as usual he was anxious to be on his way. The death of his son had interrupted his routine or whatever it was he did. Something had come up that was beyond his control, and it annoyed him: Was that what he was feeling inside? He had become a mystery to her.

Abruptly Marian found herself saying with an edge to her voice, "I don't suppose all that insurance you're always talking about having covers something like this, does it? I mean, even you probably haven't thought of that."

"As a matter of fact," Dale said, "I just took out a policy on Mark in February."

"What?"

"It was for his future."

"His future?"

"That's right. You get low rates, then you turn it over to him later. It was for his future."

"How much?"

"About forty thousand."

"And who's the beneficiary?"

"I'm the primary beneficiary, and you're the secondary beneficiary, in case something happened to me. I got to go."

Dale left the house. A disturbing idea occurred to Marian. In her mind she heard Dale's voice: "If I find out that damn Mark is involved in some dope ring, I'll kill him." He had uttered variations of that statement many times. Marian had always dismissed it as the sort of thing an angry father says, as a figure of speech. But the life insurance made Marian begin to wonder.

She had heard of parents who took out life insurance on their children and then turned the policies over to them when they married. But Dale had taken out the policy in February. In April Mark was dead. It did seem like quite a coincidence.

The disturbing idea invaded Marian. Dale had never liked Mark. Was it possible . . . ?

It was too absurd. She had nothing like proof. She would not tell anyone and she would have to try to dismiss the idea. But the more she thought about it, the less implausible it seemed and the more she heard herself saying I know it, I know he did it. She had an impulse to telephone Detective Nolen to tell him of her thoughts—but no, he would think her hysterical, and she probably was; her grief was confusing her judgment, her resentment of Dale getting the better of her reason. Fathers do not go around killing their sons.

On Monday afternoon the First Presbyterian Church, the place where Dale had gone as a child, a white wooden structure with a square bell tower, filled up with family, friends, employees from Pearce Hospital, hired hands from the farms, and many of Dale's patients. The crowd numbered close to four hundred. The Reverend Mark Porter, new to the church since Marian had left Eldorado, spoke of the tragedy of Mark's death and of how it need not be entirely a tragedy. This was the season in which we rejoice in the resurrection of Jesus Christ.

186

"Mark was a handsome young man," the pastor said, "who had a warmth toward other people. He also had a sense of love for other people that many of us experienced.

"But Mark was in a time that many of us have gone through as have many of you. He couldn't get a handle on a direction in his life and that came out in many ways."

Mark's potential would now never be realized, Reverend Porter said. He could have been run over by a car when he was five years old, or he could have had a heart attack, or he could have died in his sleep at age ninety-two. But if we believe in Jesus Christ, then we know that God is with Mark.

During the sermon Sean kept glancing over at Kevin to see if it would be all right to let go and cry, but Kevin held back. It was a brief service. Afterward Marian and Dale accepted condolences on the church steps until Marian said that she had to go back to Grandpa's house to lie down.

Mark's remains had been cremated. A plaque would be placed in the McLeansboro graveyard, but Kevin and Sean accompanied Mr. Bean, the funeral director, out beyond Herod to the Hickory Handle farm to scatter the ashes. The boys expected their father to go with them, but he drove out in his own car and lingered by the barn with his farm workers as Kevin and Sean walked with Mr. Bean, who carried the metal box, up to the top of a hill.

It was the highest point on the farm, overlooking a valley, giving an unobstructed view of the hills that rose toward the Ohio and Kentucky to the south. The spot was near the site of a graveyard dating from pioneer days, but Dale had had that bulldozed as a nuisance years before. They paused for breath, gazing over the valley. Kevin spotted a hawk riding wind currents.

"Here," Mr. Bean said, "you hold Mark," removing the lid and pushing the box at Sean, who hesitated before grasping it with both hands. Kevin could see that Sean was unnerved, having to hold his brother's ashes like that.

The boys walked along the crest of the hill, following Mr. Bean, who reached behind to scoop out handfuls of ashes and scattered them deliberately, left and right, the light breeze lifting them and letting them fall. On the wind Kevin thought he caught his father's voice from down by the barn, intermittent shouts, and he figured that the men would be drinking. He thought he heard someone laugh at something his father must have said.

They made their way along the crest of the hill in the afternoon light, saying nothing, walking and sowing the ashes.

A few days later, back in St. Louis, Marian received a letter from Reverend Porter. When he was Mark's age, the minister wrote, he had just flunked out of college and had no direction in his life. Now, however, he believed that God agonizes over us and struggles with us—with Mark, with anyone who has lost direction—rather than acting as a judge. The pastor hoped that Marian could thank God for Mark's life, even though it had been short and unfulfilled. He knew the pain she was feeling: It showed that she had loved Mark very much and had been close to him.

Marian was grateful for the letter; she believed that Reverend Porter meant well. But she did not think that anyone needed to tell her not to judge Mark; nor could she imagine that God had judged her eldest son as anything but one of the innocents. Only Dale had judged him harshly, and it sounded to her as if Dale had been denigrating Mark to the minister, making it sound as if the boy were to blame for his own death.

Mark had not asked to be murdered. He had done nothing wrong, unless being young and unhappy was wrong. One way or another, Marian blamed someone else for his death, and that someone was not God. She blamed Dale, whether or not he had pulled the trigger. But she resolved to tell no one her suspicions, not even Kevin, who was constantly asking her whether she had any theories about Mark's death. She did not even mention the insurance policy to anyone. What would be the point, when nothing could be proved and she might be wrong?

16

AFTER ONLY A FEW DAYS OF INVESTIGATION, DETECTIVE NOLEN
was able to conclude that Mark Cavaness had been for a time a
heavy drinker but only a nickel and dime marijuana user. Some of
his friends and acquaintances indicated that Mark had in the past
experimented with other drugs but that he was not in debt and
had no known enemies. All stated that in recent months, since he
had returned to southern Illinois, he had been leading a quiet and
relatively drug-free life.

With his father paying him only the ludicrous wage of two dollars
an hour, Nolen reasoned, Mark could not have afforded anything
more than the occasional six-pack and joint. He had not been a
thief and had never been in serious trouble except for the speeding
citations that had cost him a suspended license.

Mark's name had turned up on lists that the D.C.I. kept of known
drug users, dealers and hangers-on—some of them people the law
would move in on after enough evidence had accumulated, or
people permitted to remain at large because they would eventually
link up with a major drug connection and might be useful as
informers—but Mark was on these secret lists only by association.

You could get your name on such a list merely by buying a lid or by being present when drugs were bought or used. Nolen had snitches all over Little Egypt who sang rather than go to jail.

Jack T. Nolen, forty years old, the son of a miner who had died in a coal-mining accident, could have passed for a country banker or maybe a wildcat oil man, although he was too well-known in Little Egypt to engage personally in any undercover operations. He had been with the Illinois Division of Criminal Investigation all of his working life, starting out up in the Champaign-Urban area and then returning to live in his native Harrisburg and operate out of the D.C.I. office up in Carmi as the chief detective in Little Egypt. His hair, pepper-and-salt, thinning a little in front, was brushed straight back and, like his full, slightly drooping mustache, was always neatly trimmed. The dark, aviator-style glasses hid his eyes. A pink round face and a good-sized belly suggested a man who was not missing many meals, but he was portly rather than fat: "Portly gentleman" was the phrase that suited him. He chose his clothes with care. In cooler weather he favored herringbone-tweed jackets with hand-stitched lapels and leather buttons; if the jacket of the day was brown, he might wear a puce cotton shirt with a silk paisley necktie of a color poised between the shirt and the coat; light wool tan trousers neatly creased; tasseled cordovan loafers, spit-polished.

Two rectangular-cut diamond rings, good-sized, one for each hand, added to the impression of a man who was not so much looking for something as enjoying what he had already found, a man who was not to be confused with the low-life thieves, drug dealers and killers who occupied most of his attention. In his left lapel he always wore a little embroidered red rose, the crowning touch to an appearance that was disconcerting to someone under investigation. It could throw you off stride to be confronted by a detective with diamonds on his fingers and a rose in his lapel, especially in a territory where most men dressed in overalls or Sears and J. C. Penney tailoring.

Nolen put fifty thousand miles a year on his state Buick, tooling around southern Illinois gathering information. He knew more things about more people in Little Egypt than anybody else did, partly because of his carefully cultivated network of snitches, more because of his quick, retentive mind and his appearance and manner, which combined authority with an amiability that, like his

190

tinted glasses, concealed his thoughts. He was good at shooting the breeze and then suddenly zeroing in on what he was really after. His was the opposite of the typical big-city detective's approach, direct and aggressive: Nolen was circuitous, devious, as cute as a left-hander throwing junk. He might discuss the prospects of the baseball Cardinals or the migration of geese for half an hour before edging into homicide. He knew enough about hundreds of local people and their families, their debts, their secret vices, their dreams, to be able to drop something of interest to almost anybody—always with an air of courtesy, good humor and concern, so that before you knew it, you thought you were talking to your uncle—a kindly fellow with your best interests at heart who, smiling and chuckling and touching you on the elbow, was really weaseling information out of you.

Nolen had begun driving around to interview people as soon as he was finished talking to Dr. Cavaness at the murder scene that Saturday afternoon. By five o'clock he was at the house of the funeral director, chatting up Mr. Bean's son, Corwin, a friend of both Mark's and Kevin's, who supplied other names and addresses. By the time Nolen quit that night, he had spoken to seven men and to two women, both of whom had been Mark's girlfriends. On Easter Sunday he interviewed seven more people. No one had seen Mark after Wednesday of Easter week, except for one man who said that he had spotted him leaving an Eldorado restaurant with a sack of food on Thursday at one in the afternoon. A hired hand at the Galatia farm stated that he had visited the area around the Shea house on Thursday afternoon to pick up a load of hay with a tractor. He had seen nothing in the grass, no animals or vultures. The white Jeep truck had been there, parked beside the trailer.

On Easter Sunday a pathologist from Evansville issued a positive identification of Mark's remains based on Eldorado dental records and estimated, from the condition of samples of tissue taken Saturday from the lower legs and feet, that the victim had been dead for approximately fourteen hours when found. That would put the death on Friday evening or late afternoon. Nolen's original guess had been accurate. A body left out in the country did not last long.

Nor did Nolen waver from his belief that this had been a murder and that the gun had been booby-trapped with the coat hanger after the fact, probably in a clumsy attempt to make the scene look like that of an accident. As he interviewed people, however, Nolen observed that the word was getting around that the death had been an accident. He did nothing to discourage the idea, which may have originated with family members or even with one of the local deputies. It could not hurt to have the killer or killers relax.

Everyone seemed to have liked Mark. His success with the girls sometimes involved him in jealous rivalries; there was one fellow who had warned Mark to stop seeing his sister unless he intended to propose marriage. People had been killed for less in southern Illinois, but this did not feel like the stuff of homicide.

His male friends ranged from clean-cut types with whom he played basketball once a week to druggy characters who, Nolen was willing to bet, would never see the backside of thirty. Several people thought that Mark was kind of spacey; but after talking to just about everyone who had known him well, Jack Nolen concluded that Mark had been a nice, friendly kid who had a way with the girls and was probably too easygoing for his own good—which made him like almost every other young man stuck in and around Eldorado. Nolen liked to joke that the hottest thing going in Eldorado was the new electronic cash register at the IGA grocery store: You could stand around and watch the little lights flash.

After a week's poking around, Nolen isolated two suspects.

The first was Frank Stoat, a big, rough man in his mid-thirties who volunteered that he was probably as close a friend as Mark Cavaness had—a statement Nolen had no reason to accept at face value. Nolen had interviewed Stoat at his run-down house on the outskirts of Shawneetown early Easter Sunday afternoon. With him were his younger wife and a twenty-year-old boy from Eldorado who said that he had been living at the Stoats' house since leaving home several weeks before.

Stoat had worked in the coal mines, on river dredges and on various farms in the region. Mrs. Stoat had held odd jobs, but mostly she took care of the house, Stoat said.

Stoat reported that he had gone looking for Mark on Tuesday. He asked his wife to confirm the date, but she said nothing, staring into the shag carpet.

"I borried this wrench off of him," Stoat went on, gesturing. Nolen noticed that the second and third fingers were missing from Stoat's left hand. An old, deep scar ran from his left ear nearly to the corner of his mouth. With his bright red hair and watery, pale-blue eyes, he wasn't easy to look at. "I got done with the wrench and I took over to Galatia to return it, you know."

"To the Cavaness place?"

"Sure. I done odd jobs for the old man. I took and went to the Shea place to find Mark. Tried the trailer."

"You didn't see anything?"

"Not a thing."

"Is that right. Was the Jeep truck there?"

"I don't think so, I don't remember for sure."

"So you left the wrench?"

"Nosir. I figured old Mark might be over at his dad's place, you know, over by the lake. So's I took and went over there."

He had found no one at Dr. Cavaness's trailer. He had not gone inside, only knocked. Then he had gone home.

"What kind of a kid was Mark? Was he despondent or anything like that? You think Mark could have taken his own life?"

"Hell, no. He was a real good kid. He used to stay with us."

"Is that so. He stayed with you, you say?"

"Oh, yeah." Mrs. Stoat went into the kitchen. Nolen could hear her messing around in there. The young man lolled on the ratty couch. "Sure, he come and stayed with us sometime. We liked him real well. He was a good kid, wasn't he, Doyle?"

"Yeah," the boy on the couch said.

"He had his own place over there, didn't he? Why would he come and stay with you?"

"Well, him and his dad, they didn't get along real well. They'd have a fight. The old man would get on him, you know."

"What about?"

"Just the usual."

"Father and son? The boy wasn't working hard enough?"

"That's it. I think the doc kind of wanted him to go into the coal mines, you know. Mark didn't want to."

"So the doc would get on him?"

"Sure. Don't get me wrong. I like the doc real well. The doc's been real good to me."

"Is that right."

"Oh, yeah. I like the doc real well. Smartest man I ever knowed. Real good man, the doc. There's lots of folks he never charged."

"So Mark would come and stay with you. How long would he stay?"

"Off and on. A day. Two three weeks at a stretch."

"That was real nice of you and Mrs. Stoat to take him in."

"Oh, sure." Stoat pointed to the boy on the couch. "We got 'em coming in here all the time."

"A regular boarding house," Nolen laughed. "You all charge these boys for room and board?"

"They help out how they can."

Stoat said that they often had three or four boys staying at the same time. He tipped up a can of beer and wiped his mouth with his sleeve.

Nolen could see that the house had only two small bedrooms. He smelled meat frying in the kitchen. He got up to leave, handing Stoat one of his business cards, as he did everyone he interviewed. Some people would call and tell you things on the phone that they would conceal face to face, especially if there were others present. The urge to talk was a detective's bread and butter.

Nolen doubted, however, that he would hear from Stoat; but he handed over the card as a matter of routine. If nothing else, the card was a reminder that could serve to make somebody jumpy. At the upper left of the card was the gold, flying-eagle seal of the Division of Criminal Investigation. Under the name Jack T. Nolen the term Special Agent added authority.

"Seeing you were such good friends with Mark, I might want to talk to you all again."

"Sure. Anytime."

"And by the way, would you mind giving me the names of those other boys that stayed here?"

"Sure thing."

In the next few days Nolen interviewed several of the young men who had stayed with the Stoats, did some additional discreet nosing around with tavern-keepers, people who had worked with both Stoats, others in the know. The point of this line of inquiry was to learn why the young men preferred the Stoats' to their own homes. What Nolen learned filled out a picture he had already partially imagined and supplied a possible motive for Mark's murder. It suggested that Mark's sexual attractiveness and activity may have been fatal to him.

According to Nolen's informants, Frank Stoat had a sexual problem. The only thing that turned him on, from various accounts, was watching his wife make it with other men. Mrs. Stoat did not appear to mind accommodating her husband's voyeurism and engaged in sexual acts with the young men staying at the house. You could say that Frank Stoat acted as a pimp for his wife except that he declined to charge for her services, content with a spectator's pleasure.

Nolen found grim humor in the scene. People might assume that life in Little Egypt was all hard labor and churchgoing. Why, Hollywood and New York had nothing on the Stoats, who were right out there with the swingingest folks in the country. They were up-to-date.

Mrs. Stoat, people reported, sometimes taunted her husband about his bystander's approach to marriage. What with the drink and the grass and the free-form atmosphere of the house, Frank Stoat would occasionally knock his wife around and turn the young men out, only to lure them back again. Mrs. Stoat was no oil painting, as one of Nolen's informants said, but she had qualities.

Nolen had no evidence that Stoat had ever so much as turned Mark out, let alone murdered him. But if Mark had been staying at the Stoat's house for two or three weeks at a time, perhaps Mrs. Stoat had found Mark attractive enough to provoke her husband's jealousy. There were probably unwritten rules to the Stoats' arrangement. She might be permitted to savor the moment, but lingering enthusiasm could invite a reaction. It's a sad house, Nolen reflected, where the hen crows louder than the cock.

Stoat had already admitted going to look for Mark on Tuesday. Maybe it had been as late as Friday. Maybe he had gone to look for Mark not to return a wrench but in a rage; had found him in the Jeep with the shotgun; had killed him and then crudely tried to make it look like an accident.

It was nothing but a hypothesis, but it was enough for Nolen to ask Stoat to take a lie-detector test—to clear him of any suspicion, Nolen said, indicating a little of what he had learned about the Stoats' domestic arrangements, hinting that it would probably be a good idea for Stoat to cooperate. Stoat agreed to the polygraph.

He passed the test, which appeared to verify his account of having nothing but friendly feelings toward Mark and of not having seen him at all during the week of the murder. This was not conclusive proof of his innocence—the polygraph was far from infallible—but in the absence of real evidence, it let Stoat off the hook for the time being. Had he failed the test, Nolen would have begun to put the squeeze on him; now there was nothing to do but keep an eye on him, continue to ask around about him, and see if he might slip up.

With Stoat in the background, Detective Nolen turned his attention to the other prime suspect, Dr. John Dale Cavaness. Once Nolen learned, as he quickly did from the doctor's insurance agent and other sources, that Dr. Cavaness was about to collect on a forty-thousand-dollar policy which he had taken out on Mark's life only in February, the doctor naturally became an object of curiosity. Add to this the doctor's well-known animosity toward his son, his reputation for hard drinking and a violent temper, his conviction for reckless homicide, and his indictment (still pending) in 1974 on sixteen felony counts of deceptive medical practice—and the idea that he might also be guilty of cold-blooded murder was hardly inconceivable.

What was almost inconceivable was the idea that a father would actually murder his son to collect on a life-insurance policy. Nolen was sure that the identical crime must have been committed at some time, somewhere, by someone; he had been a detective too long not to believe that human beings were capable of any crime; but he had never encountered nor even heard of anything like that. Shoot-outs between feuding family members, yes—but nothing so cold and so premeditated as this appeared to be, if indeed Dr. Cavaness had committed the act or—and here Stoat remained a possibility—arranged for it to be done.

And Nolen knew that he was asking for trouble by making Dr. Cavaness a suspect. The doctor certainly had his enemies, but by and large he was probably the most respected and beloved figure in Eldorado, possibly in the whole of Little Egypt. Nolen was aware of the public reaction to the reckless-homicide charges and convictions—the support for the doctor, the indifference to the victims. In general the people of the region perceived him as a selfless humanitarian. Even if solid evidence did turn up, Nolen had doubts about indictment and prosecution. The case would likely become a social and political cause. All Nolen had to do to gauge public sentiment was to drop Dr. Cavaness's name and the testimonials would pour out: "The doc told me I had Rocky Mountain fever when nobody else knew . . . he never sent me a bill . . . Doc C.'s a regular Robin Hood . . ." and so on.

One old farmer whom Nolen engaged in conversation in a Harrisburg coffee shop was typical. Nolen brought up Mark's death, saying how hard it must be on the family, and wondered aloud whether Dr. Cavaness might take to the bottle. It was said that the doctor might have a drinking problem.

"Let me tell you something," the old farmer said, holding a finger to his mouth. "Not wine nor beer nor spirits has ever passed these lips, but what the doc does on his own time is his business. I'll tell you one thing. I'd rather have Doc Cavaness operate on me drunk than your doctor sober."

Nolen imagined what it would be like to try to find twelve impartial jurors in Saline County to listen to evidence against the local hero and then have the guts to act on it. They would all be either the doctor's patients or relatives and friends of patients. He would have delivered their babies, saved their lives, occupied a place second only to Jesus in their hearts.

Nolen knew that his only prudent course would be to investigate quietly, letting no one know that the doctor was a suspect, putting nothing in writing, confiding in no one.

If Dr. Cavaness had in fact murdered Mark or conspired in his murder, the case against him would have to be airtight before anyone got wind of it. The evidence would have to be as clear-cut as it had been when the grand jury had brought down the reckless-homicide indictments in 1971. Nolen reviewed the files on that event, noting—was it something other than mere coincidence?— that the accident had occurred on exactly the same day of the same month, the eighth of April, as Mark's murder. He was disinclined to make much of what was probably a meaningless coincidence of dates, although killers had been known to act out of obscure compulsions connected to holidays or anniversaries. What seemed more significant to Nolen was what he remembered of the doctor's uncooperative behavior and his saying, when informed of the victims' death, that everyone had to die sometime. The doctor had also talked a lot about insurance, Nolen recalled. None of this would be admitted in court as evidence, but it spurred Nolen on.

During the next few weeks, he made the Cavaness case his top priority. He gathered all the information he could about the doctor; no new suspects surfaced. He learned that Dr. Cavaness could fight like a red, roaring bull and that it did not take much to set off his temper. Nolen heard several versions of the nearly fatal fight after the poker game with Huck Gee. Numerous people recalled being challenged or attacked by the doctor: The farther Nolen ranged away from Harrisburg and Eldorado, the less willing people were to defend Dr. Cavaness. The sheriff in one county reported that the doc had been thrown in jail one night for drunken brawling in a tavern and had gone berserk in his cell, ripping out the sink and smashing the toilet. A man from Equality recalled having been at a cocktail party one summer and seeing Dale Cavaness standing by the swimming pool. Playfully the man had suggested that everybody jump in the pool with their clothes on. "You touch me," the man recalled the doctor's saying, "and I'll cut your nuts off."

A telling instance of the doctor's temper when drunk was relayed to Nolen by his own son. He had been present at a party with Dale Cavaness one evening, Nolen's son said, and had offered to give him and his girlfriend, Martha Culley, a ride home, because the doctor appeared too drunk to drive. When Dr. Cavaness refused, several people gathered around and tried to persuade him not to drive, but he grabbed a hammer from the kitchen, shoved it into his belt, and headed for his car. Nolen's son followed the doctor outside and tried to prevent him from entering his car. But the doctor shoved him aside, drew the hammer from his belt and started swiping at him with it. Nolen's son backed off.

None of the stories added up to evidence of murder, but Nolen kept probing. With his two sons grown, his normal routine was to be up at dawn at his house in Harrisburg to have breakfast with his wife, Polly, and listen to the first few minutes of *The Baptist Hour* on station WEBQ before hitting the road. His devotion to the program derived less from piety than from his half-interest in a flower shop, where Polly and his mother worked. The opening of *The Baptist Hour,* on the air since 1931, included mention of every Baptist who had died during the previous twenty four hours or over the weekend, along with news of funeral arrangements. The information enabled Nolen and his wife to adjust their flower inventory according to demand. By the time the sermon came on—always a low-key performance in keeping with the early hour, the word "hell" disallowed more than three times per broadcast—Nolen was headed for his office. From there he wheeled around through the day as investigation required.

He liked to be home by five-thirty or six for dinner, barring emergency calls. His recurrent nightmare was Shawneetown, where the miners, river rats, soldiers from a nearby base, anyone in search of whiskey and a fight would gather to hoot and holler. Some of the dirt-floored Shawneetown taverns were equipped with metal washtubs that would fill with teeth, human hide and hair, the water dark and thick with blood during a night's hell-raising. There the violent heritage of Little Egypt survived in its most traditional form. Nolen was forever getting a call in the night to head for Shawneetown to investigate a stabbing or a shooting or a head bashed in with a pool cue. One evening an arsonist torched a few of the bars; Nolen was not sorry to see them go, nor surprised to learn that locals had caught the culprit and beaten him to death. When he examined the body, Nolen counted over five hundred stitches, old and new, fresh and healed, insignia of a Shawneetown life.

But on a good evening Nolen could settle into his chair in his basement den to watch television and read and answer telephone calls—always a few and often as many as thirty from friends, tipsters, snitches, fellow detectives adding to his hoard of information. The den, paneled and immaculate, was a refuge for Nolen and his wife. Its shelves held books about the history of southern Illinois, titles like *Bloody Williamson, My Fight with the Ku Klux Klan*, and *A Knight of Another Sort: Prohibition Days and Charlie Birger*. On one wall Nolen had hung a photograph of Charlie Birger and his gang, fourteen desperadoes with their revolvers, rifles, shotguns and machine guns, posed around Charlie's armored Lincoln at Shady Rest. On another wall he had framed the front page from a 1925 edition of the Harrisburg *Daily Register*. The headlines read SHERIFF GALLIGAN'S RESIGNATION DEMANDED and SPECIAL LEGISLATIVE SESSION NEEDED TO BRING PEACE. Other stories told of coal-mine disasters and announced that the blind widow of a Klan leader was to deliver a lecture on morality and violence.

It helped Nolen to know that people had been behaving this way forever, that other lawmen had faced tough cases, mob violence and ineffective courts, and that life went on regardless. Time heals all was his motto: He repeated it often, and usually he was able to believe it.

As weeks passed without any new leads in the Cavaness case, however, another folksy phrase kept coming to Nolen's lips: "There's good times coming, but we may never live to see them." He did not seem to be making progress on the case, and he found himself sitting up later than usual thinking about it. Every time he opened the Cavaness file at the office he could not help glancing at the color Polaroids of Mark's remains; no matter how often he looked at them he felt anger along with revulsion. The ravaging of the body by animals seemed a part of the crime and suggested a savagery and also an indifference beyond comprehension. What if the boy's own father had left him to be devoured like this? If he had done it, or if he had paid someone else to do it and was now playing it cool, going on about his business, tending to the sick, chasing women, boozing—why, a man like that, Nolen said to himself, would gamble on his mother's tombstone and play poker with the corpse. There's good times coming, but we may never live to see them.

Nolen played tricks on himself to avoid thinking about the Cavaness case all day long and going to sleep with the pictures of Mark's body in his mind. He yielded to distractions. He followed the St. Louis Cardinals with greater intensity than usual. They were on the television almost every night, and he planned a weekend in St. Louis with his wife to take in a couple of games and get away from the terrible images and the accompanying frustration of not being able to do anything about them.

In June Nolen filed a long, confidential report with the D.C.I., detailing the interviews he had conducted but drawing no conclusions and listing no suspects. He did, however, identify Mark D. Cavaness as the victim of a homicide, ruling out either an accident or suicide as the cause of death.

Around that time, and regularly thereafter, Nolen began receiving calls from Kevin Cavaness, sometimes late at night after Nolen had left his den and gone to bed. Kevin wanted to know what Nolen had found out, whether there were any suspects. Nolen assured Kevin that the case was very much open, that there were some leads; but he would not give details other than that it was being treated as a murder. He did tell Kevin about the spent cartridge found on the floor of the Jeep, indicating that the gun had been fired out of the nylon case, in which no spent shells remained. Kevin, who had been permitted to examine the evidence two weeks after the murder, found this puzzling: He was sure that the case showed grooves where pellets had been fired through it.

"You're holding back," Kevin accused Nolen over the phone late one night. "You got to tell me what you know, goddamnit!"

"I wish I knew more, son." Nolen tried to calm Kevin down. "I'll keep at it."

"This is my brother we're talking about! What the shit is this? We want something done! Who else is working on this?"

Nolen remained unruffled. He let Kevin rave and vent his anger because he understood how he felt. But he was not about to tell Kevin that his own father was now the primary suspect in Mark's murder. Not only did Nolen not have any proof: He could not risk a violent reaction from Kevin, who from what Nolen could gather did not even know about the insurance policy.

Nolen continued collecting information about the doctor. The more he learned about him, the more Nolen was amazed that the man had been able not only to function but to prosper as a physician and surgeon all these years and the easier it was to imagine him killing his own son, or anyone else, whether in a fit of temper or, as it appeared, cold-bloodedly after taking out the insurance. As for how such a man, educated and, by all accounts, highly skilled in his profession, would be capable of such an act, Nolen could only resort to country wisdom and phrasing: The doc must have burned out a couple of bearings.

Kevin continued to sense that Detective Nolen knew something. He could not guess what it might be, but the feeling that Nolen was not telling him everything made Kevin wonder whether he could trust the detective. His sense of southern-Illinois justice was that it was corrupt and ineffective, and he began to wonder whether Nolen was just another bumbling, back-scratching good old boy. Kevin vacillated, because Nolen did seem to be different from other officers, above them in intelligence, aloof and independent; and the D.C.I. itself had a fine reputation for efficiency and integrity. But why wouldn't Nolen be more forthcoming? Wasn't the family of a victim entitled to know everything? Nolen promised to disclose all, but he was being enigmatic, acting more like a kindly uncle than a hard-nosed detective who was out to get his man. Kevin's rage welled up. Without a killer in sight, he had no one else to resent but the man who seemed to be failing in his task. Kevin thirsted for accusation.

He spent that summer working for Dale on the farms, or trying to work for him. His frustrations were somewhat eased by a new girlfriend, Charli Ann Haun, a nurse who had worked briefly at Pearce and was now employed by a doctor in Harrisburg. Kevin had gone to high school with Charli but had not started dating her until after Mark's death. She had known Mark. A week before his death Mark had complained to her when she was giving him a lift from Eldorado to Harrisburg that, because he was a doctor's son, people expected him to have access to narcotics. Some of his acquaintances were badgering him to get hold of speed and morphine. Mark had said that he was through with any kind of drugs except for the occasional joint.

As Kevin told Charli, he and Mark had long been sure that their father was using speed to counteract his hangovers. They had seen the bottles and packets of Fastin and Obestat squirreled away in Dale's trailer, and they had chalked up some of his irascibility to what they recognized as the "speed meanies," a short-temperedness common among heavy, long-term amphetamine addicts. It gave Kevin some solace to discuss his father and his dead brother with Charli. She was a slender, brown-haired girl whose intelligence, kindness and sympathy soothed Kevin's anguish and quickly won his heart.

Charli accompanied Kevin one afternoon over to Dale's trailer near the lake at the Galatia farm. They wanted to see how Dale was getting on with what Kevin regarded as a ridiculous plan to construct a glass A-frame over the trailer, a design that Dale said would revolutionize the mobile-home industry. They found him standing with three young men, two of whom were supposedly going to build the frame and install the glass. The third was Jim Eldridge, a male nurse from Pearce who was talking animatedly to Dale.

As Kevin and Charli got out of their car, they heard Dale curse Jim Eldridge. Dale had a drink in his hand.

"Why is he screaming?" Charli asked.

"That's just Dad," Kevin said. "It could be about anything."

"You don't even care about your patients!" Jim Eldridge shouted back. "You'll let them lay in there and die while you're out partying! I'm going to tell them what you think of them!"

"You won't tell anybody anything about me," Dale said.

It sounded like a threat. Jim Eldridge climbed into his car and roared away.

Dale turned to Kevin: "And what have *you* been doing all day?" Kevin said that he had been mending a fence. "Is that right? Mending a fence? Is that all you can think of to do? You call that doing something?"

"Now wait a minute," Kevin said. "It looks to me like you've spent the day drinking over in E-town," referring to Elizabethtown on the river, one of Dale's favorite watering holes.

"You shut your mouth," Dale said. "You're no better than your brother."

"Wait just a goddamned minute," Kevin said. "What do you mean by that?"

"I never did like him. Turkey-head. I never did like Mark. He was a no-good son of a bitch."

Kevin stepped up to his father and looked down into his face. He was big and broad and four inches taller than Dale. Kevin was holding a half-empty can of RC Cola in his right hand and he crushed it and threw it to the ground at his father's feet.

"I'm not going to stand for this shit," Kevin said, leaning into his father's face. "I happened to like Mark. I loved him. He was my brother."

"What the hell for?" Dale shouted up. "He was no good! He was nothing but a failure! Why the hell would anyone like him?"

The two remaining young men slipped away, got into their car and drove off. Kevin and his father stood toe to toe. Charli looked on from beside her car.

Dale started backpedaling. Kevin followed him step for step until his father was pinned against the trailer.

"You lousy creep," Kevin said. "You take back what you said about Mark!"

"You may be able to whip my ass," Dale said, lowering his voice, spitting out the words from between his teeth, "but I'll get you. I'll get you."

Kevin slowly turned and walked away. He told Charli they were leaving and asked her to drive.

In the car Kevin was shaking with rage. Then tears came. Charli reached over and took his hand. She told him that she loved him and that she wanted to be there for him.

That evening Kevin and Charli talked about Dale's behavior and about what he had said. Kevin confessed a terrible thought that had occurred to him. He had tried to dismiss it as too farfetched.

"Do you think there's any possibility that Dad might have had something to do with Mark's death?"

Charli at first did not answer. Finally she said yes, after what she had seen today, she thought it was possible.

They talked all night. They wondered what Detective Nolen thought, but neither Charli nor Kevin believed that they could bring the matter up with Nolen. Not now. Not yet, anyway. They had no proof.

They told each other that the idea of Dale as the murderer of his own son was too horrible and too remote to consider. He was an irrational, angry man, but they could not think of him as a killer. He had his own odd theories about Mark's death which he voiced from time to time. He said he thought that Mark was probably killed by a demented itinerant named Grolsch who had been convicted of another murder that had also occurred in 1977. He spoke of hearing about some people in a van who had been spotted by the proprietor of the Galatia cafe during the week of Mark's death. It looked as if they had had an injured man in the van; they were asking for a doctor. Probably, Dale said, they had panicked and dumped the body near the Shea house.

Kevin thought this story as preposterous as most of his father's other theories and business schemes. He felt sorry for Dale, whenever his anger at his father subsided. The poor guy had fouled up his life. He was probably half-deranged by the death of his son, in spite of his cruel, drunken words about Mark. Dale was bizarre and difficult, but underneath his aggressive, hostile manner, he had to be human, didn't he?

17

DURING THE FOLLOWING YEAR AT COLLEGE, KEVIN'S ANGER turned inward, and he fell into a depression, staying in his room and letting his studies slide. Marian became so worried about him that she convinced him to seek treatment at a St. Louis hospital. He remained there for only a couple of days, however, because the sight of the other patients frightened him and woke him up. With Charli's help he made up his lost work and managed to struggle back on track toward his degree in industrial engineering. She moved into an apartment with him at Cape Girardeau, and they began to talk of marriage. She continued working as a nurse; he hoped to land a job in St. Louis when he graduated.

Sean did not fare so well. His reaction to Mark's death was delayed; then it overwhelmed him. His moods veered from anger to despair; he frequently recalled the death scene, awakening in the middle of the night screaming from nightmares about his oldest brother's body. Kevin came up to St. Louis to try to help him and noticed that, at sixteen, Sean had already acquired a drinking problem. He lost whatever interest he had left in school and dropped out and began working at odd jobs—at a brickyard, delivering furniture, substituting off and on for workers at a landscaping outfit—still living at home with Marian and Patrick. He did not want to spend his life at manual labor, he said, but he needed time to get himself together. At home Marian would return from work and find Sean already at the booze. She tried badgering him, soothing him, warning him—nothing worked. She hoped it was a phase. Sean was the most outwardly sensitive and emotional of her boys; she could not bring herself to be harsh with him. He would take a couple of beers—probably something stronger behind her back —and burst into tears, hugging her and asking why Mark had died and when would they find out who had done this to him. He liked to stick close to her and help her in the kitchen, concocting stews, fixing breakfast for everyone on the weekends. He grew very fat and was ashamed of that.

When drunk, Sean would fall into an uncanny imitation of Dale, swaggering around the house, swearing, threatening, trying to be funny but achieving an unnerving effect. Sean was an excellent mimic anyway; his version of Dale was near-perfect. "By God," he would begin, "you can bet your sweet ass," and use all of Dale's favorite phrases. "We're going to get all the Rudies together and sit down at the roundtable and settle this goddamned thing!" He would try to telephone his father in southern Illinois and, if he reached him, tell him how much he loved him and ask when he could come down to visit. Dale usually hung up on him, and Sean would cry and wonder why his father was so cold to him. Didn't Dale love him? Was there something he had done? Did his father hate him because he was too fat? Was it because he had dropped out of school? Maybe next summer he could get close to his father again.

Dale's lawyer had succeeded in fending off the felony-theft charges against his client for six years. In November of 1980, Dale finally pleaded guilty to a misdemeanor charge of deceptive practice. He was sentenced to a five-hundred-dollar fine, seventeen hundred dollars in restitution, and one year's probation. His co-conspirator in fraud, Harker Miley, a Department of Vocational Rehabilitation counselor, received by contrast a sentence of ten thousand five hundred dollars in restitution, five years' probation, and a five-hundred-dollar fine. As the chief probation officer of Saline County wrote in his confidential report:

Having access to offense reports and conversations about the offenses with Harker Miley and Dr. Cavaness, there is no doubt in my mind that they were equally culpable but due to Dr. Cavaness' position as a doctor and surgeon, the [judicial officials] decided to reduce the charges to a level where he would not lose his license to practice medicine. . . .

Marian still invited Dale to St. Louis for holidays and tried to hold her tongue rather than to condemn him in front of the boys. She feared that to denigrate Dale to them would risk depriving them of a father. They would probably believe whatever she said of him, and she was not prepared to assume so complete a responsibility. She succeeded in burying her worst suspicions and perpetuated the necessary lies, or half-truths, or convenient fictions, whatever they were: that Kevin, Sean and Patrick had a father who, whatever his angers and peculiarities and deficiencies, had once been a wonderful man, might become so once again, and cared for them in some deep, hidden way. In the long run, she reasoned, they were better off with a distant and difficult father than with no father at all.

At Christmastime in St. Louis Uncle Eddie Bell and other guests, friends of Marian old and new, were astonished at the way Dale would talk to his sons when Marian was out of the room. Under his breath he would refer to Sean as buzzard-brain, aardvark, no-bill, deadbeat. Kevin tried to deflect Dale onto innocuous topics: How were the farms doing? Were the cattle bringing good prices?

"What do *you* want to know for?" Dale responded. "Just what are you after? Why don't you get out of my life?"

The other guests would leave early, and Dale would zero in on Sean, asking what he planned to do with his life, if he was prepared to remain an embarrassment. When Marian did witness these attacks, she would force Dale to apologize on the spot or later over the telephone; but their memory festered.

As Sean approached twenty years of age, his drinking grew worse. He would often break down when drinking, swear he was going to find Mark's killer, try to telephone his dad at all hours. He grew attached to an older couple who lived in the house next door, Elmer and Viola Eltinge, who were survivors of the Auschwitz concentration camp and had come to America in the 1950s. They had been separated from each other and from their son in 1943, reunited after the liberation in 1945. Having escaped death in the camps, they talked of little else.

Marian loved Elmer and Viola and listened to their stories with horrified fascination. Again and again she heard Viola tell of the night when they were rounded up, herded into boxcars, transported, and marched into different sections of the camp.

"They took my son!" Viola cried out. "They took my son from me!"

Marian told the Eltinges that she had lost a son, too, without going into details. At least the Eltinges could be grateful that their son had survived along with them and could come to visit them now. But Marian knew that her troubles were far less than the Eltinges had witnessed and endured. Their stories were almost unimaginable; she could stand to hear only so much about Auschwitz.

Not so with Sean. He never tired of examining the Eltinges' forearms, where the tattooed prisoners' numbers still showed, and poring over their collection of photographs taken on the day of liberation: One depicted Elmer and Viola huddled with other freed prisoners, hollow eyes telling of death.

Maybe you should not spend so much time over at Elmer and Viola's house, Marian suggested to Sean. Maybe it is too depressing for you. But Sean remained drawn to them, and when Viola died, Sean devoted hours to comforting the desolate Elmer.

While Marian could hardly fault Sean for his compassion, she perceived something morbid and compulsive in the degree of his interest in the Eltinges. He would run up to Elmer and hug him, as if by touching him he could heal the wounds of the past and his own wounds. She feared that, given his emotic.ial state, an obsession with the most hideous crimes in the history of mankind was dangerous. She tried to convince him that one had to make one's own life, find joy and hope in trivial, everyday things, as she had tried to do. The alternative was depression, madness: He could no more solve the world's problems than his brother's murder.

Sean's behavior reminded her of the way Mark would shut himself up in his room and listen to Jimi Hendrix records by the hour. Like many parents Marian had fought a losing battle against music she thought might have a baleful influence on her children. Sean's tastes were easier for her to bear—old Beatles records, James Taylor, sounds that might almost be called romantic—but the effect was similar, turning him inward, putting him in a daze. And his memories of Mark appeared to intensify over the years, especially when he drank and grew angry. Marian came home one evening to find that Sean had driven his fist through a wall in frustration.

Early in 1982, now in his twentieth year, Sean got the idea from some of his southern-Illinois friends that there was big money to be made in the oil fields of Oklahoma. It sounded like an adventure; it might shake him from his obsessions with the past; Marian encouraged him to go.

Dale supplied him with an old pickup truck and Sean headed west with a couple of his buddies to Woodward, out in the Oklahoma Panhandle, a boomtown in those days, a place as alive with drilling activity as it was rough and isolated. Sean survived the life of a roughneck for a few months, but when he was laid off as the boom began to bust, he came home, minus the truck. At Christmas in St. Louis, Dale lit into him for his failure.

Kevin and Charli, who were married in October 1982, at the First Presbyterian Church in Eldorado, were now living in St. Louis. Marian hoped that their stability might have a positive effect on Sean. Kevin landed a manufacturing engineering job at Emerson Electric Corporation, and Charli worked as the nurse and receptionist for a pediatrician. Their apartment in the suburb of Maryland Heights was only a few minutes' drive from Marian's house.

They tried to counsel Sean and to get him to seek medical help for his drinking, which was increasing. He could not stop talking about Mark, about his love for Grandpa Peck and his troubles with his father. After months of persuasion, they, along with Marian, finally convinced him to enter an alcoholic-rehabilitation center in December 1983. The program involved a month's seclusion, supervision, counseling, and diagnosis.

That Christmas Kevin and Charli, in southern Illinois to visit her parents, stayed one night at the Harrisburg house that Dale had recently bought for himself and Martha Culley. They hoped to persuade Dale to contribute something toward the costs of Sean's treatment, which was only partially covered by Marian's insurance from her nursing job.

The house was a three-story place with an impressive portico, next door to the Sullivans' on Walnut Street, filled top to bottom with antiques—mostly junk, Kevin and Charli thought, thrown together and lending the impression of a used-furniture warehouse, the rooms apparently arranged according to nationality, with a

Japanese wing here, an Italian room there, all of it dark and musty. In one room they discovered the bed and other furniture from Dale's Galatia trailer, which had burned to the ground the previous spring, supposedly a total loss. Evidently Dale had had the foresight to remove everything of value beforehand.

"I knew it," Kevin said to Charli as they lay in bed after a difficult evening trying to make conversation with Dale and Martha, everyone except Charli, who seldom took more than a single beer, ending up pie-eyed. "The son of a bitch burned that trailer and collected on the insurance. He told me he got eighty thousand or something. Son of a bitch."

They found themselves unable to sleep in the house and wished they had not stayed there. Marian, in her usual effort at diplomacy, had urged them to try to be friendly with Martha. She herself would never speak to the woman again, but after all, it looked as if Dale planned to stick with her, for God only knew what reasons. There was no sense in having more ill feelings in the family than there already were.

But Kevin could not stomach an evening with Martha. He told Charli, who held him as he squirmed in the bed, that he wished he had grabbed Martha's wig and flung it in the fire. He boiled with resentment at the house which, though it needed paint and smelled of wood-rot, was just the sort of elegant old place Marian would have loved to fix up. It dated from the early 1920s, the end of Little Egypt's only prosperous modern period, and qualified as a Harrisburg landmark. To Kevin the house symbolized everything that his family had lost through Dale's indifference and Martha's complicity in his ways.

"I don't suppose you could cough up something to help Sean," Kevin said to his father the next morning. "That treatment program is going to cost a bundle."

"Can't promise anything," Dale said. "Things are tight."

He'll send something, Kevin thought. He'll send a couple of hundred dollars, cry poverty. He'll probably take it out of Grandpa's trust fund, if that isn't already gone.

During that same period, from the middle of December 1983 into January 1984, Jack Nolen dared to hope that he was finally closing in on the doctor. He had discovered no new evidence regarding Mark's murder. Frank Stoat had separated from his wife and was living somewhere in the Deep South; Dr. Cavaness was behaving as usual but had betrayed nothing that would tie him to the killing. Yet the case remained open, Nolen had not given up, and now he thought that he might have something on the doc that would land him in jail, perhaps for a good long stretch.

Nolen organized an undercover drug bust that led to the biggest narcotics dealer in southern Illinois, a man known as the Panther, who operated out of Old Shawneetown. In a sting operation, D.C.I. agents were able to purchase cocaine and other drugs from the Panther who, in return for leniency, agreed to inform on other dealers. He named names and one of them, Johnny Weingarten, Nolen recognized as a close acquaintance of Dr. Cavaness's.

Weingarten worked for the doc on the Galatia farm and had built a house on property acquired from Dr. Cavaness on Harrisburg Lake. (Where Weingarten, who had been a promising youth, valedictorian of his high school class, but had amounted to nothing since, had acquired the money to buy land and build a house was an interesting question; the property deed indicated a price of fifty-five thousand dollars for the land alone.) Weingarten's former marriage to Martha Culley's daughter was another link to the doctor.

None of these connections proved any criminal behavior on the part of Dr. Cavaness, but Jack Nolen had them in mind when he planned a setup in which the Panther would attempt to buy drugs from Johnny Weingarten. It was not a matter of guilt by association but rather of suspicion by association, so often a fruitful approach in any investigation. The target of the bust was Weingarten; if he could be shown to have any criminal ties to Dr. Cavaness, who as a physician had access to drugs, that would be a bonus.

When the Panther told Nolen that a meeting to buy drugs had been arranged with Weingarten at a spot out in the country near Galatia, Nolen directed that the Panther be wired with a transmitter. Nolen knew the location well. It was on the Cavaness farm, near the Shea house, where Mark Cavaness's body had been found.

On a clear December night Nolen placed the recording equipment in his Buick and followed the Panther out to the Galatia farm. He let the Panther proceed up the dirt road to the Shea house; Nolen switched off his headlights and pulled up on the main road beyond the entrance to Dr. Cavaness's property, safely out of sight and hearing.

Nolen adjusted the recorder and his earphones. He heard the

Panther and Weingarten exchange greetings. Weingarten introduced another man.

"You sure there's nobody else around here?" Nolen heard the
Panther say. "Who owns this place?"

"Our friend the doctor," Weingarten said. In the darkness Nolen
turned up the volume and smiled. He heard Weingarten go on to
say that he had done a little favor for the doctor a few months back.
He had torched the doctor's trailer for him.

"This is pretty good stuff," the Panther said. "Where'd you
get it?"

"The doctor," Weingarten said. "Our buddy the doctor."

"You don't say. So what if he gets raided? Here you are. He
could tie you in."

"No sweat," Weingarten said. "We don't have nothing to do with
him, see? We just say we've been working for him on his catfish
farm. Which is what we have been doing."

When the evidence was analyzed it included 29.3 grams of liquid
morphine. With five milligrams as the normal dosage given to a
heart-attack victim or other patient suffering excruciating pain, this
was a considerable amount, worth upwards of ten thousand dollars
on the street, capable of providing several thousand highs.

Nolen tried to trace the morphine and other drugs, including a
morphine substitute, to Dr. Cavaness. They were pharmaceutical
substances, on hand in every hospital, accessible to the doctor.

These particular drugs turned out to have been manufactured
several years before; they had perhaps been in Dr. Cavaness's
possession all that time. But Nolen was unable to trace them directly to Dr. Cavaness.

Nolen still had Weingarten's word on tape that he had "torched"
the doctor's trailer, on which Nolen was able to verify that the
doctor had collected insurance.

He presented all the evidence to a judge, asking for arrest warrants to be issued against Dr. Cavaness, Johnny Weingarten, and
the third man present at the deal, who turned out to be Weingarten's younger cousin.

The judge agreed to the warrants for the Weingartens on the
drug charge, but refused to issue one against Dr. Cavaness. There
was not sufficient probable cause against the doctor, the judge
rightly determined, because Weingarten could hardly be consid-

ered a "reliable informant," a precondition for arresting someone on the word of another. If either of the Weingartens could be persuaded to name the doctor fully and to trick him into giving them drugs in a deal observed, recorded, or in some way proved by officers, then there would be probable cause and Nolen could arrest him.

The age of the drugs suggested that Dr. Cavaness was a novice at dealing, making use of substances no longer on inventory at the hospital, and that he might not deal again. Nolen decided that he would have to go ahead and arrest the Weingartens and hope that they would implicate the doctor. He was prepared to make them a sweet deal if they would cooperate.

When confronted with the tape of the conversation with the Panther, the younger Weingarten at first named Dr. Cavaness, then retracted his statement. Johnny Weingarten refused to talk at all.

The cousins were tried, convicted, and sentenced to ten years each. Nolen felt sorry for the younger cousin, who appeared to have been only marginally involved and seemed remorseful; but as Nolen liked to say, recreation can be mighty expensive. As for why neither cousin was willing to finger the doc, Nolen could not be sure. He wondered whether the Weingartens feared Dr. Cavaness. Johnny and the doc had been close over the years, Johnny might know about other activities in which the doctor had been engaged, and surely he must have witnessed many instances of the doc's violent temper. He might know more than was healthy for him.

But all this was speculation. For now Nolen could only continue to wait and watch, carry on with his daily routine, wheel around Egypt pursuing other cases and absorbing information. Six years after Mark's death, Nolen could not be absolutely certain that Dr. Cavaness was responsible for the murder, but he felt in his bones that it was so. The doc was one hell of a clever little guy. Everybody in Eldorado and half of Harrisburg still swore by him. It was probably a good thing that Kevin and his brothers were living away from southern Illinois.

In St. Louis Marian was able to discern signs that her burdens were beginning to lighten. Sean, released from the treatment center, joined Alcoholics Anonymous and seemed to be coping much better with his problems. He had a new girlfriend, Tina Crowley, a sympathetic young woman with a child of her own. He was talking about taking classes at a technical college.

Even Dale gave indications of mellowing. He had come up with a scheme to provide for his sons' futures, an investment program to which he would contribute a thousand dollars per son per year that was tied to the stock market and could be worth a great deal of money, so he said, in a few years' time. All the boys had to do was to sign some papers; he would take care of the rest. It was a new type of investment program established by the Equitable insurance company: By making the payments through the company, Dale said, he would be able to get a tax deduction.

Kevin thought the plan sounded a little goofy. He called Dale's insurance agent, Harry Bramlet, who assured Kevin that the plan was sound and would be of great benefit to him and his brothers. The payments would be deducted automatically from Dale's checking account. Kevin noted that the plan was actually a life-insurance policy and that it included a nonsmoking clause, even though both Kevin and Sean smoked. But he and his brothers went ahead and signed. What the hell, Kevin figured, if the old man wants a tax deduction, let him have it.

Marian meanwhile was making plans to marry again. She had been surprised late in 1982 to receive a telephone call from Les Green, a man whom she had not seen or heard from in thirty years but whom she remembered as the fellow who had married one of her roommates from her Washington, D.C., days as an airline stewardess. Les contacted her after his wife died of cancer and he learned from the third roommate that Marian was divorced and living in St. Louis, where one of Les's married sons also lived. Les told her that he was president of his own advertising agency in Wausau, Wisconsin; he was coming to St. Louis to visit his son and would love to see her and reminisce about the great times they used to have together in Washington.

Marian went to dinner with Les and his son and daughter-in-law at Al Baker's, a popular Italian restaurant that Marian had not been able to enjoy for years. Being with Les was like escaping decades of unhappiness. He was a quietly humorous, conservative man, close to his children, successful in his business, ten years older than Marian but still handsome, elegantly dressed, with beautiful manners. Soon he and Marian, as Les said, became the best thing that ever happened to the airline business between St. Louis and Wisconsin. He called her Skip; her old nickname made her feel like her fun-loving self again.

"I guess we've found out that we can bear each other's company," Les said to her when she was visiting him at his house in Wausau. That evening he proposed to her. He had a spare room where Patrick could live while finishing high school.

Patrick resisted, and Marian worried about leaving Sean, but marrying Les seemed to her a godsend. She knew that she would be a fool to turn down a man whose company she loved and who offered her peace and security. Les made every effort to befriend her boys; for a man at his age to agree to live with someone else's teenaged son was a sign of generous character. Wausau was not a metropolis but it was attractive and orderly, and Les's friends welcomed her.

Putting Sean on his own seemed the best choice for him. At twenty-two, it was time for him to stop living with his mother anyway. He cried at the prospect of her leaving, but she helped him find a spacious apartment across from the Botanical Gardens on Arsenal Street, only seven blocks from Tina Crowley's. Kevin and Charli would watch out for him, and Marian could fly down if there were any crises. Dale agreed to send the hundred and fifty dollars monthly rent until Sean could establish himself.

Marian was puzzled when, in order to obtain a marriage license, she requested a copy of her divorce decree from the St. Louis County clerk and was told that none could be found. She hired a lawyer from Marion, Illinois, to investigate. It turned out that, although the judge had pronounced Dale and Marian divorced thirteen years before, the final decree was conditional on Dale's signing and filing the settlement papers. He had neglected to do so.

Isn't that typical, Marian thought. Anything having to do with Dale meant problems. It crossed her mind that he might deliberately have contrived to leave the divorce unsettled, as a final gesture of control over her or as an expression of his indifference or contempt; but she kept her thoughts to herself. Les took the matter lightly. He laughed that it was the first time that he had gone steady with a gal only to find out that she was married. Imagine a man of my years, he said, ending up engaged to a female bigamist.

Marian's lawyer drove over to Eldorado to obtain Dale's signature. He reported that the doctor had kept him waiting for an hour and a half but that Dale had seemed to be a terrific guy, warm and down-to-earth.

"That's Dale," Marian said. "He could charm the birds off the trees. That's why I married him. The charm wore off after a while."

She said no more. She saw no reason to burden Les with her tales of the woe that had been her marriage. If you were going to start over, you had better be prepared to leave the past behind. All Les knew was that Marian's marriage had soured after many years and that her eldest son had died under tragic circumstances. The important thing was, Les liked to kid her, that she had survived all those years without losing her looks.

Les and Marian were married in June 1984 at the Central Presbyterian Church in St. Louis, with her boys and his three children in attendance. Pat and Betty Ray Sullivan drove up from Harrisburg, and Marian's brother, Bill, flew back from California for the event. Bill invited the boys to visit him and his family at their house in the Bay Area. They should consider moving to California, Bill said, where there were plenty of opportunities. Privately he told Marian that he had surmised some years before that she might be having trouble with Dale. He had been on a business trip in the late 1960s, he said, checking into a hotel in Nashville, when he noticed that the man signing in next to him at the registration desk was from Eldorado.

"I've got a sister living in Eldorado," Bill had said. "She's married to a Dr. Dale Cavaness."

"That's not something I'd brag about," the man had snapped and turned his back.

The minister spoke of how Les and Marian had found each other after thirty years. Now they would be able to love and care for one another in their maturity. Their story was an inspiring one, an instance of benign providence.

At dinner afterward at The Coal Hole, a cheerfully opulent restaurant in Clayton, everyone toasted the newlyweds.

18

THROUGHOUT THE LATTER HALF OF 1984, WITH MARIAN AND
Patrick living up in Wisconsin, Sean and Dale were in closer touch
than ever before, as Sean reported happily to Kevin and Charli.
There were phone calls two or three times a month, and once early
in November Dale dropped by Sean's apartment unexpectedly
when, he said, he happened to be in St. Louis on medical business.
Sean was not at home but the downstairs neighbor put Dale on
the phone with Tina Crowley, who said that Sean was with her
and gave directions to her place. Dale had stayed at Tina's for
several hours, talking and drinking.

Kevin was glad for Sean that he was getting closer to Dale,
although Kevin worried that Dale would encourage Sean to drink.
Around Kevin and Charli, Sean drank little or not at all, being
anxious, they understood, for them to see that he was making
progress. They worried about him. They were never sure whether
to believe him when he told them that he had a job doing one
thing or another, and he had dropped out of the classes he had
been taking at St. Louis Community College at Forest Park. He

seemed to enjoy being with Tina Crowley, but he also spent a lot of time alone, walking through the Botanical Gardens across from his apartment and going fishing out at the Busch Wildlife Center, which reminded him of southern Illinois.

As winter came on, Sean's only job was shoveling snow for a landscaping company. Dale paid his rent, but his telephone was shut off—temporarily, he assured Kevin and Charli; he had forgotten to pay the bill. He did not tell them that his gas and electricity had also been cut off. They asked him to dinner as often as they could and gave him a few dollars when they had something to spare.

On Saturday, December 8, Sean came to dinner at their apartment, bearing Christmas cards for Marian, Les, Patrick and some friends, wrapped gifts for Kevin and Charli. He asked them to mail the cards for him—to save the postage, Kevin presumed, figuring that Sean must have pawned something to afford the gifts, however small they probably were. But he seemed cheerful, hugging them as he always did and asking whether he could ride down to southern Illinois with them for Christmas; he did not think his Olds would be able to make the trip. He was looking forward to seeing his dad and to spending the rest of the holidays in St. Louis with Tina. The old man had been acting pretty decent lately. It would be a drag, staying with Dale and Martha as Sean planned to do, but it would be worth it, he said.

After dinner they watched a World War II documentary on television. If he ever had to go into combat, Sean said, he would want to have Poncho (his pet name for Kevin) by his side.

"Poncho would ride shotgun," Kevin said. He had been reading Ernest Hemingway and had placed a bust of Papa, with sunglasses perched on the bearded face, on top of the television set. Kevin liked to kid Sean by talking in Hemingway lingo to him. "Poncho would pick off the bastards one by one. Then we would catch a fish and cook it and eat it and drink plenty of the good white wine they serve in the clean café by the river. You stick with the old Poncho. We'll have good times, and the women will be fresh and pretty after we're finished with the killing."

Kevin and Sean talked about other Christmases, laughing about the bad times and trying to remember the good ones. That Christmas in the trailers after the house had burned down had been the worst, they agreed. When they saw that it was after midnight, Sean decided to sleep over. He headed home after watching some football on television the next afternoon.

One Monday evening Dale telephoned to ask whether Kevin had seen Sean. He wanted to talk to him; it was nothing important, some papers to sign. Kevin said that he would relay the message. On their way over to a St. Louis Blues hockey game the following evening, Kevin and Charli stopped by Sean's apartment, but he was not home, so they left a note saying that they hoped to catch him after the game. When Sean was still not at home—they assumed he must be with Tina—Kevin left a second note:

Sean,
    Give me a call as soon as you can. Nothing wrong. Just a relay from the Honcho [Dale].

Luv,
Kev.

P.S. Do you really live here?

On Wednesday evening at about eight-thirty, Kevin and Charli were watching *Dynasty* on television when Sean telephoned. Kevin told him to get in touch with Dale and made final plans for the Christmas-week trip to Eldorado.

Kevin and Charli were preparing for bed at ten-thirty the next night, Thursday, December 13, when the telephone rang and Charli answered it. She did not recognize the caller, who asked to speak to Mr. Kevin Cavaness. She put Kevin on.

"Mr. Cavaness?"

"Yes. Who is this?"

"This is Detective Dave Barron of the St. Louis County Police Department. Do you have a brother by the name of Sean?"

"Yeah. Why?"

"There's been a problem."

"What kind of a problem?" Kevin asked. He was irritated. It was late and he wondered whether this call might be some kind of a prank. "How do I know who you are? How do I know you're a police officer?"

"I'm sorry, Mr. Cavaness. It's very serious. Can you come down and meet me at the County Hospital?" The man's voice was mild and courteous. To Kevin it did not sound like a cop's voice. "Your brother has been shot," the man said.

Kevin felt his knees weaken.

"Is this some kind of a joke? This better not be a joke! You're telling me he's been killed? You better be for real!"

"You'd better come down to the hospital," the man said. "I'm very sorry. I'm afraid that your brother Sean is dead."

Charli drove; Kevin could not. He sat in the car slumped down, unable to speak or to feel anything except bewilderment. He prayed that there was a mistake. It could not be true. Not after Mark. That kind of thing could not happen twice.

At the hospital Detective Dave Barron ushered them into a small office. He was a big, tall fellow, nearly six feet five, in his early thirties, slightly balding, dressed in a brown suit. He had a large, pained, kindly face with small features. In his soft, almost sweet voice he offered his apologies for having to call them and upset them.

"I didn't mean to be rude over the phone," Kevin said. "It's just—you see, I've been through this before."

"What do you mean?" Barron asked.

"It so happens, I had another brother who was killed. Seven years ago. He was—" and Kevin choked up. Detective Barron shoved a chair over to him.

"My God, another brother? Seven years ago? Was he shot, too?"

Kevin nodded, covering his face with his big square hands.

"What was his name?"

"Mark."

"If you don't mind my asking, how old was Mark when he was shot?"

"Twenty-two."

Detective Barron said that Sean's body had been found early that morning in a remote, western part of the county on Allen Road, which was near Lewis Road, off Highway 44. It was not far from the entrance to Times Beach, Barron said, which was the place that had been sealed off because of dioxin poisoning. Sean had been shot twice in the head. Unfortunately, the body would have to be identified so the police could proceed with their investigation.

Kevin got up to go perform the awful task but sat down again when Charli volunteered. Kevin thanked her. He said that he would hate to have to remember Sean as he was now. He wanted to remember him alive.

Afterward, at around midnight, they accompanied Barron over to his office at the South Central Police Station in Clayton. The station was quiet at that hour, Barron's office clean and orderly: two steel desks, some filing cabinets, a hat rack. The county police covered serious crime in all the municipalities and unincorporated areas beyond the limits of the actual city of St. Louis. Theirs was a suburban operation. The South Central station in Clayton, a prosperous area eleven miles from the city center and headquarters of the county's judicial apparatus, handled only a dozen or so homicides a year. All of the high-crime areas were within the city of St. Louis itself.

Dave Barron's first questions had to do with whether or not Sean had been on drugs or associated with people involved in drugs. He pressed Kevin and Charli on these points, staring into their eyes as they answered, but they assured him that Sean's problem was alcohol, never drugs. They described their last meeting with Sean at their apartment on Saturday and their telephone conversation with him on Wednesday and said that he had not indicated in any way that he was in fear of his life. They had no idea why he was murdered or who would wish to murder him. Everyone had loved Sean.

Barron turned to the matter of the other brother who had been killed. That murder had taken place in southern Illinois in April of 1977, Kevin said, and he described the circumstances of Mark's death, the shotgun in the truck, the body lying out in the open. So far as Kevin and Charli knew, no suspects had ever been identified. Detective Jack Nolen of the Illinois D.C.I. had told them that Mark's case remained an open homicide.

Dave Barron wrote down Jack Nolen's name, along with Tina Crowley's and the names and addresses of every friend or acquaintance of Sean's that Kevin and Charli could supply. He also got Sean's address and the make and model of his car from them. Barron had known little more than Sean's name and a former address before talking to Kevin and Charli.

Twice while they were talking, Kevin asked to use Barron's telephone and attempted to call Dale at the house on Walnut in Harrisburg. There was no answer. They were out partying, Kevin figured. He would have to keep trying. He was not ready yet to call Marian. He would have to get himself psyched up for that one.

After being with him for an hour and a half or so, Kevin found himself drawn to Dave Barron. He seemed so calm, straightforward and understanding, he was like a big brother.

"I'm real sorry about the way I acted on the phone," Kevin said.

"Hey," Dave Barron said. "Forget it. You should hear some of the people I talk to."

"It's just . . ." Kevin faltered. "It's just that I've been through this before."

The second that Kevin had said that he had another brother who had been killed seven years before and indicated the circumstances of that murder and Mark's age in 1977, Dave Barron immediately thought that there must be a connection between the two homicides. A quick calculation showed that Sean was also twenty-two. Like Mark's, his body had been abandoned in a remote area. More than that, Barron could not discern, but he kept the similarities in the forefront of his mind. What a lot for one family to suffer, he thought. They must have a curse on them like the Kennedys.

By the time Barron let Kevin and Charli go home, it was after midnight, Friday morning. Barron had been on the case since about eight A.M. Thursday when, having breakfast at home with his wife and two daughters, he was called to proceed on the double to a place near the southwestern corner of St. Louis County.

He took Interstate 44 some twenty miles to Lewis Road, passing by the sealed-off entrance to the evacuated town of Times Beach, where a guard was stationed to prevent people from driving into the dioxin-contaminated area, and turned right onto Allen Road. There, about three tenths of a mile ahead, other officers were gathered around a body, which lay beside the gate to a pasture. Two stone pillars framed the gate.

This was the Meramec River Valley, farm country, rolling hills and trees, the grass already faded from the first frosts, a low morning mist dampening the area, the air about thirty-eight to forty degrees. Dave Barron spoke to the man who had discovered the body. He was Charles Goad, a retired quality-control inspector at a Chrysler plant, who had been driving out to feed the filly he kept at the end of Allen Road. It was about seven-forty-five when he drove past the body, stopped to examine it and saw no signs of life. He telephoned the police from a house at the corner of Allen and Lewis.

Barron looked more closely at the body and noted down the details: white male, dressed in brown corduroy slacks, a cream-colored V-neck short-sleeved sweater and blue tennis shoes, lying on his back with his head pointing in a northerly direction, feet pointing in a southerly direction, both arms parallel with the body. There was one bullet wound to the lower right back of the head, another on the right side of the head; a third wound on the left side under the eye appeared to be an exit wound.

A search of the victim's pockets revealed no personal identification of any kind, no personal effects whatever.

Barron was struck by the freshness of the body, still warm to the touch. At nine-fifty A.M. an investigator from the St. Louis County medical examiner's office arrived and took the body's temperature by means of an electronic thermometer with a long needle probe, which he inserted into the liver. The thermometer registered ninety-five degrees Fahrenheit. Based on this and on subsequent readings taken at twenty-minute intervals, which showed that the body's temperature was dropping at the rate of approximately one degree every twenty minutes, the surgeon who performed the autopsy later that afternoon determined that death had occurred anywhere from three to five hours before the time of the first temperature reading. That put the time of death at anywhere from five to seven o'clock that morning, perhaps as little as an hour or less before the body had been discovered by Mr. Goad.

The cause of death had been two gunshot wounds, either of which could have been fatal. Powder stipplings indicated that the shot to the back of the head, which exited below the corner of the left eye, had been a close shot, fired from an inch or less away. The other shot, which entered beside the right ear and, as X rays showed, had lodged in the brain, had been fired from a distance of eighteen to twenty-four inches. The weapon had been a pistol, probably a .357 magnum or possibly a .38: Fragmented bullets were often difficult to identify.

It was not until after six that evening that Detective Barron finally thought he could identify the victim. In the absence of a driver's license or any other personal effects—no abandoned automobile that could be connected to the crime had turned up—Barron had to rely on the fingerprint bureau. A set of prints matching those of the victim was at last dug up from the county police files. They belonged to Sean Cavaness, who had been stopped more than a year before for failing to yield to an emergency vehicle—only a misdemeanor, but Sean had been booked and his fingerprints taken.

When the name Sean Cavaness did not appear anywhere else in police records, Dave Barron cursed. He and his fellow detectives at South Central had managed to clear every other 1984 homicide off the books; now it looked as if he would have an open case hanging over him as the New Year approached. With only a piddling misdeameanor on his record, Sean Cavaness, whoever he was, seemed unlikely to have criminal associates who would be or could lead to suspects. The case was beginning to look like a bitch.

The address given on the Cavaness arrest record was for a house in the Shenandoah development in Chesterfield. Barron drove out to the house, but the family in residence had never heard of a Cavaness. A check with the local real-estate salespeople, however, told Barron that Marian Cavaness, who was now living in Wisconsin, had owned the house and raised three sons there, including Sean, who had lived at the address with his mother and younger brother, Patrick, until the previous June. Another brother, Kevin, was supposedly married and living somewhere in St. Louis. Barron returned to his office and, by ten-thirty, was on the phone to Kevin.

Barron was inclined to believe everything Kevin and Charli told him. Their statement that Sean was not involved with drugs but had a drinking problem was corroborated by the blood-alcohol level in the body, 0.26, which was enough to render someone Sean's size (five feet eight, a hundred and eighty pounds) incoherent and possibly unable to walk.

Who would wish to kill him? The girlfriend? From what Kevin and Charli said, Tina Crowley was hardly the homicidal type, just a poor young woman trying to care for her child, drawn toward Sean out of mutual sympathy. She might know something or someone, however, that Kevin and Charli did not.

As Barron sat in his office trying to piece what little he had together, he noticed that it was two in the morning.

Barron decided that he had enough energy left to check out Sean Cavaness's neighborhood. It was a difficult area to classify—a Bohemian kind of place made up of veterans of the counterculture, teachers, aging students, a sprinkling of the elderly: not a high-crime area but unpredictable. Unlike many of St. Louis's neighborhoods—the black areas shunned by white taxi drivers, the

Italian Hill, the lush enclaves of *Fortune* 500 executives and doctors and lawyers, the suburbs peopled by aspiring whites—Sean's district had no distinct ethnic or sociological character. Most of the buildings were two-story brick houses designed to accommodate four families, built late in the last or early in this century. It was a pleasant part of the city, full of trees, a refuge for moderate- to low-income people who shunned the suburbs.

Sean's building at 4170 Arsenal was at the corner of Bent Drive, across the street from the park, called either Shaw's Gardens or the Missouri Botanical Gardens; and there on Bent Drive sat the Olds Cutlass that Kevin and Charli had described as Sean's.

A break? Maybe.

"Please let there be blood in this car," Barron said to himself as he took his flashlight and approached the Cutlass. It was unlocked.

In the car Barron found neither bloodstains nor anything else that looked like evidence. He had been up for more than twenty hours working on this case. He knew that he could not last another twenty; better to get some sleep and start here again tomorrow.

Kevin telephoned Wausau at about half past midnight. He was hoping that Les would answer; he could not bear the idea of breaking the news to Marian. When she said hello, Kevin disguised his voice and asked to speak to Les, who sounded half-incredulous, half-appalled when Kevin told him that Sean had been murdered, with no clues as yet to a suspect. Les agreed to tell Marian. There were no words of comfort or hope possible, only the fact of death. Kevin said that he would call again in the morning to speak to his mother.

At about one-thirty Kevin reached Dale at the Harrisburg house Kevin thought that his father sounded drunk and gathered that Marian had already telephoned him.

"He's dead, huh?" Dale said.

Kevin asked his father to come to St. Louis the next day. He could stay at Kevin and Charli's apartment. He said he would.

Kevin and Charli were up all night, trying to imagine who would have or could have murdered Sean. They could not name a soul.

19

BY NINE-THIRTY THAT MORNING DAVE BARRON HAD RETURNED
to 4170 Arsenal. With other officers he surveyed Sean's apartment,
which proclaimed alcoholic depression: an empty quart of vodka
left on one of the few pieces of furniture, a round coffee table; a
little Coleman kerosene stove which with the electricity and gas
shut off must have served for heat and light; the telephone dead;
dirty clothes heaped in corners of the two bedrooms and the bathroom, which had seen no scrub brush for many weeks.

The scene made Barron melancholy. From Kevin and Charli he
had already formed an image of Sean as a sad young man eager to
love and be loved, swamped by miseries, facing a doubtful future.
It was easy to imagine him in these dark, bare, rudimentary rooms.
Kevin by contrast, devastated though he was, seemed strong—
angry but determined. Kevin had Charli. Barron had been im-
pressed by Charli when she had volunteered to spare Kevin the
task of identifying the body. In conversation she revealed an intense, coherent intelligence, a kindly nature, and powers of endurance. A woman like that probably meant the difference between
the two brothers' lives.

Barron had been a cop long enough to know that family members with the same background could turn out radically different. Like most homicide detectives, he was a believer in both heredity and free will: People made their own heavens or hells, although some had to overcome longer odds than others. Barron had extricated himself from poverty in a tough St. Louis neighborhood. He gave his wife much of the credit for his being able to handle a difficult and depressing job with equanimity. He also tried never to neglect his marriage, sharing his cases with his wife, making sure to telephone her during the day, more often when he was working nights, to see how the kids were doing and to ask whether she was having any problems. He had seen too many cops' marriages break up, and even a brief conversation with his wife helped his perspective, reminding him of normal life.

While other officers photographed the apartment and dusted for fingerprints, Barron went downstairs to talk to the neighbors, who, Kevin and Charli said, were Sean's friends. They were Ralph and Peggy Kroeck, in their late twenties, married with two young children. Mrs. Kroeck answered the door; her husband emerged in his bathrobe, rubbing his eyes.

Barron identified himself and Detective Larry Fox, his partner. Mrs. Kroeck, a short, heavy woman dressed in a meter-maid's uniform, said that she had seen the officers come in and had heard them go upstairs to visit Sean's place. She had not wanted to wake Ralph, who had worked last night, but he had heard the footsteps. Why were the police visiting Sean? Was something wrong? Surely Sean hadn't done anything.

"Sean is dead," Dave Barron said.

Peggy and Ralph Kroeck, who was as wiry and tall as she was neither, looked shocked. When Barron told them that Sean had been shot to death and found early the previous morning, they grabbed one another and started crying. They could not understand why anyone would want to kill Sean, he was such a loving, wonderful person. They had come to think of him as a brother or even as a son. They described him as a young man who drank too much but was a happy drunk, around them anyway. They had last seen Sean two nights ago, late Wednesday evening.

"Did you speak to him?" Barron asked.

Mrs. Kroeck said that Sean had come down to use the telephone sometime after six that evening. He had been excited about his plans for the holidays, going to Illinois with his family for part of the time.

"Did he seem drunk? Was he acting intoxicated?"

"No, not at all. He had not been drinking from what I could tell," Mrs. Kroeck said.

Somehow he managed to get up to 0.26 before dawn, Barron thought, but he did not doubt Peggy Kroeck's perceptions.

"So that was the last time you saw him?"

No, Mrs. Kroeck said, Sean had gone out after that. He had said that he was going over to his girlfriend's, Tina Crowley's. Mrs. Kroeck said that Tina was her best friend and that she had introduced Tina and Sean when he had moved into the building; he and Tina had been close ever since. Then Mrs. Kroeck herself had gone out, to visit a funeral parlor. Her husband's grandfather had died.

Ralph Kroeck added that he had come home from work—he was a truck driver—after nine, when his wife was still at the funeral parlor.

Mrs. Kroeck said that she was driving back from the funeral parlor at about ten-thirty when, only a few blocks from home, she noticed what she thought was a dark car acting very strange, staying close to her, following her as she turned east on Arsenal from Morganford and right on Bent Drive from Arsenal, where she parked at the corner. As she stopped, she said, the other car pulled up next to her for a moment and then drove on, heading slowly south on Bent.

Mrs. Kroeck said that she hurried out of her car and ran into her apartment and told her husband, Ralph, that she was afraid she had been followed home. She and Ralph had run to their daughter's bedroom window, which looked out on to Bent Drive, and she noticed the strange car make a U-turn in an alleyway and then come back toward Arsenal. The car was going very slowly. When it reached Arsenal, it made another U-turn and headed back south again on Bent.

At this point Ralph Kroeck picked up the account. He had been alarmed, he said, at the behavior of this car, and he hurried out the back door of the apartment to get a better look. He saw the car make yet another U-turn at Hartford, one block south of Arsenal, and head back, slowly as before, again toward Arsenal on Bent. As the car approached, Mr. Kroeck took up a position at the rear of his building and was able to get a clear view as it passed under a streetlamp. He read the license plate and rushed back inside and wrote down the number.

"You wouldn't still happen to have that number, would you?"

"I think so," Ralph Kroeck said. He went into his kitchen and produced a brown-paper grocery sack. "Here it is. Illinois, AVT-one-eight-three."

"Illinois. You're sure it was Illinois? Okay. Then what happened? Did the car go away?"

Mr. Kroeck said that the car parked under a streetlamp at the corner of Bent and Arsenal, facing north. By this time he and his wife were watching it again from their daughter's window and then through the front windows. They watched the driver, who was the only person in the car, get out and reach back in on the passenger side and take from the glove compartment a flashlight and some other object, they could not tell what. The car was a dark-colored Oldsmobile Toronado, Mr. Kroeck said, with a spare-tire kit on the back, like a Lincoln Continental. The man walked to the corner of Bent and Arsenal.

Just then Sean Cavaness appeared on foot. He was coming from the direction of the 7-Eleven store several blocks away. He walked right up to the man, and the two embraced.

Mrs. Kroeck said that at this point she finally recognized the man she thought had been following her. He was Dr. Cavaness, Sean's father from Illinois.

Mrs. Kroeck had recognized Dr. Cavaness because he had come to the apartment once before, about a month earlier, looking for Sean, and she had put him on the phone to Tina Crowley, who gave him directions to her apartment. He had introduced himself at that time, and she was able to see that it was the same person because he was standing under the lamp. Then from their front window she and Ralph had watched him and Sean walk together up the porch steps, talking and embracing; and they heard the two men go up the stairs to Sean's apartment. Ralph Kroeck said that he did not recognize Dr. Cavaness, because he had never seen the man before; but he described him as white, between fifty and sixty years old, short and stocky. The porch light had been on. They could see both men clearly.

Mr. and Mrs. Kroeck said that Sean and Dr. Cavaness had been upstairs in Sean's apartment for a couple of hours or more. They could hear them up there, talking and laughing and singing; they assumed that father and son were sharing drinks, the laughing and the singing got pretty loud. And they could hear them walking around up there: two distinct sets of footsteps.

So we're on the way to 0.26, Barron thought. Then we take a ride out of town, and that's it.

Mr. Kroeck said that he and his wife had watched television and gone to bed sometime before one o'clock on Thursday morning. They were able to fall asleep, but later—he could not name the hour; he had not looked at the clock—he was awakened by footsteps, again two distinct sets, coming down the stairs. He was a light sleeper, and he always heard Sean coming in or out. The stairs ran right past his bedroom, and the hallway echoed. That night he heard the footsteps clomping all the way down the stairs and the front door being opened and shut. Peggy had not awakened. It was unusual, Mr. Kroeck said, for Sean to have late-night visitors, except for Tina Crowley, and very unusual to hear him go out after midnight. That was entirely unlike Sean.

Neither Mr. nor Mrs. Kroeck had heard or seen anyone enter or leave Sean's apartment since Thursday morning before dawn. There had not been a sound from up there. They had assumed that Sean must have been with Tina, with whom he had been staying off and on.

Barron had Mr. and Mrs. Kroeck go over their story again. He checked out the places from where they said that they had observed the car and the man who Peggy was sure had been Sean's father, and he took with him the grocery bag with the license number on it. He thanked the Kroecks, telling them that they had been very helpful and that he would be in touch with them again. They agreed not to discuss what they had told him with anyone else for the time being.

Back in his car with Detective Fox, Dave Barron whistled in amazement. It was usually only on television cop shows that people wrote down license numbers; unless there was an automobile accident, it just did not happen. Over his radio he ran a check on Illinois license AVT-183: The car was a 1983 Oldsmobile Toronado, two-tone gray, registered to Dr. John Dale Cavaness at 210 Walnut Street, Harrisburg, Illinois.

"I don't believe it," Barron said. "The Police Fairy must be looking out for us."

231

He drove directly to the Clayton station and deposited the grocery bag for safekeeping with the evidence custodian. Then he telephoned Kevin and Charli. They said that they had been able to reach both of Kevin's parents. Marian would arrive the next day, Saturday; Dr. Cavaness was expected at Kevin's apartment sometime later that day or early evening.

"I'm glad the family can come," Barron said, trying to sound as casual as possible. "This is going to be pretty rough on everyone, I know. Listen, Kevin, do me a favor, would you? Give me a call when your father arrives, okay? You have my number? Good. They'll reach me if I'm out of the office. And here's my home number. Just give me a call when the doctor arrives. I'll come over."

Now he wanted to talk to Tina Crowley. On the way out of the station, he passed a sergeant who asked him kiddingly whether he had solved the murder yet.

"Sure," Dave said. "Don't tell anybody. It's the victim's father. A doctor."

"A doctor?" the sergeant laughed. "The hell you say. Get the fuck back on the street."

Tina Crowley was in a bad state when Detective Barron interviewed her at her apartment on Wyoming at half past two that afternoon. She had heard the news of Sean's death from Peggy Kroeck and from Charli Cavaness. She was worn down from weeping. Sean was the first person who had ever truly loved her, she said, and they had even begun talking about getting married. She had last seen Sean on Wednesday, December 12, and had spent the early evening shopping with him. She had dropped him off at his apartment at about eight and had neither seen nor heard from him since.

Tina, whom Barron observed as a forlorn creature who had obviously been in love with Sean, a single mother who had glimpsed some hope for her future only to have it dashed with Sean's death—Tina Crowley said that Sean had seemed happy about his Christmas plans to visit his father in southern Illinois.

"Did Sean say anything about his father coming up to visit him? Coming to his apartment?"

"No."

"Would you have been aware, do you think, if he had been expecting a visit from his father on Wednesday evening?"

"Sure I would've." Had Dr. Cavaness visited? She wanted to know.

"I didn't say that." Barron said. "I was just wondering if Sean mentioned anything."

Tina then told Barron about the only occasion on which she had met Dr. Cavaness. He came over to her apartment, she said, and sent Sean out for some vodka and Bloody Mary mix. That had upset her, because she was trying to help Sean stop drinking, but she did not say anything because she knew how glad he was to see his father, and she knew that Dr. Cavaness was a heavy drinker. Sean had told her he loved his father very much but that he could be difficult. Dr. Cavaness had not been difficult that evening. He and Sean had sat in the kitchen drinking and talking and laughing, while Tina had played Monopoly with relatives in the living room.

Sean had no enemies, Tina said, breaking down. She had no idea who had killed him or why. He was such a good person.

Difficult as it was for Dave Barron to imagine, Dr. John Dale Cavaness was now the major, indeed the only, suspect in the murder of Sean Cavaness. As yet Barron could discern no motive, but he had placed the doctor with his son within three to five hours of the murder. What had brought the doctor up from southern Illinois and when he had returned there remained unknown; but neither he nor Sean had gone back to the apartment that night. Sean was dead by seven Thursday morning. The doctor would have some explaining to do.

The toughest thing for Barron was not the evidence, which had been thrown into his lap by the miracle of the Kroecks' having seen the doctor and having written down the license number. What bothered him was the idea of a father's shooting his son—twice! —in the head. Barron and his wife, after having two children of their own, girls now in their teens, were in the process of adopting an eight-year-old orphan boy. They wanted a son and agreed that it would give them added pleasure and satisfaction to rescue a homeless child. They were now making regular visits to the boy before taking him home. Their daughters were enthusiastic. Barron and his wife knew that the boy would be frightened and would probably resist their love at first, but they welcomed the challenge and the chance to do something worthwhile for an unfortunate kid. To conceive of a father who would murder his own son—that was the hard part of this case as it was developing. What a weird world,

Barron thought, with me adopting a son while I'm trying to catch a guy who murdered his—or who certainly appears to have done so.

And who may have murdered yet another son. The connection to Mark, the similarities of age and circumstances of death, had never been absent from Barron's mind.

It was time to tell his superiors about the case. Barron met with a sergeant, a lieutenant, and Major Tom Moonier in the major's office.

"The doctor is suspect number one right now," Barron told them. He went through the evidence and said that he was expecting a call from Kevin Cavaness when the doctor arrived in St. Louis. He planned to go to Kevin's apartment, have a chat with the doctor, and ask him the big question—when was the last time he had seen his son Sean. Everything hung on how he would answer that one.

"If he doesn't admit that he was in town Wednesday night," Major Moonier told Barron, "book him."

"I don't want to do that," Detective Barron said. "I figure he's probably going to admit that anyway. He'll say he took Sean to dinner and dropped him back at the apartment—something like that. Or he left him off somewhere. And even if he lies about being in town, I need more time. I need more on him."

Barron reminded the other officers that, only a few weeks before, he had locked up a wife too soon for killing her husband, and she had been able to get released for lack of evidence and had subsequently escaped trial. He said that he would also prefer to spare the family more trauma than was necessary. He told the other officers about the connections to another son's death in 1977. If he could wait until after the funeral to arrest the doctor, more evidence might turn up in southern Illinois. He did not want the doctor to think he was a suspect, not for a couple of days anyway.

Major Moonier asked Barron to leave the room. After about ten minutes the major summoned him again. They were worried, Major Moonier said, that this doctor might try to kill someone else. He might try to blow the whole family away.

"The M.O. would be too different," Barron said. "I don't think he kills people when there might be witnesses. I'll just make sure nobody takes a scenic drive with him."

"Okay, Barron, we'll do it your way. Go talk to him. See what he says. See what you can dig up. But take somebody with you and put some men out there. We better watch that son of a bitch."

*   *   *

Kevin and Charli had sat all day in their Maryland Heights apartment waiting for Dale to arrive and feeling uneasy. Not having any idea who had murdered Sean made them wonder whether there was some nut out there who for some reason had it in for all the Cavaness children. When they spoke of Mark, they could see no other possible connection to Sean's death.

Kevin recalled that every time he visited southern Illinois, some idiot or another came up with a so-called theory about Mark's death, one more ridiculous than another, some involving the Mafia, as if mobsters would bother with someone like Mark Cavaness. Kevin hoped to God that at least the St. Louis police would be able to catch the killer this time.

By late afternoon Kevin was beginning to become irritated that his father had not yet appeared. There was no answer at the Harrisburg house; he left messages at Pearce Hospital. Finally at six P.M. Charli reached Martha in Harrisburg. Dale had been seeing patients all day, she said. She would see that he got on his way. She expressed what Charli thought were tepid condolences. But this was no time to be concerned with Martha.

Dave Barron telephoned twice more to ask whether Dale had arrived. Finally Dale showed up at about half past nine. He walked through the door mechanically, saying nothing.

"Hi," Kevin said.

"Oh, hi," Dale said, "how're you doing?"

"You haven't seen this place before."

"Yeah. It's nice."

Kevin telephoned Barron, who said he would be right over.

Thinking about interviewing Dr. Cavaness, Dave Barron had grown nervous; yet he knew that he would have to try to appear nonchalant. Barron believed himself to be a good detective, but in his mind he had conjured up the image of the doctor as someone who must look like Marcus Welby, M.D., silver-haired, distinguished, suave, brilliant and fabulously articulate. From what he had gathered from Kevin and Charli, Dr. Cavaness was chief of surgery at his hospital. Who am I, Barron wondered, a cop with less than three years' experience in homicide, to try to take on some medical whiz? If I'm not careful, he'll bullshit me and wrap me around his finger. I'm not even a college graduate.

His regular partner was otherwise occupied, so for support Barron took along Detective Tim Nisbet, a friend whom he could trust to be quiet and cool; this was no time for strong-arm tactics. They arrived at the apartment complex, modern two-story buildings set in a wooded, landscaped tract, rather like a college campus. Barron knocked at the door of Apartment F and offered a last prayer that he would not screw this up.

Kevin answered the door and led the detectives through the living room to the open kitchen, where Dale and Charli sat at the table. One look at Dr. Cavaness soothed Dave Barron's nerves. This little guy, over whom Barron loomed like a giant, did not seem like any threat. His clothes looked like thrift-shop stuff. His curly gray hair was sparse and dirty-looking, his lips thin and tight. He showed a boozer's bloat and all in all looked more like a traveling vacuum-cleaner salesman just in from the road than a physician.

Dale greeted the detectives in his folksy way. He held a drink between his hands on the table. Barron noticed that there appeared to be something the matter with the doctor's hands. They were gnarled, misshapen. They looked like claws. They certainly did not appear to be the hands of a surgeon.

Dale had for the past few years been suffering from carpal-tunnel syndrome, a narrowing of the tunnel in the wrists which induced pinching of the nerves serving his fingers. The syndrome caused the muscles of the hands to knot up and atrophy and made the fingers separate, two on one side, two and the thumb on the other. He had inherited the condition from Noma.

Dale offered the detectives a drink, which they declined.

Barron had rehearsed his opening questions. He had had plenty of time to think about them, waiting for the doctor to get to town. He hoped to catch him off guard by bringing up Mark's death first: Throw him a slider when he's guessing fastball was the way Barron thought about it. He began soothingly.

"Dr. Cavaness, I'm just here to pick up a little background information on Sean."

"Fire away," Dale said.

"I understand there was another death, another son killed, some years ago. Do you happen to know what's happened in that case? Has it ever been resolved?"

"I think it's closed," Dale said. "They ruled it an accident."

"No, it isn't," Kevin broke in. "I understand it's still open. It's still an open homicide. Jack Nolen—"

Barron told Kevin to hold it.

"Come here, come here," Barron said softly to Kevin and Charli. "I think this would work better if you guys go into the bedroom for a while so we can talk to the doctor here. It might get too confusing otherwise." He ushered them into the bedroom, thanked them, said he would not be too long, and closed the door on them.

When Barron returned to the kitchen he noticed that Dr. Cavaness's glass was empty. Barron brought the quart of vodka from the kitchen counter with some ice and fixed the doctor another, saying that if he had lost a son, he'd be drinking too. He and Nisbet sat down at the table, and Barron got right to business.

"When was the last time you saw Sean, Dr. Cavaness? When was the last time you were in St. Louis?"

"Oh," Dale said, "it must have been, let's see, about four weeks ago. I was up here for a medical convention. Yes, it was four weeks ago. I can check the date."

That's it! Barron thought to himself. He strove to keep his composure; his heart raced. I've got you, you lying son of a bitch. So you don't turn out to be so smart after all. All you had to say was that you saw Sean on Wednesday, took him out to dinner, dropped him back, and I'd have been in trouble. But you've lied. I hope you just keep on lying. Dig yourself into a real good hole.

Dale went on to describe, accurately, his previous visit to Sean's apartment, how he had talked to Mrs. Kroeck, how he had gone over to Tina Crowley's and visited with Sean. It was nice of the doctor, Barron thought, to volunteer that he had met Peggy Kroeck. He was confirming her ability to eyeball him.

Dale said that perhaps once, since his visit four weeks earlier, he had talked to Sean on the telephone. He could not recall the content of the conversation. Kevin and Sean and Charli, he said, had been planning to come down to southern Illinois for the holidays.

Barron asked a few more questions, mainly in order to continue to appear totally in the dark about the murder. It was cat-and-mouse stuff now.

Dale said that, as far as he knew, Sean had no drug problem but that he did have a problem with alcohol. Sean did not own any handguns but should have had a couple of shotguns and a muzzle-loading rifle.

From Tina Crowley, Barron already knew that the guns had

been pawned. When he asked the doctor about whether he was aware of any money problems Sean might have had, Dale said that he was not aware of any. This Barron took as another lie, since the doctor had visited the apartment on Wednesday and would know that the telephone, electricity and gas were shut off.

"I'm just so shocked and saddened by this thing," Dale said. "I want to cooperate with you guys in any way I can. I want whoever did this brought to justice."

We'll do our best to accommodate your every wish, Barron thought. He thanked the doctor for his cooperation and told Kevin and Charli that they could come out of the bedroom now. He said that he would like to talk to Kevin's mother when she arrived tomorrow, if that was all right.

Dr. Cavaness was up and fixing himself another drink. From the kitchen he called to the detectives, who had reached the front door:

"Dave, Tim, you sure you don't want one? You know, Dave, something I think you may want to check out more, come to think of it, is drugs. You know, I'm a doctor. I see things. You know how these young people are."

"Yes," Dave Barron said. "Drugs are a real problem."

"You know how it is," Dale said. "Desperate people do desperate things."

I'll be asking you about that one in three or four days, Barron said to himself. It was thoughtful of the doctor to offer advice. He must think that he sailed through the interview just fine. All the better. That's just the way we want it. Let him be cocky as hell.

Barron told Kevin and Charli, making sure that the doctor heard him, that the police had nothing new on the case, but they were working on it.

After the detectives were gone, Kevin and Charli sat at the kitchen table with Dale and watched him fill his glass again. The quart was finished, so he poured from the half-gallon he had brought in from his car—a Chevy Blazer this time, not the Toronado. Kevin helped himself to a bourbon and Coke.

Dale asked Kevin whether he thought that whoever had killed Mark had also killed Sean. Kevin said that he did not see how that could be possible. Seven years had passed; southern Illinois was far from St. Louis; Mark had been killed with a shotgun, Sean with a pistol, from what the detectives said. Dale agreed. There could not be a connection.

"You have any ideas?" Kevin asked.

"No," Dale said. "What about the family? The people got killed when I had that accident. You think they could be coming back to haunt me? I mean, taking revenge against me by killing Sean?"

Kevin thought that idea was pretty farfetched. He decided to change the subject. He asked whether Dale knew anything about how Johnny Weingarten had gotten busted.

Dale hesitated. As he finally replied, he held his chin in his hand, a characteristic gesture of his, so that his mouth was covered by his lumpy fingers. The effect was as if he spoke from behind a veil, but Kevin and Charli had no difficulty in understanding him.

"Yeah," Dale said slowly, "I know something about that." He paused again. Then, with steady eyes, he looked up at Kevin and Charli. "But if you tell anybody, I'll kill you."

They were too startled to say anything. Both of them, as they confided to one another afterward, sought some hint of kidding in Dale's voice or eyes but could find none. Dale said that he had concluded that Johnny Weingarten had been set up for a bust because Johnny had told him that he was selling some pills to a guy at fifteen dollars apiece. The only person who would pay that kind of money for those pills must be a cop. He decided to help out the cops, Dale said, so he asked Johnny to move a safe for him that had some drugs in it. The safe came from the hospital, so what was in it would be obvious. Johnny wasn't stupid.

Dale taped the combination to the back of the safe, where Johnny would see it, knowing that Johnny would steal the drugs and try to sell them. That way he would be caught with some real stuff, morphine, a Class A felony, and really do some time.

"You mean that old safe that was at the clinic?" Kevin asked.

"That's it. The drugs in there must have been fifteen or twenty years old."

"Hell, no wonder you don't want anybody to know about it. They were bad drugs. You sure wouldn't want people knowing that bad drugs came from you."

"No," Dale said. "That's not the point. That's not it at all. They'd probably just kill me."

That was enough. Kevin and Charli showed Dale the bed in the spare room and said good-night. Alone they talked about what Dale had said about Weingarten and the safe and could not make any sense of it. Why would Dale be so anxious for the cops to set up

Johnny Weingarten? The only thing that Charli could figure was that Weingarten had something on Dale, so Dale wanted him put away. The whole business was confusing and disturbing. Maybe Weingarten knew about Dale's medical scams or some of his livestock flimflams. Kevin had long suspected his father of forging cattle pedigrees and selling bull's sperm that had not come from its labeled source.

But the story of the safe did not make sense. It sounded like drunken rambling—nothing new with Dale. Between Sean's death and the vodka, the man did not know what he was saying, Kevin and Charli told each other. They decided to try to forget it.

In the morning they found Dale in the living room, passed out in a reclining chair.

20

DAVE BARRON ARRANGED TO HAVE A COUPLE OF PLAINCLOTHES officers watch Kevin's apartment. Barron was not worried about Dr. Cavaness's violence—he was sure to be on his best behavior, unless he was a homicidal maniac, a hypothesis Barron rejected— but he wanted to make sure that the doctor stayed in town. If the Cavanesses spotted the men as cops, they would assume that they had been assigned to protect them against the unknown killer or killers. Kevin and Charli had already told Barron that they were frightened.

On Saturday, waiting for Marian Green to arrive, Barron decided that it was time to dig up what he could about the murder of the other son. He wondered about Detective Jack Nolen, of whom Kevin had spoken with some misgivings. Barron knew nothing about southern Illinois, but he gathered that Dr. Cavaness was a local hero there. In a small, rural place, everybody would know everybody. If this Jack Nolen could not keep his mouth shut or, not an inconceivable possibility, if Nolen was on the take, Dr. Cavaness could be tipped off and the whole case blown out of the water.

Barron decided to check Jack Nolen out before contacting him. He telephoned an officer whom he knew over at the Illinois D.C.I. office across the river in East St. Louis and asked for a run-down. He would not find a better man, Barron was told. Nolen was savvy, honest, and he knew more about southern Illinois than anyone else. If Barron could not rely on Jack Nolen, he would be up shit creek down there.

Barron reached Nolen at home in Harrisburg. Nolen had already heard about Sean's death; it was in the local papers.

Barron conveyed his instincts about connections between Sean's death and Mark's. The M.O. was similar: shot and left out in a lonely place.

"Is that right?" Nolen said in his enigmatic way. "Well isn't that interesting? What do you know? Kind of makes you wonder, doesn't it?"

What was the status of the earlier case, Barron asked. Nolen said that it remained an open homicide. He had been unable to arrest anybody. "Kind of a sore point, if you want to know the truth," Nolen said. "Bugs the hell out of me. Kevin Cavaness still calls me. I can understand it. The guy can't sleep, thinking about his brother. How's he holding up? Hell of a thing, another brother gone. It's not like your everyday situation. No, it's not."

Barron told Nolen that he needed his help. Could he keep a secret? If this got out, the St. Louis case would be fucked. Nolen assured him that he was very good at keeping secrets. One of the best.

"We've got him," Barron said. "We haven't booked him yet, but we know who he is."

"Is that right, well, I'll be damned," Nolen said. "I guess you fellows work pretty fast up there. Don't keep me hanging here with my mouth open. Who the hell is it?"

"The father," Barron said. "The doctor. Dr. Cavaness. No question."

"Son of a bitch. Everything's coming into focus."

"Yeah? Everything's coming into focus?"

"Now I know the doc killed Mark."

Dave Barron and Jack Nolen were on the phone for more than an hour. They exchanged everything they knew. When Nolen described the drug bust and his frustration at not being able to arrest the doc, Barron quoted what Dale had said the night before about drugs being a factor in Sean's death and desperate people doing desperate things.

"He knows what he's talking about," Nolen laughed. "Think he's giving you a hint? He's pretty clever, I can tell you that. He's a cute one. And he doesn't think anybody else is good enough to shine his shoes. I wish I could make the arrest myself."

Barron said that in the long run he hoped that he could get the doc to admit to both killings.

"He might," Nolen said, "and he might not."

Early Saturday evening Dave Barron drove alone over to Kevin's apartment to interview Marian. Barron relished the situation, knowing who the killer was while everyone else was in the dark, but he was on edge. He felt like an actor in a murder mystery, the kind that was not supposed to happen in real life; he was the sleuth toying with family members, acting cordial, casually indifferent. He worried that his secret was written on his face.

Dale greeted him like an old fraternity brother, introduced him to the ex-wife. A classy lady, was Barron's impression of Marian. He found it difficult to imagine that Dale and Marian had once been married, the contrast between them was so great. He met Patrick, quiet and withdrawn, and Charli's sister and brother-in-law. Kevin offered to take his father, Patrick, and Charli's relatives out for pizza, so Barron could talk to Marian alone.

Charli stayed behind. Barron escorted her to the bedroom, where he noticed a pistol lying on the bedside table. It was Kevin's, Charli said. He had been worried that somebody was after them. She asked Barron quietly if the police had anything concrete. Were they making any progress at all? Feeling that he had to tell her something, Barron chose his words carefully.

"Keep this to yourself, Charli. But if finding the killer is what it will take to give you and your family a merry Christmas—well, then you'll have a merry Christmas. If that's what it'll take."

He was tempted to confide more in her, but he decided that he had said enough. It would be too much to ask of her to tolerate having Dale in her home if she knew the truth.

He sat down with Marian in the kitchen. He began asking her about Sean and learned that he had been very upset at first about Marian's second marriage but had seemed finally to accept it. She talked of Sean's treatment for alcoholism. Barron asked her if Sean had ever indicated contemplating suicide. Only once, Marian said. Sean had been drunk and had talked about blowing himself away. He had been terribly affected by the death of her other son. But she did not consider Sean suicidal. Confused, yes.

Suicide had never been a possibility in this case, with two shots to the head, but Barron was trying to cover all the bases. There was no telling what a defense attorney would come up with. Barron's own view, which he kept to himself, was that anyone who drank the way Sean apparently had was suicidal; and the slovenly condition of his apartment indicated a seriously depressed young man; but that was irrelevant. He had been murdered, denied the chance to change and fulfill his life.

Marian said that she had had misgivings about leaving town, knowing that Sean was not in the best of shape; but she did not think that continuing to live with her would do him any good. And he still would have Kevin and Charli in St. Louis. Perhaps she had made a mistake.

It was ridiculous for her to blame herself, Barron told her. Her leaving had nothing to do with Sean's death. He said that he was sure that her new husband would agree.

She had told Les Green not to accompany her on this trip, Marian said. There was no sense in putting him through all this. He had not known Sean well; he had never met Dale; it would be too much of a strain.

It was about Dale that Barron wanted to hear. He began asking a few questions about Marian's marriage to the doctor. His guess was that Dale had been a bastard to her: A woman with four children did not divorce a wealthy doctor without good cause; she had struggled on her own for years before marrying again. But he needed to hear her version and hoped that she would be able to repeat some horror stories in court.

Marian bristled as soon as Barron asked her about Dale.

"That's my business," she said, her voice icing over, "and it has nothing to do with Sean's death. I'll tell you one thing. I loved that man, very, very much. And if you want me to prove it, I will."

Barron backed off. He saw that Marian was in such an emotional state that she was probably not thinking clearly and might not even remember what she said to him now. Evidently she still had feelings for Dale, or thought she did. He wondered what on earth she had in mind to prove it. Whatever love for him she had left was going to receive quite a shock in a couple of days' time.

Barron wound up the conversation. It had been an unproductive interview, but he was sure that Marian would have more to say later.

Over at Buster Murphy's pizza restaurant, Kevin and Charli's sister and brother-in-law were reminiscing about Sean—how good he was with children, how affectionate he was, how thoughtful, how willing to give his time to others. Dale, who had been silent throughout the spontaneous eulogies, broke in.

"Now wait just a minute, he said. "Let's not make Sean into something he was not."

"What do you mean by that?" Kevin asked.

"He was an embarrassment to me," Dale said.

Kevin demanded that Dale take back his remark. He said that he could not believe that his father would say such a thing at a time like this.

"Sorry," Dale said. "Just talking."

Dale was supposed to stay in a motel room that Charli had reserved for him, but the Cavanesses ended up together in the apartment, talking through most of the night. They all agreed that the funeral should be in St. Louis, rather than in Eldorado, but Dale raised objections to just about everything else that anyone suggested. He could not afford a big funeral, he wanted no flowers and no music, he could not spend the money.

At this Marian, who had been sentimental, saying that she was glad to have the family together at this time, grew livid.

"You can do something for him this once," she said. "You never did anything for him when he was alive. You wouldn't give him the time of day."

Dale protested. Why was he being attacked? What was going on here? What was the point of having a big funeral when Sean had no friends anyway?

"That's bullshit," Kevin said. "Sean had lots of friends in St. Louis. Everybody loved Sean. What the hell are you driving at?"

Charli calmed everybody down. Dale relented. The funeral, including music and flowers, would be held on Monday at the Fitzinger funeral home in Kirkwood which had taken care of Marian's mother and other family members. A minister from the Central Presbyterian Church would conduct the service. When they began discussing which songs or hymns would be appropriate to Sean's memory, Dale suggested "Onward, Christian Soldiers" and "The Battle Hymn of the Republic." He was overruled. Marian said that she had never heard of anything so bizarre in her life as the idea that someone would sing "Onward, Christian soldiers, marching as to war" at a funeral.

The Reverend John P. Splinter chose Proverbs 14:32 as the text for his eulogy: "The wicked is thrust down by his wrongdoing, but the righteous has a refuge when he dies." Dale wept throughout the sermon. Marian, sitting beside him, patted him and tried to comfort him. In the rear of the chapel, which was crowded with family friends from St. Louis and southern Illinois, Dave Barron observed Dale's performance with amazement. Barron felt like rushing to the front and telling the assembled mourners the truth; he listened as the minister, reading from notes supplied him by family and friends, described Sean as sweet, kind, considerate, gentle, a lover of people, a man who never met a stranger.

"A favorite poet of mine," Reverend Splinter said, "has described the death of a young man, such as Sean, by comparing the death with '. . . a stupid fool, slamming a foolish door.' Sean's death was senseless."

Barron stood near the family afterward as they greeted people. Dale had turned off the tears and now seemed almost ebullient, shaking hands, slapping people on the back, behaving as if the occasion were a wedding rather than a funeral. He spotted Barron and waved him over.

"This is my buddy, Detective Dave Barron," Dale announced to everyone. "He's the best damned detective in St. Louis. He's going to catch whoever did this to Sean. He is one fine detective, let me tell you."

Dale greeted Pann Beck with a hug and a kiss on the cheek.

"I'm so sorry, Dale," she said.

"Now don't you worry, dear," Dale said. "Meet Detective Dave Barron. He's going to solve this thing. They have the first team on this. It isn't like the Saline County Mounties, you know. Give us a kiss. How about coming around to Kevin's afterward for a drink?"

Barron had decided to wait to make the arrest until the doc was alone in his car, headed back to Illinois. He understood that Dale did not plan to leave town until the next day, Tuesday, December 18. He followed him back to Kevin's apartment and stationed men to watch his car all night in case he tried to take off early. Barron instructed the officers not to let the doctor cross the Mississippi.

That evening after the friends who had gathered to visit and eat and drink had left, Charli said that Tina Crowley had mentioned that someone had been seen hanging around Sean's apartment on Wednesday, the night before he had been killed. Tina said that Peggy Kroeck had told her that the man looked something like Sean's father. It seemed strange. Peggy had not said anything else to Tina.

"That's weird," Kevin said. "You weren't up here then, were you, Dad?"

"No," Dale said emphatically, throwing up his hands.

Kevin wondered what the appropriate thing would be to do with Sean's ashes. Perhaps they should be scattered with Mark's at the Hickory Handle farm.

"I think you ought to let Tina Crowley have them," Dale said. "She loved him. You saw her at the funeral. She was real torn up."

"I think that's a terrible idea," Charli said, and Kevin joined her. In no time Kevin and Dale got into a furious argument. Dale insisted that Tina should have the ashes, while Kevin demanded that he trash such a ridiculous notion, asking why in hell someone who had only known Sean for six months should be given possession of his remains. Father and son shouted back at one another. Marian and Charli were afraid they would come to blows.

They did not reconcile until the next day, as Dale was preparing to leave. Kevin extended his hand, and they shook, but Dale continued to sulk, saying that he had been surprised that Kevin could get so angry at him. He had not known that Kevin could feel that way about him. He had been hurt.

Kevin and Charli apologized for having lost their tempers in the argument over the ashes. They did not back down, however, insisting that they still felt strongly about the impropriety of Dale's suggestion.

They saved their farewells for the funeral parlor, where they returned to pick up the flowers. Dale followed Kevin and Charli in his Blazer, flashing his lights and stopping at a liquor store on the way to buy some vodka for the trip.

Dale helped them put the flowers in their car. Charli was crying, and Dale confronted her, saying that he was sorry for causing the ashes controversy. She had been right, he told her.

"Last night—it never happened, okay?" Dale said, exchanging hugs and kisses. He would be in touch. He would see them in Illinois at Christmas. He told them that he loved them, got in his car and drove away.

Kevin noticed that a police car, which had been parked up the street, took off in the same direction as his father. He hoped that Dale would have the sense not to speed until he got clear of the city.

Throughout that night Marian, who was not leaving until early Wednesday morning, came into Charli and Kevin's bedroom several times, weeping, hoping that Patrick, asleep in the living room, did not hear her. She was having terrible nightmares, she said. She kept dreaming about an infant with Sean's head. The body was that of a newborn baby, but the head and the face were Sean's as he was before he died.

"It's my fault," Marian wept. "It's all my fault. I never should have left just to get married. I never should have left poor Sean."

Kevin and Charli tried to reassure her. Charli said that she thought everyone would feel a little better when the police had the killer in custody. Dave Barron had promised her that they would make an arrest by Christmas.

The arrest had already been made, just before five that afternoon. Dave Barron stopped Dale's car less than half a mile from the funeral parlor. Dale seemed completely surprised but offered no resistance. Barron did not bother to handcuff him.

"Dale," Barron said in the police car, deliberately addressing him by his first name to let him know that things were different between them now: There would be no more Dr. Cavaness courtesies. "Dale, I know you were just blowing smoke up my ass at the funeral, when you were telling everybody what a great detective I am."

"Hey, no, Dave," Dale said. "I know you're a great detective."

"Let me tell you something, Dale. I am a fucking good detective, and you're going to find out just how good I am."

21

DAVE BARRON BROUGHT DALE INTO A WINDOWLESS, EIGHT-BY-seven-foot interrogation room on the second floor of the South Central station in Clayton and made sure that he understood his rights as established by the Constitution and defined by the Miranda decision. He presented him with a St. Louis County Police Department Warning and Waiver form and directed him to read over carefully his rights not to speak and to have an attorney present. Dale initialed each clause and signed the form stating that he wished to waive each right and was willing to answer questions concerning the investigation. Detective Nisbet joined Barron for the interrogation.

Dale stated again that he had last seen Sean four weeks before, in November, and had had no more than one telephone conversation with him since then.

"Dale," Barron said, "we have witnesses saying that they saw you at Sean's apartment on Wednesday evening. That was December 12, the night before Sean was found."

That was impossible, Dale said. He was in southern Illinois that night.

Barron showed him a photostatic copy of the grocery bag with his license-plate number written down by the witness. Dale said that he had no idea who had given Barron that information, because it was false. He said that he had worked all day in Eldorado at Pearce Hospital and had eaten dinner at the hospital. He had gone out to his Hickory Handle cattle farm that evening to change the dressing on a heifer's leg, was home in Harrisburg watching television by ten, and after that was in bed asleep with his lady friend, Martha Culley, who was living with him. He had left his house, he said, at about nine the next morning, had driven to the K mart store to buy medical supplies for the heifer and then spent most of the morning at the farm.

"We're going to check out your alibi," Barron informed him. "I think you ought to know that we have two St. Louis detectives waiting in southern Illinois for word to start talking to people. I am going to go call them right now. They'll talk to your girlfriend and to other people. So while I'm calling them, maybe you'd like to think over what you've told me."

Barron left the room and telephoned the detectives, Jack Plummer and Larry Fox, who were with Jack Nolen at the D.C.I. office. He told them Dale's alibi and directed them to interview Martha Culley first. Nolen had already taken them to the state's attorney, who had issued a complaint for a search warrant for the house on Walnut to see whether a .357 magnum or a .38 pistol, a red-colored flashlight, and Sean Cavaness's wallet and keys were there. Judge Michael J. Henshaw of the First District Court, Saline County, had issued the warrant by three o'clock that afternoon. A second judge was prepared to issue a warrant to seize the Oldsmobile Toronado. The detectives were ready to roll. Jack Nolen would escort them.

When Barron returned to the interview room and informed Dale that the detectives had been contacted, Dale repeated that he had nothing to hide.

Barron drew a map of the area around Sean's apartment and referring to his conversations with Peggy and Ralph Kroeck—Barron had reinterviewed them on Sunday; their account had not changed—described to Dale the exact movements of his Toronado that night, noting the U-turns and the various passes in front of Sean's apartment. Barron told Dale that two witnesses saw him hug his son under the streetlamp, heard him go upstairs and leave again with Sean in the early hours of Thursday morning. His license number, moreover, had been confirmed.

Barron kept going over the Kroecks' account for two hours. At around seven-thirty, Dale finally broke.

He had been lying, he said, throughout the investigation.

"Why have you been lying to us, Dale?"

"Because I didn't want to be thought of as a suspect."

"Why did you think you would be a suspect?"

"It just seemed logical."

When Barron asked him why he thought that the St. Louis County Police Department would think that somebody who was truthful would be a suspect, Dale had no answer.

Dale admitted that he had driven up to visit Sean and had arrived at approximately ten-thirty. When he saw that there were no lights on, he drove around as Mr. and Mrs. Kroeck had described, finally parked, and took his flashlight so that he could see the doorbell. Sean had walked up. They had embraced. He entered Sean's apartment with him and stayed until about one-thirty in the morning, when he drove his son to a Quick Shop convenience store for a pack of cigarettes. He brought Sean home and watched him climb the porch steps and disappear into the door of his apartment building. He then headed home to Harrisburg.

He had come up to St. Louis on the spur of the moment, Dale said, to check on Sean's welfare. Sean had seemed entirely normal during the evening. They had discussed holiday plans. They had not been drinking, only a little beer which he had brought with him in a plastic container.

Barron could see that the interview had reached an impasse. Dale had changed his story only enough to cover his tracks in view of the irrefutable evidence that he had been seen by the Kroecks that night. He could stick to that version indefinitely. Barron excused himself to take a call from Detectives Plummer and Fox in Illinois.

They had interviewed Martha Culley at her home. At first she had said that the doc had been with her, and that she had used the Oldsmobile herself early in the evening to go to a beauty-shop appointment. But when she was told that the Oldsmobile had been seen in St. Louis and that at that very moment, as she was being interviewed, John Dale Cavaness was being questioned about his participation in his son's murder, she changed her story. Dr. Cavaness had not been at home when she returned from the beauty parlor, and he had stopped by the beauty shop to exchange cars with her. He was not at home when she went to bed, and the next morning she had found him asleep on a couch downstairs. She did not see him again until they went to a party together that night, Thursday. He had appeared to have a good time at the party; they had stayed late. He had said nothing about going to St. Louis to visit his son.

The detectives reported that they had found none of Sean's belongings in either the house or the garage. From the Oldsmobile they had taken a flashlight but nothing else relevant to the case; Martha Culley had turned over to them a .357 magnum pistol which she said was kept in the house for security purposes.

Barron returned to the interview room and had Dale run through his story several more times. He had sandwiches, coffee and soft drinks brought in, tried chatting amiably with Dale, got nowhere. He asked Dale whether he would voluntarily submit to a lie-detector test. Dale said that he gladly would.

Just after midnight Sam Yarbrough, chief polygraph examiner for the St. Louis County Police Department, arrived with his machine to administer the test. Yarbrough advised Dale of his constitutional rights and presented him with a second waiver form, making sure that he read and understood each right, initialed each paragraph, and signed his name without coercion. When Dale said that he suffered from buried cataracts and could not see the print clearly, Yarbrough read the form aloud.

Yarbrough, a man in his early thirties whose entire professional life was devoted to administering lie-detector tests, did not believe in the infallibility of the polygraph but saw the device as a useful police tool which, if properly interpreted, could indicate in a general sense whether or not the subject was a reliable witness to his own or to others' crimes. Yarbrough treated Dale with elaborate courtesy, acknowledging that as a physician he probably understood better than most people what the polygraph entailed. He asked Dale whether he was taking any medication—Dale said that he was on a regular dose of thyroid pills and nothing else—and ran through the principal questions in advance. Yarbrough presented himself as a sincere, friendly professional who was concerned only with the truth.

"Let me tell you about something, okay?" Yarbrough said. "There' a lot of suspicion here, Dale, not only because of the unusual circumstances of you coming to St. Louis on this particular night, but because most of us have children ourselves, you know? We have sons and daughters. Our children aren't as old as yours, I mean Dave Barron's kids and my own kids, but we're all fathers. Let me say to you that I project, if I can use that term, project a few years on down the road, to where my son is Sean's age and I'm the father visiting the son. Then a few hours later my son is found dead. I think my reaction would be first of all shock, and after that I would want to catch the person who did it, especially given the manner in which your son died. Being shot. And the only way to catch the killer is to cooperate with the police. But here we have you lying about where you were, whether you were in St. Louis and so on, and you can understand, the investigators are going to say whoa, wait a minute, this guy is lying to us.

"Why, Dale, why did you not say, oh, my God, I just saw my son, and the last time I saw him was one-thirty, two o'clock in the morning on Thursday? Why didn't you say that? You understand —there's a lot of suspicion here. It's out of character, if I may say so, for a father to deny when he last saw his son, when the son has been killed. Those of us with children, Dale, children we love, we just don't understand why you've responded in this way."

To this and to other extended, friendly-sounding inquiries, Dale replied that he had simply not wanted to appear a suspect.

"I'm not talking to a fool," Yarbrough said. "You may be from a rural part of Illinois, but you're a medical man, an intelligent man. I'm sure you're a very perceptive man. You've got to realize that if you lie, it's going to cause suspicion in our minds. We're not fools either, see what I mean? Why did you lie? Were you afraid?"

"I suppose," Dale said. "I just had the feeling that if I leveled with them, they would involve me unnecessarily."

"Let me tell you something, Dale. These investigators—Dave Barron, the rest—they are going to find the person who's responsible for your son's death, because they are that tenacious. You've got to believe this. You can't bullshit these guys. Maybe you don't understand, even though I know you're an intelligent man. These guys are for real, Dale. They're that dedicated. They are smart enough to smell it when something's not right. Do you understand this? Do you understand that you are dealing with a bunch of guys who are totally honest and are going to find the killer? This is the way it is in St. Louis, Dale. There is no bullshit here, do you understand that?"

Dale said nothing.

"You're a physician," Yarbrough said. "Let me make an analogy, if I can. It's just like when you make a diagnosis. The disease here is murder. When somebody smells of murder, our guys are excellent diagnosticians, understand me? Your symptoms are everything you've lied about. You tried to fool us, but you couldn't. You know that now. If you smell of murder, Dave Barron is going to smell it, see what I mean? like some patient of yours who stinks because he's rotting away from something. Dave Barron is going to arrive at a diagnosis sooner or later. If you want to help, this will all be over sooner. If you don't want to help, we are going to arrive at a diagnosis eventually. Don't you think it would be beneficial to us if you helped us in making the diagnosis just like you make a diagnosis as a doctor?"

"I understand now, yes," Dale said.

Dale Cavaness, the man of a few thousand words, the fellow who had always been able to survive on a raft of countrified rhetoric, gave minimal, terse answers to all of Yarbrough's questions about his whereabouts on the night of the murder, his feelings about Sean's death, and his reactions to Mark's death years before. Yarbrough's bluntness had the effect of rendering Dale nearly speechless. Confronted with his past—the reckless-homicide and deceptive-practice convictions, everything that Dave Barron had learned from Jack Nolen—Dale could only mumble:

"Well, don't you know, I don't, for you to start with the past, I—"

"You and I and everybody else on earth," Yarbrough told him in concluding the interview, "that is what we are in our lives. We are our past lives. The occupation, the profession that you have as a doctor, the legal complications that you have gotten yourself into. I am not sitting here playing war games with you. You know what your past is. Your past is you. You add it all up, and what do you come up with? We are all a sum total of everything that we have experienced and everything that we have done. Right, Dale? Do you understand that? Just a sum total over the years of everything that we have experienced and everything that we have done, good or bad."

Yarbrough reported to Dave Barron that, in his professional

opinion, the doc was a liar. Dale had firsthand knowledge of Sean's death, but was concealing it. Yarbrough thought Dale's coldness extraordinary. In all of his experience as a polygraph examiner, he had never before dealt with such a cold person, a man apparently devoid of normal human reactions.

It was also noteworthy, Yarbrough thought, that Dale had confused the identities of his two dead sons throughout the interview, calling Sean Mark and Mark Sean, mixing up their ages and personalities. He did not seem to have an emotional commitment to either. Yarbrough also gathered that Dale thought both boys an embarrassment to a man of such professional competence and accomplishment. It was as if the doc had decided at some point that both boys were indistinguishable and expendable, like two animals tagged for slaughter.

One of the keys in determining whether or not someone is lying during a polygraph examination is the tone of voice, something not always within the power of the machine to evaluate with the necessary subtlety. Dale's tone had been monotonous throughout. He might have been discussing the price of eggs rather than the death of his son, or two of his sons. The doc was encased in a cake of ice, the kind of guy you would not want to play poker with. You would lose.

Barron tried questioning Dale again. It was getting on toward dawn. Barron was feeling the strain, but Dale appeared to be willing to go on indefinitely. I've got to hand it to the son of a bitch, Barron thought. This is like dealing with the Bionic Man.

By seven that morning, Kevin and Charli had returned from taking Marian and Patrick to the airport and were facing the necessity of going to work. Charli set the alarm for seven-thirty and fell into bed with Kevin for a few minutes' sleep. But before the alarm could go off, the telephone rang. It was Dave Barron.

"Charli, we've made an arrest."

"Great!" Charli said. "Don't tell me who it is yet. I've got to tell Kevin."

"We need you down here."

"We'll be right down!"

Charli switched off the alarm and told Kevin the news. They were speculating on the identity of the killer—probably somebody Sean had worked with, some kind of a redneck nut case—when

255

the phone rang again. Hap Dawson, the manager of the Hickory Handle farm, sounded hysterical. He was yelling into the phone.

"Charli! They've arrested D.C.!"

"What? Who?"

"Doc C. They've arrested him!"

"Oh, no," Charli said. "What for?" She remembered that Dale had stopped at a liquor store before leaving St. Louis yesterday afternoon. "What is it? D.U.I.? Was he speeding?"

"I don't know," Hap said, and as he spoke, Charli's mind slipped into gear.

"Oh, Hap," she said, "we just got a call from the St. Louis police. They've made an arrest. Who told you about Dale? How did you find out?"

"Martha called me."

Charli said that she would call back. She told Kevin what Hap had said. Kevin immediately telephoned Martha.

"Yes," Martha said. "He's been arrested." Kevin thought that Martha sounded rather snippy, as if he had intruded on her privacy.

"What's he been arrested for?" Kevin asked.

"I don't know."

"Well, how did you find out?"

"You better call Murphy's office." Martha's voice made Kevin want to spit. "Murphy knows what's going on."

T. R. Murphy was Martha's son-in-law, a lawyer who had married Martha's daughter after her divorce from Johnny Weingarten. T. R. Murphy was a big-boned man with a ponytail who had handled Dale's legal affairs for the past few years; Kevin did not relish the prospect of having to contact him to find out what was going on. But he dialed Murphy's number and reached an assistant. Had Dale Cavaness been arrested? Kevin asked. What were the charges?

"It's the big one," Kevin heard the twangy voice say. "Murder One."

Dave Barron was on the phone when Kevin and Charli walked into his office at the Clayton station. Kevin, standing at Barron's desk, scanned a yellow legal pad on which Barron had been making notes. "Suspect admits arriving in town," Kevin read. "Suspect goes upstairs to victim's apartment. Suspect leaves with victim." Barron hung up the phone and grabbed the pad.

"You been reading my notes?" Barron said.

"It doesn't matter," Kevin said. "We know who you've got."

"Oh, yeah? Who?"

"My dad."

Barron leaned back in his chair.

"Well, you're right. You're too quick for me. You've ruined my spiel."

"What have you got on him?"

Barron went through the evidence and described to Kevin and Charli how Dale had reacted to the charges. It was then just after eight in the morning. Dale had been questioned for nearly fifteen hours. He had not asked for an attorney, had waived all his rights. Apparently he had the idea that the St. Louis police were stupid and would not be able to check out his alibi and trace his movements.

"I get the impression," Barron said, "that Dale is a guy who's used to having his own way. It sounds to me like he's been able to do just about anything he wants in southern Illinois."

"That's putting it mildly," Kevin said.

He had changed his story once, Barron said, but had admitted to nothing. Martha Culley had more or less confirmed Dale's absence on the night of the murder. The case was becoming clear-cut, even with his stonewalling.

Barron said that he understood what a shock this must be to Kevin and Charli. He did not envy them, having to call Marian with the news. But he wanted them to understand that he had not acted without being sure of what he had. It was a difficult thing to face, but everything pointed to Dale's having murdered Sean. The only question left was, why?

Barron explained the MOM theory of probable cause: Means, Opportunity, Motive. Dale certainly had the means; he was known to carry loaded guns around in his car. He had the opportunity, because he was in St. Louis with Sean that night. But what about a motive? Barron said that he had some ideas, but they were a little too hypothetical and abstract to stand up in court. If they did not get more evidence as to motive, they were going to have to release Dale. A judge was going to have to issue a proper warrant for his arrest. The police could not hold a suspect for more than twenty hours without probable cause; that was Missouri law. They had only four and a half hours left. Why had Dale done it?

Kevin and Charli looked at each other. Simultaneously they uttered the word: insurance.

257

Kevin described what his father had talked Sean and him into signing earlier that year, back in January as Kevin recalled. He had thought that there was something hokey about it at the time, but Dale's insurance agent had assured him that the scheme was sound and potentially very lucrative. Kevin thought that the amount was something like a hundred thousand dollars each on all three sons, with Dale as the primary beneficiary and Marian as the secondary beneficiary.

"I don't see how we could have been so naïve, signing something like that," Kevin said. "I can't believe this."

Barron said that he could easily understand. If Kevin had seriously suspected that Dale would take out insurance in order to kill him or one of his brothers, he never would have signed and he probably would have kept his distance from his father. But it was too difficult for a son to imagine. It was hard enough for anyone else to imagine: Barron himself had had trouble at first accepting Dale's guilt. He had never run across anything comparable before, nor had any of his fellow officers.

Barron asked Kevin and Charli whether they were aware that Dale had also had an insurance policy on Mark, around forty thousand dollars' worth, taken out just a month before Mark's death. Kevin and Charli were stunned.

"Then you think he killed Mark too?" Kevin asked, finding it painful to pronounce the words condemning his own father, his flesh and blood, the man with whom he had just spent four days and nights in close confinement.

"Jack Nolen thinks Dale killed Mark," Barron said. "He's thought so for a long time. As soon as I told him about Dale being a suspect here, he said that he was sure then that Dale had killed your other brother, too."

After letting all this sink in, Kevin and Charli agreed that they had more to tell Dave Barron. They described how Dale had threatened to kill them if they told anyone about the safe and Weingarten. They had not known whether to take the threat seriously; now they did. And Charli told of a suspicious incident which had occurred a couple of years before when they had been visiting at Thanksgiving, staying in one of the Galatia trailers because there was not enough room for them at Charli's parents' house. They had gone to sleep one night in the trailer with the door locked. Dale had the only other key.

They were awakened in the morning by Charli's sister and her husband, who had stopped to say good-bye.

"And when they walked in," Charli said, "the trailer was full of gas. Every gas burner on the stove, all four of them were turned up full blast. I know we had locked the door. When my sister arrived at the trailer, the front door was unlocked. I woke up and the smell of gas was heavy. It was sickening. If Kevin had lit a cigarette that morning, we would have blown up."

"We could have just plain been gassed out of existence," Kevin said, "in our sleep."

"I was sick to my stomach all day from the gas," Charli said.

Charli added that they had told Dale about what had happened, but that he had just shrugged his shoulders and said that the same thing had happened to a girlfriend of his one time. But all four burners? It was possible that one of them had bumped up against one of the knobs and turned it on, but not all four.

They had thought that the whole thing was very strange at the time, but they had more or less forgotten about it until now. In a way it did not fit with Sean's murder, because the insurance on him and Patrick and Kevin had not been taken out until the winter of 1984, yet . . .

"It's worth remembering," Barron said, "but the polygraph examiner picked up on something I agree with. He thought that Dale confused Mark and Sean in his mind, I mean sort of lumped them together, and that he thought they were an embarrassment to him, because he didn't approve of their life-style."

"That's true," Kevin said, and he recounted some of the numerous occasions when Dale had denigrated Sean and Mark. Dale had even said hostile things about Mark right after his death, in the summer of '77. It was as if he had not thought Mark worthy of the Cavaness name, Kevin said sarcastically. It was the same with poor Sean, who had tried so hard to get Dale to love him. So he had taken out insurance and gotten rid of both of them.

Kevin remembered the time that Dale had shot the prize bull because it would not follow orders. His dad was obsessed with bovine genetics. It looked as if Dale felt the same about humans. Maybe he thought that Mark and Sean just did not measure up, so he got rid of them. It was like a science-fiction horror story or something the Nazis had done. Purifying the race. Kevin took a deep breath and emitted a long, weary, grieving sigh. "I guess he was culling the herd."

Barron thought the remark apt. Mark and Sean were to their father, the master breeder, nothing but a couple of culls.

Suddenly Kevin remembered that he had asked his father about the insurance when Dale had said that he could not afford to pay for a decent funeral for Sean. Couldn't that money be used or borrowed on to pay for the funeral? Dale had said that the policy was not in effect, because of Sean's drinking problem. Kevin had not thought anything more about it until now.

Barron left the office and hurried down the hall to the room where Dale was being held. He asked Dale about the insurance, and Dale denied that he had ever paid any premiums on it or that the policy had ever actually been issued on Sean, because of his treatment for alcoholism.

Barron rushed back to the office and told Kevin and Charli that the motive was in danger of going out the window. He checked the clock. It was nearly eleven A.M.: Dale had already been held for eighteen hours. In two hours they would have to release him.

"Jesus," Kevin said, "he'll head right for southern Illinois. If he gets back down there, you may never get him. Charli and me, we'll have to leave the country."

Barron asked Kevin to walk over to the holding cell and talk to Dale. Kevin said it would do no good. Couldn't Kevin just go in and look at him, shake his head, try to shame him, break him down?

"It won't work," Kevin said. "You cannot intimidate my dad that way. He's got an iron will."

Barron said that Kevin was probably correct. They would have to find out on their own about the policy in the little time they had left.

Kevin called work, where he had his copy of the policies stored in his desk, and had someone read him the policy numbers and the name of the company. Barron telephoned Jack Nolen, who would check with Dale's insurance agent. Then Barron reached the head office of the Equitable company. Nolen called back with the information just as Barron was learning it from the company.

Dale had lied again. The policy was in effect on all three sons; the premiums, a thousand dollars a year on each, were paid up. The payoff was a hundred thousand.

Nolen also reported that Dale had two other policies, with different companies, amounting to another forty thousand on Sean's life.

There was now less than an hour left before Dale would have to be released. Barron told Kevin and Charli that they could go home and raced from his office down to the booking sergeant, charging Dale with murder, first degree. The Prosecuting Attorney's Office for St. Louis County, located just up the street in the County Courthouse, quickly issued a criminal-information sheet when Barron presented the facts. Barron hurried the papers over to the chambers of Judge Samuel Hais of the Circuit Court who, with about ten minutes to spare, issued a warrant and ordered the prisoner held without bond when Barron explained that John Dale Cavaness remained a menace and a threat to the surviving family members. Barron had no difficulty in believing that, if Dale were released, he might well try to kill Kevin and Charli, especially once he discovered that they were cooperating with the police and had supplied the most important evidence of all, the insurance policies.

Barron believed that he now had everything he needed except the murder weapon. When Dale was arrested the police had found a loaded pistol under the seat of his car, but when tested it did not appear to be the right gun.

As soon as Charli and Kevin got home early that afternoon they opened an attaché case Dale had left behind. Marian had glanced into it for only a second when she had noticed the case lying behind a chair in the living room, after Dale had hit the road, or so the family had believed, for Illinois; but she had snapped it shut again, not wishing to pry and saying that there was nothing inside but books and papers. Kevin and Charli now decided to open the case again. They thought that they might find a gun in it.

Inside they discovered no gun but an equally frightening collection of objects underneath some tax statements, medical brochures and a letter demanding payment of a debt: a ten-inch butcher's knife, a two-pound sledgehammer, and a length of nylon cord knotted with a hangman's noose.

"Looks like he wanted to have several options," Kevin said. "Holy Christ. Were we next, or what?"

"He'll probably just say he needed this stuff for the farm," Charli said. She telephoned Barron, who said that he would send someone over to pick up the case.

* * *

When Kevin telephoned Marian, she had only just arrived from the Wausau airport. Les answered the phone and said that Marian would call right back. Kevin did not tell Les what had happened, feeling that he should inform his mother directly.

"I have some good news and some bad news," Kevin began.

"Yes, dear. What on earth?"

"The good news is that they have the killer. They've arrested somebody."

"That's wonderful. But who is it? Who?"

Kevin then began reading Dave Barron's notes, which the detective had given him: Suspect admits arriving in town, goes upstairs to victim's apartment, and so on. He asked Marian to say whether she thought the police had the right guy.

"It certainly sounds convincing," Marian said. "Who is this person?"

"That's the bad news," Kevin said. "It's the old man."

"It's what?"

"It's Dale. They've arrested Dad for killing Sean."

Marian at first could not accept it. Kevin referred again to Barron's notes, and Marian acquiesced reluctantly, then affirmed her belief in Dale's guilt. For the first time she confessed that seven years before she had suspected Dale of killing Mark. She had known about the insurance on Mark, but she had repressed the idea. It was too terrible.

Kevin admitted that he had also had his suspicions and had also repressed them, for the same reasons. He of course had not known about the insurance on Mark. He was kicking himself now, Kevin said, for not seeing through Dale's latest insurance fraud. There had been one after another. They all fit together.

Marian had to get off the phone. She had to tell all this to Les. She had to lie down.

That evening the phone rang constantly at Kevin and Charli's— Marian, friends who had seen the news on television. Tomorrow, Kevin knew, it was going to be in all the papers, in St. Louis and all over southern Illinois. He would probably have to get an unlisted phone number to keep his sanity, if indeed he could get through all this without cracking. The horror of what his father had done —and might have wished to do to him—weighed him down, sending his emotions from anger to despair. He caught himself wondering whether he had done something, along with his brothers, to earn Dale's hatred. Charli told him to banish such thoughts. They were poison and totally irrational.

One of the callers was an old girlfriend of Dale's, the one to whom he had given a few acres of Hickory Handle. She was living in the northeast now but had heard about the arrest from southern-Illinois friends. It was absurd, she said. What did the St. Louis police think they were doing? It was outrageous to think that they could hold Dale just because they had found a gun in his car.

"If that's all it is," Charli told her, "I'd have to agree with you." Barron had instructed her and Kevin not to discuss the evidence with anyone except Marian and the prosecutors, who would soon be contacting them. Charli was not pleased to be talking to one of Dale's old girlfriends about anything anyway. Her loyalty to Dale and her faith in him were not surprising, but they were unsettling. Charli told her to talk to T. R. Murphy, who was acting as Dale's lawyer for now.

"She didn't ask about Sean, did she?" Kevin said. "All she cares about is the old man."

"She won't be the only one," Charli said. "We better be prepared."

22

STEVE GOLDMAN, ASSISTANT PROSECUTOR FOR THE COUNTY OF St. Louis, was a wry, scholarly man of Barron's age, dark and birdlike in appearance—he had a way when he was thinking of crooking his neck downward and dropping his chin onto his shoulder that made him resemble a heron. Law-enforcement circles knew him for his thoroughness and his sardonic wit. After reviewing the facts of the case, Goldman declared that if a book was ever written about Dr. Cavaness, it should be entitled *Family Practitioner*.

On the afternoon of Christmas Eve, Goldman and Barron were chatting about the doc, who had been sitting silently in his cell since the nineteenth. They wondered what he was thinking and when he was going to get himself a lawyer, or whether the Public Defender's Office would have to handle his case. The doc's finances were a question. The check that he had written, postdated, for Sean's funeral expenses had bounced; the funeral director was holding on to Sean's ashes as a kind of security deposit.

"I've got an idea," Barron told Goldman. "From everything we've learned, the holidays are a pretty rough time for the doc. He always went wacko at Christmas. Sean was killed practically on Christmas. Mark was killed at Easter. The reckless homicide happened at Easter. The guy might be in the mood to spill something. I'm going to wait until tonight and go talk to him again."

"You can try," Goldman said. "Maybe you should bring him a tree."

It was after five in the afternoon when Barron went to see Dale where he was now being held, in a cell on the top floor of the St. Louis County jail in Clayton. Barron took Detective Sergeant Frank Foan along to witness the ritual reading of the rights and resigning of the waiver forms, which Dale completed without complaint. Barron noticed with satisfaction that from Dale's cell window you could look out over Clayton, a prosperous, fashionable part of St. Louis, and see the Christmas lights and the hurrying last-minute shoppers. He hoped that Dale had been staring out the window and feeling sorry for himself. I should have brought a cassette, Barron thought, and played him some Bing Crosby.

"It's Christmas Eve, you know," Dale said, much to Barron's satisfaction.

"We know," Barron said. "We thought you might be wanting a little company."

Dale said that he had been thinking. He wanted to make an additional statement about Sean's death. It was true that he had driven to St. Louis, stayed at Sean's apartment, and left the apartment with Sean at about half past one in the morning. Neither he nor his son had, however, ever returned to the apartment.

"Is that right?" Barron asked. "Well, tell us what happened, Dale."

Dale said that he had taken Sean down to Laclede's Landing— a restored part of old St. Louis on the Mississippi waterfront, full of restaurants and bars—and drunk with him until after closing time at approximately three A.M.

That explains Sean's 0.26 blood-alcohol level, Barron thought. The two of them were really hitting it.

Dale said that, rather than go back to Sean's apartment, they decided to drive around for a while. They passed through various areas of the city and ended up driving west on Highway 44. He did not know what time it was by then, Dale said, but the sun was coming up.

As they approached the Lewis Road exit, Dale said, Sean suggested that they turn off and drive through some of the countryside because it reminded him of southern Illinois.

They exited at Lewis Road and drove until there was a dead end, with a group of trailers blocking the way.

Barron noted, silently, that this must have been the sealed-off entrance to Times Beach.

They turned around the other way, Dale continued, stopped for a school bus that was loading children, crossed some railroad tracks and took a side road.

Allen Road, Barron thought.

It was farm country, and it did look like southern Illinois. Dale had driven down the side road for a short distance when Sean asked him to stop the car so they could get out and look at some cows. He did stop, next to a pair of stone pillars that might have been hand-carved. As they were standing by the car, Sean all of a sudden asked Dale if he had a gun with him. Could he see it?

Dale opened the trunk, took out a pistol, a Smith & Wesson .357 magnum that he carried there, and handed it to Sean, who was standing near the passenger-side door. He did not know whether Sean wanted to fire the gun or not. They were out in the country, so it would not have mattered.

Dale said that as he returned to the trunk of the car to get himself a can of soda, Sean said:

"Tell Mom I'm sorry."

Dale heard a shot and looked up to see his son crumple to the ground. He ran to Sean's aid but found him lying there lifeless. He showed no vital signs.

Dale said that he immediately felt that his ex-wife, Marian, would have a terrible time dealing with a suicide, so, in order to save Marian from emotional stress, he picked up the gun from Sean's hand, backed up a few feet, and fired another shot, striking Sean in the back of the head.

"Where did the bullet hit him?" Barron asked.

Dale pointed with his index finger to a spot just to the right side of the lower portion of the back of his head. The autopsy report did indeed show a wound at that exact spot. The examining surgeon, however, had determined that this was the first shot, not the second, which was to the side of the head, just in front of the right ear. The shots had occurred in reverse order from Dale's account of them; and the pathologist had determined that the first shot, the one to the back of the head, had been fired from behind, while the victim was still standing.

Barron could not think through these discrepancies in the midst of the interview. He made a note to check Dale's version of what had happened against the forensic evidence.

"It must have been tough to hit that spot on Sean's head," Barron said quietly, concealing his disgust at the image of a father firing a bullet—a second one—into his dead son's head. This was some story.

"It was a lucky shot," Dale said, as though describing target practice, showing no emotion whatsoever. He spoke as if his actions had been logical, even thoughtful, with his supposed concern for Marian. "I didn't have my glasses on and I have buried cataracts. It was a lucky shot, that's all."

"You know, Dale," Barron said, "that our Bureau of Criminal Identification is going to be able to verify whether or not Sean had fired the weapon. They did a gun-residue test on Sean's hands."

"Any test you did would come back negative," Dale said.

"Why is that, if he fired the first shot himself?"

"Because I took a damp cloth. After the second shot, I took a damp cloth and wiped his hand clean so nobody would find gunpowder residue there. You see, I wanted it to look like a homicide and a robbery."

Dale said that he had for that reason taken his son's wallet, keys and coat and driven back to southern Illinois that morning. He had hidden Sean's things on some property he had down there.

"What about the gun?" Barron asked.

"I have that," Dale said. "It's hidden in my garage."

Barron asked for exact directions to where the items could be found. He gave Dale pen and paper, and Dale drew two maps, showing where Sean's belongings were at the Galatia farm and where the gun was hidden in the garage on Walnut Street in Harrisburg.

Barron telephoned Steve Goldman to convey this latest of the doc's stories. The idea that Sean had committed suicide was preposterous, Goldman said, and Barron agreed. Barron thought that he might have put the suicide business in Dale's mind during the previous, marathon interview, when he had asked him whether Sean had died of murder or suicide or what, just to try to get him to say something and admit that he had been present at Sean's death. It had taken Dale a few days to dream up this version.

"The autopsy should disprove it," Goldman said, "but I don't like to have an entire case hanging on forensic evidence. I hope you can come up with something else. We may not have enough here."

"Don't worry, Steve," Barron said, "I'm going down to southern Illinois the day after Christmas. I'll come back with everything you need."

Dave Barron drove down to southern Illinois on Wednesday, December 26, with detectives Larry Fox and Ted Kaminski and met Jack Nolen at the Saline County Courthouse on Shawnee Square in Harrisburg.

Nolen had warned Barron not to expect a warm welcome from the people of Little Egypt, especially not from the citizens of Eldorado. They were up in arms about the doc's arrest. Nobody, nobody who was talking anyway, believed that Dr. Dale, as they called him, had murdered his son. Barron had better understand that Doc Cavaness was the local hero. His patients worshiped him, and just about everybody was a patient or a relative of the patient. Nolen had talked to one man, the owner of an Eldorado shop, who had told him that he did not think that Doc Cavaness had done it, but that if he *had* murdered his son, the boy had probably deserved it and, the man said, he hoped that the doc got away with it and was acquitted whether he was guilty or not.

Nolen had always had good relations with the people of Eldorado. Now he was no longer welcome there. He could feel it. He could see it in the faces and hear it in the voices. The word was out that he was still investigating Mark Cavaness's murder and that there might be a connection between the two killings. Publicly he was still denying that Dr. Cavaness was a suspect in the earlier death or had ever been a suspect. He had to tread carefully. His new name for Eldorado was the City of Hostility. The people were organizing a defense fund for the doc, asking for donations to hire a hotshot St. Louis attorney. They planned to hold fund-raising bean suppers and to place canisters in stores, so people could donate to the doc the way they did to conquer diseases.

Nolen had sent Barron a copy of an edition of the Eldorado *Daily*

Journal so that he could get a better idea of what he would be up against when he came down. REACTION TO ARREST IS ONE OF DISBELIEF the headline read. The article said that local reaction was "overwhelmingly supportive" of the doctor and quoted a cross-section of the community as affirming that they were one hundred percent behind their beloved Dr. Dale. A nurse at Pearce Hospital who had worked for the doctor for twenty-five years vehemently denied that he could be guilty of murder. "I've seen him work too hard to save lives," she said. Another hospital employee stated that the doctor's patients believed that "the sun rises and sets with him." "If he did do it, I hope and pray that they can't prove it," somebody else told the reporter.

When Barron met Nolen at the County Courthouse, he asked whether public reaction was calming down or changing. Some of the evidence had come out. The prosecutor's office had publicly stated that they could place Dale with Sean on the night of the murder.

Nolen said that public support for the doc was stronger than ever.

"I don't get it," Barron said. "What about Sean? What about Marian and Kevin?"

"People think the doc's a kind of Robin Hood," Nolen said in his jovial way. "Don't worry," he laughed, "I'll stick by you boys. I'll ride shotgun. Folks around here aren't used to big-city cops. They won't be sorry to see you leave town, either."

Barron studied Nolen's round, ruddy face, his natty clothes, the embroidered rose in his lapel, and hated to think what it would be like down here without him. Barron already had a gloomy impression of southern Illinois. He felt as if he were in another country in another century. He did not enjoy being without his gun, but he was out of his jurisdiction. From what Nolen had told him, the folks in Egypt liked to settle an argument with a bullet. Nolen handled as many homicides a year as Barron did, with only a fraction of the population of St. Louis County.

At the courthouse Nolen escorted the St. Louis detectives as Barron signed an affidavit noting probable cause for a search warrant to be issued for the garage at 210 West Walnut and another for Dale's Galatia farm.

Nolen drove them out to the farm and, following Dale's hand-drawn map, they discovered in a pile of rubble not far from the

Shea house the pathetic belongings of the dead Sean: a red nylon jacket, a set of keys, a brown leather wallet containing his driver's license. All had been stuffed into a white plastic bag and hidden under a plastic tarp covered with bricks and trash, just as the doc had described.

Handling Sean's things, Barron felt nausea. Seeing these objects brought the reality of what Dale had done into sharper focus. Even in the company of Nolen and the other detectives, it was lonely out there on the farm, and the loneliness and sadness of Sean's life were present in a young man's wallet and keys and jacket, left by his father in a trash heap. Had any human being in the history of the world deserved such a father? Had anyone had such a father?

Detective Kaminski took photographs of the site and of the objects. The men, guided by Nolen, explored the area. Nolen pointed out the spot where Mark's remains had been found seven years before.

"I'll send you the photographs of Mark," Nolen told Barron. "I've never seen anything like them. I'll bet you haven't either."

They headed back to Harrisburg along Route 34. Nolen showed the others where Dale had hit the McLaskeys' car in 1971 and killed the father and daughter. Barron said that the former Mrs. McLaskey had telephoned the police and had been put in touch with Steve Goldman right after the doc had been arrested. She was married again, Barron gathered, and living in St. Louis. Evidently she had neither forgotten nor forgiven the doc. She wanted the chance to testify against him at the trial.

"Well, I'll be damned," Nolen said. "Now isn't that something. What do you know. I'll bet the doc'll be mighty surprised to see her," he chuckled. "How do you do. That's what they say, what goes around comes around. Isn't it the truth?"

Nolen pulled his Buick in behind the garage at 210 Walnut, and they began the search for the gun, following Dale's diagram of its location. They found the blue-steel, four-inch-barrel .357 magnum pistol, exactly where Dale said it was, jammed between a wooden strut and the drywall. Kaminski took photographs.

The St. Louis detectives stayed the night at the Holiday Inn in Marion, twenty-five miles west of Harrisburg, and spent the next day interviewing people who, Nolen suggested, would be able to account for Dale's movements and his behavior during the period immediately after Sean's murder. They talked to nurses, a lab technician, and the administrator at Pearce Hospital. Barron remembered telling Steve Goldman that he was going down to southern Illinois and would come back with everything needed for the case. He had retrieved the murder weapon and Sean's belongings, but he could see that he was not going to get anything else.

The atmosphere at Pearce Hospital was so palpably hostile that Barron commented to his colleagues that he wished he had brought along his bulletproof vest. Nurses, secretaries, administrators, doctors—everyone was defensive about Dr. Cavaness. Their responses ranged from a formal, unrevealing courtesy on the part of Ann Pulliam, the chief administrator and the chairman of the hospital foundation that now ran the place, to outright resentment and rudeness from the nurses. According to everyone, Dale did not appear to be acting strangely at all on Friday, December 14. He had made his rounds as usual. Only the doctor's laboratory technician, Russell Anderson, said that Dale had looked tired, possibly ill. Mrs. Pulliam said that he had been his usual attentive self, inquiring about the well-being of Mrs. Irma Pearce, the widow of the hospital's founder.

"They don't want to believe anything has happened," Barron said afterward, relieved to be back in Nolen's car. "They think we've invented all this. They despise us."

"I told you they wouldn't be friendly," Nolen said. "It's the same all over Eldorado. I feel sorry for Ann Pulliam, though. She's a nice lady. It's not her fault the guy on her staff who was supposed to be taking out gallbladders was a killer."

Barron wondered whether Dale had killed other people in addition to his sons. A story had surfaced just before Christmas, by way of an anonymous phone call to the St. Louis police from McLeansboro, that Dale might have killed a widow in order to inherit her estate. The woman had been a patient of Dale's since his McLeansboro days and, after her husband had died, she had made Dale her executor. The widow's neighbors, according to the anonymous caller, had begun noticing that Dr. Cavaness was keeping company with her. He would show up at her house late in the evenings, starting in late 1982 and into '83, and sometimes take her out and bring her back in the early hours; on other occasions he would spend the night. The neighbors, watchful like everyone in small towns, would see his car leaving at six or seven in the morning.

"Martha Culley won't be real pleased if she hears this," Nolen said.

One evening in the summer of '83 Dale brought the widow back late at night and the two of them were laughing in her driveway, with drinks in their hands, before disappearing inside. It was a hot night and a woman across the street was sitting out on her porch from where she could see and hear everything. In the morning Dale's car was gone.

The widow had a regular bridge game the next night. When she didn't show up, the other players wondered, but they did nothing until two nights later, when the widow had still not come out of her house and the neighbors noticed that the paper had not been picked up for two days and lights were burning. The police found her dead in her bed.

There was no autopsy. No one had said anything until now, but the story was that Dale had inherited her jewelry and antiques and that she had also loaned him money over the years.

"I think he killed that old woman," Barron said. "Kevin tells me that he did inherit some jewelry from her but that it was just junk, from what Kevin could see. I think he got jewelry and antiques and sold the good stuff."

"We'll never know now," Nolen said. "That old lady was nearly eighty when she died. If Dale really was seeing her, she might've died of joy. She might just've keeled over in ecstasy."

At Hickory Handle the detectives interviewed the farm manager, Hap Dawson, who said that Dale had appeared to be in a completely normal emotional state on Thursday, December 13, when he arrived at the farm at about noon, driving the Oldsmobile, and stayed until after four.

Barron went alone to see Martha Culley. At her request he interviewed her in the presence of her attorney at his law office in Harrisburg. Barron began by telling her that she was in no way considered a suspect nor someone with firsthand knowledge of the homicide.

Martha said that she had known Dale for twenty-five years, had been seeing him romantically for fifteen years and living with him off and on throughout that time. Barron identified her on his notepad as "Doc's live-in girlfriend." He saw her as someone who had once been attractive but was now pretty well worn. She described how Dale had traded cars with her on Wednesday night, taking the Toronado, but stated that she had no idea where he was going and had never known that he had driven to St. Louis. On Thursday evening they attended Peggy Ozment's annual Christmas party, which was held at the Gateway Holiday Inn in Muddy. It was a big bash, and they had had a good time, staying till one in the morning.

After they had come home from the party Dale received a phone call. He did not tell her about the nature of the call.

"He didn't tell you that it was his ex-wife or Kevin calling, saying that Sean had been killed?" Barron asked.

"No," Martha said.

"Don't you think it's kind of unusual, his getting a call saying that his son was found murdered and not telling you about it?"

"I don't see anything unusual about it," Martha said.

"Not unusual that he didn't tell you about going to St. Louis or what he had been doing?"

Martha said that she found nothing unusual about it. Dale lived his life and she lived hers. She hoped the charges against Dale were not true.

Dave Barron had not expected Martha Culley to be an eager witness. Aside from her connection to Dale through romance and a house, her son-in-law, T. R. Murphy, was the doc's lawyer. Her former son-in-law was a convicted drug dealer linked to the doctor. Everyone in Little Egypt seemed to be related or connected to everyone else. The judge who had issued the warrant authorizing the police to seize the Toronado turned out to be the son of a state's attorney from the 1920s who had served time for his association with the Charlie Birger gang and had been the target of assassination attempts by gang members who considered him an informer. Jack Nolen had all the links and genealogies in his head. Martha Culley herself was the daughter of another judge.

"Now you see how tough it is," Nolen said, "to get an impartial jury down here. The doc's big mistake was killing Sean in St. Louis. I seriously doubt whether we could get a conviction in southern Illinois."

But Martha had accurately, it seemed, described the doctor's movements and behavior after Sean's death. Along with everyone else's statements and the St. Louis evidence, Barron now believed he could form a picture of Dale as a man capable of murdering his son one morning after being up all night drinking, then driving a hundred and fifty miles back to southern Illinois to go about his business, tending to a sick heifer, having a whale of a time whooping it up at a party, and spending the next day caring for patients— to say nothing of driving back to St. Louis and staying up most of the night talking to the police and putting on an act for his family.

"He's not your run-of-the-mill, everyday guy," Nolen said. "You can see why people admire him, can't you? He's got a whole lot of unusual qualities."

By the second week in January the Dr. Cavaness Defense Fund, coordinated by a group of Eldorado business people, friends and employees of the doctor, raised approximately thirty-six thousand dollars to hire a lawyer to defend him. The money came in amounts ranging from substantial to as little as a dollar and included donations from most of the eleven counties of Little Egypt. Pictures appeared in the papers showing children breaking open their piggy banks. People offered to mortgage their houses for the cause, although that would not be necessary, the committee assured everyone. Considering the population of the area and its poverty, an extraordinary amount of money was flowing in. Much was made of the doctor's having treated the sick for free over the years, and patients were urged to pay their outstanding medical bills.

Early in January T. R. Murphy contacted attorney Arthur S. Margulis of St. Louis, who agreed to represent Dr. Cavaness through his trial and possible appeal for a flat fee of fifty thousand dollars, as Murphy announced in calling for more donations. (Criminal defense lawyers in St. Louis, unlike those in many other parts of the country, do not charge on an hourly basis.) Margulis, one of the top criminal defense attorneys in Missouri, was highly regarded enough to have been one of two lawyers elected by the fifty-five hundred members of the bar in his circuit to a committee which advised the governor on judicial appointments. Margulis was at the doctor's side as the grand jury brought down its indictment.

When Dave Barron announced to the press that the gun believed to be the murder weapon had been found in Dr. Cavaness's Harrisburg garage, the revelation was denounced in Eldorado as a smear and an attempt to dry up the defense fund. "No one on our committee believes Dr. Cavaness is guilty," declared Bertis Herrmann, the proprietor of Herrmann's Tin Shop, a hardware and heating and air-conditioning business, and the self-appointed, unofficial spokesman for the fund committee. "Everyone I have talked to feels he is innocent," Herrmann told the Harrisburg *Daily Register*.

Several people wrote lengthy letters to the Eldorado, Harrisburg and other regional papers, defending the doctor as the victim of a big-city frame-up. One such letter, written by a woman, spoke of the "decadent, abominable and deplorable grand-scale character assassination of Dr. John Dale Cavaness by those who perpetrated the diabolical plot to frame him for the murder of his son. . . . People are sickened and angered by this whole provarication [*sic*]. . . . To the St. Louis detective who described Dr. Cavaness as being the most cold-blooded and unemotional person you have ever seen, then just how long have you been in your field (two seconds?)? And what cave have you been hiding in? What would you do if your son was killed and you were framed for the murder, dance in the Follies?"

Not a single letter appeared suggesting that the doctor might possibly be guilty or that citizens ought to wait to see what a jury decided. As more evidence piled up, the letters grew more strident. The police had planted the gun in the doctor's garage. Sean's St. Louis neighbors were part of the frame-up. Someone had lured the doctor to St. Louis that night and told the neighbors to watch for him. Reviving talk of Mark Cavaness's death after all these years was nothing but St. Louis "hype and vilification." The doctor had been framed in 1971, one letter said, when witnesses changed their stories and lied, to get him convicted of reckless homicide. Now he was being made a scapegoat for the rottenness of big-city life. The people of St. Louis wanted a hanging: "If Dr. Cavaness were the worse [*sic*] criminal you had in St. Louis, your fair city would be well off beyond imagination."

A story in the Evansville, Indiana, *Sunday Courier and Press* ran on February 3, 1985, under the headline HOMICIDE STIRS ILLINOIS TOWN'S EMOTIONS. Eldorado residents were "deeply suspicious of authorities in St. Louis who are trying to convict one of their own of murder."

Articles telling of the defense fund and the support for Dr. Cavaness soon appeared in papers all over Illinois, in the *Chicago Tribune* and the *St. Louis Post-Dispatch*. Television news broadcasts featured the controversy. The popular theory in Eldorado was that Sean had been killed by drug dealers for gambling debts; the criminals had ties to St. Louis bigwigs, who were framing Dr. Cavaness to protect themselves. Detective Barron took most of the heat and publicly replied with as much diplomacy as he could muster: "I admire people who stick up for him but I think they're putting blinders on. They see one side. They do not know what I know about this case."

The story quickly became national news. A reporter in the Chicago bureau of *People* magazine, Giovanna Breu, realized that the Dr. Cavaness imbroglio was of more than local interest, especially because of the vehemence and seeming unanimity of the doctor's hometown support. She did a thorough job of research, interviewing Bertis Herrmann and others in Eldorado and the authorities in St. Louis, and obtaining a taped interview with Dr. Cavaness in his cell at the county jail.

Steve Goldman, learning of the interview and assuming that the doctor would tell the *People* reporter his latest version of Sean's death, the suicide story with the doc's firing a second shot to make it look like a murder-robbery, leaked that material to the Evansville *Courier* before the *People* story could come out. When he subpoenaed Giovanna Breu, she refused to produce the tapes of her interview.

The *People* story, accompanied by a chilling photograph of Dale Cavaness sitting in a chair in shackles and another, poignant photograph of Sean, Kevin and Patrick in 1980, was meticulously accurate and fair. Breu did include the doctor's version, but she also quoted Kevin as saying that the people who supported his father were those who knew him least. "I was reared in his shadow and I know," Kevin said.

The *People* story brought the first wave of writers and movie and television producers from Hollywood and New York. Kevin and Charli hoped that their side of the story would come out at the trial. Their emotions were too frayed for them to think about sharing their thoughts with strangers who, as Goldman advised, should not be trusted with evidence before it was presented to a jury.

Kevin, Charli and Marian were offended by all the support Dale received. (As for Patrick, Marian did her best to shield him from the publicity and, except for the *People* story, was mostly able to do so, since the Cavaness case did not get much play in Wausau.) Rumors reached them that a relative of Martha's, a woman who was a lawyer in Oklahoma City, planned to write a book about Dale from his point of view. Supposedly he was filling his hours in jail writing letters about his life and talking into a tape recorder about the wrongs he had suffered. Vicious remarks about the doctor's ex-wife and elder surviving son surfaced in southern Illinois, characterizing them as disloyal and out to crucify a decent man.

What about Sean and Mark? Kevin wondered. Didn't anyone care about them? About Marian and what she had gone through, was going through? Did the credulous citizens of Eldorado and Harrisburg not believe that Marian had had good reasons for leaving Dale years before? In Little Egypt the double standard reigned. A man like Dale could do just about anything he pleased—apparently including getting away with murder—and his wife was supposed to keep her mouth shut and stick by him. It was all in the Bible, people said. The only public sympathy for the family came in the form of an announcement that appeared anonymously one day in the *Daily Journal*. Framed in black it read simply "In Memory of Mark Dale Cavaness and Sean Dale Cavaness" with their dates of birth and death. Kevin learned that the tribute had been placed by two young women, friends of his and Charli's from Eldorado. He was grateful for the gesture, which he hoped might prick a few consciences.

As Kevin maintained, Dale's vocal supporters were people who knew him least. The Sullivans and the Becks were publicly silent; others, like the Leonards and the Davenports, had moved from southern Illinois. Kevin wished that dissenters in Eldorado and Harrisburg would speak out, but he understood why they did not. They had to live and work down there.

One of the most bewildering of Dale's supporters was a Baptist minister, the Reverend Staley R. Langham, who appointed himself Dale's spiritual counselor and principal personal spokesman. A letter from Reverend Langham, pastor of the College Heights Baptist Church in Eldorado, appeared in the *Daily Journal*, stating that he had visited Dr. Dale Cavaness in jail and that the doctor was well and in a good state of mind. Dr. Dale wished to thank everyone for their letters and support, which proved what a kind and loving place Eldorado was. He was looking forward to returning to his practice and was certain that he would be cleared of the charges against him.

Reverend Langham went on to report that Dr. Dale had revealed what had really happened to Sean. Even his attorney did not know the true story at first; now the attorney wanted it kept quiet, so Reverend Langham was required to maintain the secret. Everyone could rest assured that the doctor was innocent and would be cleared.

This letter was only the first of many public statements by Reverend Langham, who said that he had gone to see the doctor as a Christian act of mercy and had discovered an innocent, persecuted man. The minister would not abandon Dr. Dale until he was freed.

Kevin had never heard of Staley Langham, and he was sure that Dale had never had anything to do with him until now. The idea of Dale's so much as giving a minister or a priest the time of day was ironic; he had not set foot in a church for years except for funerals and for Kevin's wedding. But Dale was clever, Kevin knew, and would be prepared to try anything to save his own neck. Talking to a minister who then blabbed to the public was a good strategy; it had worked for other criminals.

The Sullivans, like most of Dale's longtime friends, were so shocked and depressed by what had happened that they could hardly speak about it between themselves, aside from the wisdom of keeping a public silence. Once the evidence began to come out, especially Dale's tale of a suicide and a second shot, they assumed that their old friend had finally gone crazy. They were sorry to conclude that they had so misjudged a man whom they had considered difficult, eccentric and irresponsible toward his family but hardly a murderer.

Lou and Pann Beck could not talk about Dale and his sons without crying. Over in the Missouri Ozarks, where Marilyn and Chuck Leonard had retired to a cottage beside a lake, Marilyn had been sure that Dale was guilty the minute that she saw the news of his arrest on television; and she telephoned Marian often to comfort her. Dale's guilt was more difficult for Chuck to accept; he became silent and depressed, finding it difficult to reconcile all the good times he and Dale had spent together with Dale's being a father who had murdered his son. Marilyn was more inclined to see what had happened as the logical extension of the megalomaniac behavior she had endured working for Dale.

Marilyn's successor, Eddie Miller, never for a moment doubted Dr. Cavaness's guilt; but he kept silent for his own health and safety, in case the doctor managed to wriggle free. Eddie had heard the rumors about the widow in McLeansboro and believed that the doctor had also killed her. Back in 1977 Eddie Miller was one of the few who assumed that Dr. Cavaness had committed the perfect crime in killing Mark. Eddie thanked God that he had taken Dr. Cavaness's threats against him seriously and had quit his job before being killed or driven insane. He was surprised that the doctor had not killed his wife when she dared to leave him. He admired Marian and hoped that she would be able to survive.

Privately Eddie Miller thought it amusing that Bertis Herrmann was so prominent among Dr. Cavaness's supporters. Eddie remembered when the doctor had ordered him to fire Herrmann, who Dr. Cavaness had said was incompetent and incapable of repairing the office air-conditioning. Herrmann had blamed Eddie, of course, who took responsibility for the dismissal, preserving the myth of Dr. Cavaness's good-fellowship.

Among those who had known Dale Cavaness well, one of the most shocked was Greg Sullivan, Pat and Betty Ray's son, who had always been one of Dale's favorites. Greg had heard his parents say that, if Dale had paid as much attention to his own sons as he did to Greg, Mark and Sean would have turned out happier and better-adjusted kids. His father had often urged Dale to be a more responsible parent.

Greg was now the manager of the Marion Holiday Inn, the largest and best-run hotel and entertainment complex in Egypt, a hugely profitable operation; he was also a successful racing-car driver and the pilot of his own plane. He rightly considered himself more sophisticated than the typical admirer of Dr. Cavaness, yet he realized he too had been fooled, dramatically so.

Greg had attended Peggy Ozment's Christmas party and with his wife had spent almost the entire evening, well over two hours, at a table with Dale and Martha, laughing and drinking and reminiscing about old times—hunting trips, parties, excursions. To Greg, the fact that Dale had only that morning either murdered Sean or watched him commit suicide and then shot his own son in the head was astounding.

Greg knew Dale as crafty, someone who showed you only as much of himself as he wanted you to see; he had also known him as a warm, funny guy, who could encounter you in the street and sit down with you on a corner to chat for half an hour just for the hell of it. He had seen Dale explode on many occasions over the years; he had also heard him give wise, confidential advice. When Greg had been experiencing some troubles with a girlfriend several years back, it was Dale who had gone out of his way to help him.

Greg had believed Mark's death to have been an accident until the papers began quoting Jack Nolen as saying that the case was an open homicide seven years later. As for Sean, Greg's theory was that Dale might well have bitched and taunted him into suicide. He could hear Dale's voice, vicious and loud, telling Sean that he was no good and that he ought to do everyone a favor by killing himself. But what was beyond imagining, almost, was what had certainly happened: that Dale had casually conversed and laughed for hours at Peggy Ozment's party.

Wherever they were, whatever they were doing with their lives, people at all close to Dr. John Dale Cavaness and his family were puzzling over what had happened. In south Florida, where he had retired, Marian's uncle Eddie Bell thought he understood why Dale had murdered both Mark and Sean. Eddie was a combat veteran of World War II and a successful businessman. He was not a sentimentalist and was no more surprised by what human beings did than a homicide detective was. He had observed Dale during those Christmases in St. Louis when, usually with Marian out of the room, Dale would attack Kevin and Sean, telling them that he wanted them out of his life. Marian would try to pass off Dale's behavior as drunk talk, but Eddie had seen the hatred in Dale's eyes and was glad that his beloved Marian had divorced this tyrant and was not living near him.

To Eddie, Dale Cavaness had a threefold motive for killing his sons. The first was greed: Dale was a business failure and wanted the insurance money. The second was hatred: He had contempt for Mark and Sean and wanted them out of the way, as embarrassments. He also despised that part of himself that was a failure—in business and in his first marriage, as a father and a husband—and he saw Mark and Sean as living proof of his failures. In a twisted way he must have thought that by killing them he was getting rid of that part of himself that he hated.

The third motive was revenge. Eddie knew Dale Cavaness well enough to see that he was the sort of man who never forgave and never forgot. He had married Marian and gone back to Eldorado to spite his first wife, Eddie thought; and when Marian also left him, he had to find a way to get back at her. No matter that Dale had brought the divorce on himself by his behavior: No woman was going to rebuff Dale Cavaness and get away with it. He had hurt Marian by killing the one thing she cared most about in life, her children.

For Eddie, all three motives were intertwined, greed and hatred and revenge. He wished that he could explain them to the jury. He did not think that Dale Cavaness was crazy, just a son of a bitch and a doctor who thought that he could get away with anything.

23

DALE'S TRIAL DATE WAS INITIALLY SET FOR FEBRUARY 11, 1985, but Arthur Margulis needed time to assess the evidence and to interview potential witnesses in St. Louis and in southern Illinois, as well as to prepare his client on the crucial question of what had actually happened on the morning of and the night preceding Sean's death. Margulis's various motions postponed the date to July 8. Justice moved swiftly in Missouri. Protracted delays and the lengthy, histrionic trials that characterized the sluggish pace of the courts in such states as California were unknown in Missouri. There were several reasons for this efficiency, perhaps the most important being that the state's criminal lawyers did not charge by the hour and so had no incentive to drag out a trial.

The Eldorado defense fund had raised thirty-eight thousand dollars, twelve thousand short of the amount needed to cover Margulis's expenses and fee; but Margulis was willing to proceed. Dale wrote many, many letters home to southern Illinois thanking and encouraging his supporters and bolstering their belief in his innocence. In his bold hand, a cross between script and printing notable for the long tails on the *f*s which carried downward into the following line, he wrote of his initial panic and confusion at being arrested. He felt like a drop of water, he said, going down the drain, as if he had been in "a sort of psychodelic [*sic*] vortex," and he worried about how confused all his friends and patients must have been. But the letters, calls, cards and notes from all the "Rudies" had cleared his mind. If he failed of eloquence in expressing his gratitude, he would have to blame his English teachers, he said lightly. In some of the letters he digressed about his fellow prisoners, the nut cases, the blacks who could not read the newspaper, one man who, Dale said, looked exactly like Jack Nicholson after shock therapy in *One Flew Over the Cuckoo's Nest*. One inmate liked to take showers with his clothes on; another was indignant that the police had taken away his cocaine. Since the *People* magazine story, he had been receiving letters of encouragement from all over the country, but the most important to him were from southern Illinois. The love he was feeling from everyone was keeping him from being bitter and depressed.

Some of the recipients of these letters talked to the press about them, saying how glad they were that the doctor was in such good spirits. Emma Lou Mitchell, Dale's faithful nurse, wrote to him every other day. But Dale, in an epistolary frenzy that lasted throughout the entire period of his incarceration, sent letters to many people who were not pleased to hear from him and considered his postal onslaught nothing more than an attempt to manipulate the public in the hope of influencing the outcome of his trial.

Dale wrote to a friend of Eddie Miller's, wishing her well, asking her to please give his regards to Eddie, and signing off by saying that all things were possible in Christ. The letter, written on stationery decorated with a cartoon of Garfield the cat, repelled its recipient who, well-known to be active in her church, considered its closing burst of piety transparently false; it certainly did not impress Eddie Miller, who shuddered at the idea of what the doctor was thinking about him. A doctor who had been a medical-school classmate of Dale's and was now a specialist in St. Louis received one of Dale's letters, which included a request for a donation to the defense fund. The St. Louis physician, who happened to be a friend and golfing buddy of Arthur Margulis, was disgusted. He had despised Dale in school as a belligerent know-it-all and had a low regard for Dale's professional competence. Dale had been referring patients to him for years and, like several other St. Louispecialists, he had the impression that Dr. Cavaness cared more about cattle than people, if the number of misdiagnoses among his referrals was any guide. Playing golf with Margulis one day, the St. Louis doctor told the lawyer that he did not envy his having Dale Cavaness as a client. He would find him very difficult to deal with. Dale was a guy, the doctor said, who thought he knew more about everything than anyone else did. He would try to tell Margulis how to handle his case. Margulis, who never talked about his clients to anyone except his wife, did not reply.

Publicly Margulis expressed his confidence that Dr. Cavaness would gain an acquittal, pleading innocent to the charge of capital murder. In Missouri capital murder was defined by section 565.001 of the penal code:

> Any person who unlawfully, willfully, knowingly, deliberately, and with premeditation kills or causes the killing of another human being is guilty of the offense of capital murder. . . . Persons convicted of the offense of capital murder shall, if the judge or jury so recommends . . . be punished by death. If the judge or jury does not recommend the imposition of the death penalty on a finding of guilty of capital murder, the convicted person shall be punished by imprisonment by the division of corrections during his natural life and shall not be eligible for probation or parole until he had served a minimum of fifty years of his sentence.

There was in Missouri, in other words, no way out for someone convicted of capital murder—no forgiveness, no possibility of parole for at least fifty years, no chance of swaying a parole board by being a model prisoner and behaving as if one were rehabilitated, no advantage to finding Jesus behind bars. If Dale was found guilty, he would either die in the gas chamber or wait for his first parole hearing at the age of a hundred and nine.

As a defendant, Dale had as his strongest suit his credibility as a doctor and the extraordinary nature of the crime with which he was charged. Could twelve impartial jurors believe that a successful man who had devoted his career to saving lives would stoop to murdering his son for insurance money? Against him would be the testimony of his own family and the ballistics which, as Steve Goldman would argue, showed that he had shot his son twice in the head.

Jury selection began on Monday, July 8, in Clayton at the St. Louis County Courthouse, a large, modern building that contained the prosecutor's offices as well as those of all the other legal officials of the county. Goldman and Margulis took only a day and a half to agree on a jury of nine women and three men. Neither man believed in courtroom theatrics nor in so-called scientific jury selection: You challenged those obviously hostile to your side, excluded those who said that they could not vote for the death penalty, and took your chances. Judge Margaret Nolan scheduled the opening arguments for Tuesday afternoon. Margulis and Goldman agreed that the trial should last about a week.

In court Dale appeared haggard and drawn. He had lost a lot of weight in jail; his dark suit fit loosely. Standing and sitting side by side, he and Margulis formed a striking contrast. At fifty Margulis, who was two or three inches taller than his client, looked fifteen or twenty years younger than Dale. Margulis was vigorous, athletic, fashionably dressed and handsome, his sky-blue eyes and thick silvery hair his most striking features; Dale, in the words of Jack Nolen, who was present in the courtroom with his wife, looked like a bad stretch of nine-mile road. Apparently his lawyer had been unable to spruce him up.

Dave Barron, who was prepared to testify and was present throughout the trial, told Nolen during a recess that the main thing to worry about was Art Margulis, not Dale Cavaness. He knew Margulis and respected him. After receiving his law degree from Washington University and before beginning his criminal defense practice, Margulis had joined the F.B.I. on the East Coast, back in the days when agents had to be either lawyers or accountants. He was possibly the most skillful defense lawyer in St. Louis, but the cops held him in high regard because he was honest, would never pull anything unethical and relied on his brains rather than theatrics to sway a jury. In hiring Margulis, T. R. Murphy had shown more savvy than Barron would have credited to him. That Margulis had four sons, just like the doc, was an interesting coincidence. The difference was that all four of Margulis's boys were in good health.

But in this ball game Dave Barron was betting on Steve Goldman, who was just as smart as Margulis and this time had the stronger case. The ballistics evidence would show that the doc had blown Sean away, snuck up behind him while he was standing beside the car and shot him once, then shot him again as he lay already dead on the ground. And the doc's lies to the police would work against him. Thank God for the Kroecks and their fabulous grocery bag. If it weren't for them, the doc might be in southern Illinois, cutting people up and screwing widow-women. Barron just prayed that the doc's family, who were scheduled to take the stand, could hold up. He was especially worried about Marian.

Dr. Ronald Turgeon, who had performed the autopsy on Sean, testified on the second day. Questioned by Goldman, he stated that the first shot, which powder residue and searing on the flesh showed had been fired from a distance of within an inch or less but not in actual contact, had entered at the back of the head just to the right of center, had traveled upward at an angle through the brain, and had exited at the corner of the left eye. Blood and flesh fragments found on the left shoulder and in the crook of the left arm showed that the victim had been standing, with his left arm slightly raised, as the first shot was fired. There was no way for blood to have splattered in that particular pattern on the left shoulder and arm if the victim had been lying down.

The second shot, Dr. Turgeon said, had been fired from a distance of twelve to eighteen inches when the victim was on the ground. It had entered near the right ear and had not exited, lodging in the brain. Either shot had been lethal. The victim had been brain-dead when the second shot was fired.

Margulis did his best to refute Turgeon and brought on a medical expert to argue that the ballistics evidence was inconclusive. The key question was whether Sean had fired the first shot into the side of his head. If Dr. Turgeon was correct in saying that the shot to the back of the head had been fired first, as the blood on the left shoulder and arm seemed to confirm, for Sean to have inflicted this wound on himself was, if not impossible, nearly so, and an act inconsistent with suicide.

When Kevin, Charli and Marian testified, they had to face Dale, who fixed them with a steady, hostile gaze, and a courtroom packed with his supporters from southern Illinois. The Cavanesses recognized most of the faces and knew that these people regarded the family as a trio of Judases. But Charli, whom Goldman chose to testify first because she seemed to be in better emotional shape than Kevin or Marian, came through strongly, accounting for Dale's behavior during the days following Sean's death. She managed to slip in her story about finding gas escaping from all four burners on the stove at the Galatia trailer. Margulis, who had not heard this anecdote before and was caught off guard by it, was unable to stop her.

Charli gave a coherent, articulate picture of Dale as an uncaring father who showed no concern for his troubled son and who at first had been unwilling to pay for his funeral expenses. Charli was six months pregnant at the time of her testimony, and Steve Goldman hoped that her condition would add to her credibility as a devoted relative of the victim.

Kevin heartened Goldman by his dignity and precision of description. He came across as angered and tortured by his ordeal; he spoke of how his father had resented paying for the funeral and how Dale had acted at the service, behaving like the host at a wedding reception. Kevin conveyed his understanding of his father's financial problems and revealed how the doctor had lied about whether the insurance on Sean's life was paid up and in effect.

Kevin's testimony, together with Goldman's documented evidence showing that Dale had declared a two-hundred-thousand-dollar negative net income on his 1983 income tax, added to other indications of a man in financial trouble despite the large income from his medical practice.

Marian, whom Goldman cautioned beforehand not to mention Mark's death—it was irrelevant to this trial and would trigger a motion for a mistrial if introduced—described how Dale had told her, when she had been six months pregnant with Patrick, that he did not love her or want her or need her. She recalled Dale's hostile behavior toward Sean at Christmas in St. Louis in 1982, saying that he had chased Sean down the block and shouted, "I'll kill him. I don't care if I go to prison. I'll kill him." She said that Dale had been unresponsive when she had called him to inform him of Sean's death and that he became surly and hung up on her before she could finish talking to him. She described Dale as loud and abusive toward his family.

"His patients loved him, apparently," Marian said, "but he didn't have any use for us."

Marian found testifying against Dale traumatic. She could feel Dale's eyes boring into her—especially when she stated her name as Marian Green, as if he still refused to accept that she was no longer his wife. She was sure now that he had deliberately contrived to delay their divorce decree, to exercise a last power over her.

Steve Goldman was optimistic about a conviction. The family had performed admirably; the financial evidence showed Dale in debt for at least half a million dollars, with assets of about a hundred and fifty thousand and creditors hounding him; and the ballistics evidence weighed strongly against the doctor's bizarre version of events. It remained for Dr. Cavaness to take the stand and testify in his own defense. Goldman hoped that the jury would see him as a cold-blooded villain. To Goldman, who had two children of his own, the doctor was the most sinister defendant he had ever prosecuted.

Saturday, July 13, was the worst day of Steve Goldman's professional life. The jury was examining evidence—Sean's clothing, the murder weapon, the eloquent contents of the doctor's briefcase left behind at Kevin's apartment—when suddenly Goldman realized that one of his assistants had mistakenly included Sam Yarbrough's report of the results of the lie-detector test. Polygraph evidence was inadmissible in Missouri: The machine was not considered sufficiently reliable. The introduction of polygraph evidence was sure grounds for a mistrial.

Goldman took the bad news to the chief county prosecutor, Buzz Westfall, who agreed that they had an ethical obligation to report this lamentable mistake to Art Margulis. The polygraph results, which showed that Dale had failed the examination and lied repeatedly to Yarbrough, were certainly prejudicial to the defendant.

Goldman contacted Margulis, who expressed his appreciation for Goldman's honesty and said that he would recommend to his client that they move for a mistrial.

"I'm sure he'll agree," Margulis said. "I'll explain to him that a second trial usually works to the advantage of the defendant."

"Sure," Goldman said. "Tell him he's going to get a second shot. He'll appreciate that."

Margulis replied that he would put the matter in less colorful terms.

On Sunday Judge Nolan ruled in favor of a mistrial and, on Margulis's urging, set the date for the new trial in November.

Polled by the press after they were dismissed, all twelve jurors said that they had been prepared to vote guilty and were sorry to have been deprived of the chance to convict Dr. Cavaness.

The doctor's supporters were undaunted. They would raise more money, Bertis Herrmann said, and the Reverend Staley R. Langham declared that he had new evidence to present to Dr. Dale's attorney which would assure an acquittal.

Margulis moved for a bail hearing, a normal procedure after a mistrial. Steve Goldman told Kevin that he would have to stand before the judge and in the presence of the defendant state his reasons for believing that Dale Cavaness should be denied bail. Kevin found this the most difficult moment so far in the legal proceedings, but he went through with it, saying that he feared for his life and those of other family members if the defendant was released on bail. The judge agreed, ruling that Dr. Cavaness would have to remain in jail while awaiting the new trial.

"My dad wanted to kill me right there," Kevin told Goldman afterward. "I could see it in his eyes. Did you see the look he gave me?"

Dale resumed his letter-writing campaign. He was hurt, he wrote to a woman in Eldorado, that Kevin, Marian and Charli had turned against him and were telling such lies about him. Sure, he had not been a perfect father, but he had always provided for them and had never been the stingy sort of person that they had made him out to be. How could Marian say that he had no use for his family, when, among many other acts of selfless generosity, he had paid in full for a two-hundred-and-fifty-thousand-dollar house for her, after she had divorced him, so that she could live in Chesterfield with the boys in the style she preferred? It was sad, how ungrateful people could be.

The declaration of the mistrial was devastating to Kevin, Charli and Marian—as well as to Les Green, who had not planned on having his second marriage start off with a murder trial and revelations about Marian's life with Dale that were almost beyond belief. He did the best he could to help Marian and admired her strength. He tried not to think about what might happen if Dale got off, fearing that Marian would crack and amazed that she had not broken down already. She was putting up a brave front, but she was not sleeping well. Her nightmare about a baby with Sean's mature head kept recurring, sending her wandering through the house in the dark.

Kevin and Charli worried about the effect on Charli's pregnancy of the anxiety of waiting and dragging through the entire wretched business again in the coming weeks. Fortunately the baby was due in September, before the new trial would begin.

Charli was at full term when, on September 27, she gave birth to a stillborn girl. Losing the child, whom they named Kelly Ann and buried formally in a St. Louis cemetery, hurt more than anything else in the string of tragedies that beset them. The baby had become their symbol of hope and renewal, to Kevin a way of defying and overcoming everything that Dale had tried to do to them. Now, only ten months after Sean's death, the baby was dead. The two deaths seemed linked.

In Charli's second month of pregnancy they had taken Sean's ashes, finally recovered from the funeral home when the Cavaness defense fund paid the outstanding expenses, and driven them to southern Illinois, as they believed Sean would have wished. For all that he had suffered there, Sean had always been drawn back to the land between the rivers. Under the circumstances they did not think they ought to risk driving onto the Hickory Handle farm to scatter Sean's ashes with Mark's. The farmhands, loyal to Dale, might make trouble.

In a snowstorm they slowly made their way along Route 34 past Herod, up into the Shawnee hills to a spot called the Garden of the Gods, a scenic lookout point in good weather, enshrouded that day by the blizzard.

They walked to an obscure, rugged place on the edge of a bluff. Kevin poured the ashes out of the urn in a thin stream, letting the cold, wet wind take them; and Charli said quietly, "God bless him and keep him."

On the road home to St. Louis they talked of Sean and of their baby, hoping that Dale's trial and conviction would be past before it was born.

Now she too was gone, and Dale still defiant, still, it seemed, bringing death. Charli could not help but think that the agony of the trial and its failure to reach a resolution had drained the life from Kelly Ann. Kevin in despair wondered whether they were forever cursed. Did his father somehow have the power to ruin their every hope?

They placed a vase on their baby's grave and brought fresh flowers when they could.

24

THE REVEREND STALEY R. LANGHAM PESTERED ART MARGULIS during the four months between the first and second trials, saying that he had new evidence proving that Dr. Cavaness's story of Sean's suicide was true and that the State's ballistics evidence was as phony as a three-dollar bill. Margulis accepted the minister's frequent telephone calls and listened to his argument about the first shot's being the one near the right ear, inflicted by Sean himself, and the second being the shot to the back of the head, inflicted by the doctor, exactly as Dale had said, the reverse of Dr. Turgeon's testimony; but Margulis could not make sense out of the Langham's reasoning. Margulis knew about Langham's public defense of the doctor and took an indulgent attitude toward this man of God who, favoring string ties and cowboy boots with his suits, had stood out among spectators at the first trial.

In addition to his ministry for Christ, Reverend Langham also claimed to be a "photographic lab specialist" and said that he could prove that the evidence used by Dr. Turgeon at the trial had been altered. Langham had a photograph of himself holding a .357 magnum pistol in his right hand with his thumb on the trigger, his arm outstretched and the gun pointing at the side of his head. He would have no trouble shooting himself in the head that way.

"I'm sure you wouldn't," Margulis said, "but I'm still not sure what you're saying."

"You have to see the picture," Langham said. "I know Dr. Dale is innocent and I can prove it. I've got other pictures."

"You do?"

"I am so sure because I shot a sheep head that had been killed to butcher."

"You what? *A sheep's head?*"

"I shot a sheep head with a magnum. Yes, I did. And we took and had X rays made of the sheep head, exactly like Sean's head."

"You think the sheep's head is exactly like Sean's head?"

"We shot it at close range and had X rays made to compare with the X rays of Sean's head. You see the X rays of the sheep head and the debris and soot found prove that the shot to the back of the head was not a close-range shot. It was the second shot. And the first shot to the side of the head was the one went out the eye, a fragment of it, not like Dr. Turgeon said."

Reverend Langham had performed other ballistics tests. He had also shot a pork roast and a baloney-roll.

"You shot baloney?" Margulis said.

The baloney-roll experiment, Langham said, had not worked as smoothly as the others. Baloney was full of water and it had exploded when he shot it, and the water had gone all over the place. Margulis would have to examine the photographs fully to appreciate the conclusiveness of this new evidence. It would be just what was needed to shoot the State's case full of holes.

Margulis, not wishing to offend one of his client's most vigorous supporters, made an appointment to meet Reverend Langham in Clayton at his law offices, which were just down the street from the courthouse.

Reverend Langham arrived bearing slides and a projector—no animal remains. Margulis let him set up the projector in the office of a junior member of the firm, who watched the show without uttering a sound.

"Now do you get it?" Langham asked when he was through showing photos and X rays depicting a bullet-torn sheep's head and brain.

"Sort of," Margulis said. "I'm not sure."

Langham asked whether Margulis would permit him to testify at the trial. Margulis said he would have to think the matter over. There might be a problem with the jurors' thinking that the defense was comparing Sean's head to a sheep's and to a pork roast or other objects. They just might be offended by that and fail to grasp the subtlety of the argument.

Unfazed, Reverend Langham brought out a tape measure and got down on his hands and knees on the office floor.

"Here, Art," he said, "take this here tape measure and measure the distance over my head from the right ear to my left eye."

Margulis did as he was asked, wondering what this experiment was supposed to prove.

"What do you see?" Langham asked. "What's the measurement?"

"I'd say it's about a fifteen and a half—thirty-four," Margulis said.

His feelings only slightly ruffled, Reverend Langham gathered up his things. He hoped Margulis would let him testify. It could mean the difference between life and death.

"You're probably right," Margulis said.

Dave Barron spent time between the trials comforting Kevin and Charli after their latest loss and assuring them that this time the trial would reach its proper conclusion. If they and Marian could go through their testimony once more, everything would be fine. The doc was stuck with his incredible story. A second panel of jurors would be no more likely to believe it than had the first. The state was planning to call a new forensic expert, Dr. George Gantner, who had examined the autopsy report and the photographs and agreed strongly with Dr. Turgeon's conclusions. Dr. Gantner was the chief forensic pathologist for both the city and county of St. Louis and one of the most respected men in his field in the world. Barron doubted that Art Margulis would be able to find anyone able to refute Gantner.

Barron also tried to dig up more information on Mark's murder. The photographs of Mark's remains were, as Jack Nolen had promised, the worst Barron had ever seen, and he was as convinced as Nolen that Dale had committed both murders. He was intrigued by a meeting he had had with a relative of the Weingartens, who had contacted him and told him that she believed that Johnny Weingarten knew something about Mark's death: The property on

Lake Harrisburg that Dale had deeded to Johnny Weingarten in 1978, supposedly for fifty-five thousand dollars, might have been a payoff to keep Weingarten quiet. The younger Weingarten cousin had told her that Dale had once threatened both Weingartens and Mark late in 1976, when they were climbing out of their boat after doing some night fishing on the lake. Dale had sprung out from behind a tree, held a shotgun to the younger Weingarten's neck, and said that he could blow his head off and nobody would know anything about it. Dale had been drunk, of course, but he had scared hell out of the boys.

The woman believed that Mark had known about his father's dealing narcotics to the Weingartens and had wanted no part of it. Dale had killed Mark to shut him up.

Barron, while accepting that there was no proof that Dale had dealt any drugs other than the stuff found on the Weingartens when they were busted years later, and understanding that not even that would stand up in court, nevertheless believed that Johnny Weingarten just might know something about Mark's murder and Dale's involvement in it. If he did, that would explain why Dale, as he had told Kevin and Charli, wanted Johnny locked up.

It was only a slender lead, but Barron contacted Jack Nolen and went with him to visit both Weingartens at the state penitentiary at Vienna, about twenty-five miles south of Marion. Neither Weingarten would talk to the detectives, and Johnny refused even to come out of his cell.

Barron, guessing that the Weingartens might not want to talk in the presence of Jack Nolen, whom they surely blamed for their arrest and conviction, returned to Vienna on his own. Johnny again refused to leave his cell; his cousin again said he knew nothing, and Barron believed him. Whatever Johnny knew, if anything, he was not telling. Barron felt frustrated, sensing he was missing something, but he had to give up on that lead.

Because of the enormous amount of publicity surrounding the Dr. Cavaness case in St. Louis—the first trial had been front-page news in the *Post-Dispatch* and the lead story on the television news every evening—the judge assigned to the second trial, the Honorable Drew W. Luten, Jr., of the Circuit Court of St. Louis County, determined that the jurors should come from Kansas City,

Missouri, where the case had been reported with less intensity. The judge reasoned that, rather than move the entire trial away from St. Louis, it would be less expensive to bring jurors in from across the state who had not formed an opinion about the defendant's guilt. Although the crime had occurred in St. Louis County, capital murder was a crime against the State of Missouri, so the case could appropriately be tried by jurors from Jackson County.

The judge's plan was for himself, Goldman, Margulis and Dr. Cavaness—who by law had to be present during all phases of his trial—to be in Kansas City on Tuesday, November 12, to select a panel. The twelve jurors and three alternates would then be escorted to St. Louis and sequestered at a Clayton hotel for the duration of the trial.

Goldman and Margulis agreed to this plan, which seemed the most sensible means of gaining an impartial panel at reasonable cost to taxpayers. They considered Judge Luten fair, learned and experienced. The judge planned to retire after the Cavaness trial; over the years he had merited respect, having been but rarely reversed by a higher court.

Jury selection took one day. On Wednesday the jurors, whom the judge instructed to be prepared to remain a week or perhaps more in St. Louis, were bused from Kansas City to the Clayton Holiday Inn, where bailiffs would see to it that they did not read about the trial or watch relevant portions of the television news. The jurors and their alternates were ten women and five men and included a second-grade teacher and a high school principal, secretaries, salespeople, a carpet cleaner, a pest-control worker, a housewife, a food porter, a kitchen manager, a liquor sales representative, and a Hallmark Cards handler—about as various and representative a group of Missourians as one could find.

The second trial began at the County Courthouse on Wednesday, November 14, with the scene in the courtroom the same as before: thirty or forty southern Illinois supporters, including the Reverend Staley R. Langham, who arrived equipped with slides and projector, hoping for his moment on the witness stand; the press; the detectives, among them Jack Nolen and his wife; members of the public who could find a seat.

One interested spectator was the former Mrs. Dorothy Mc-Laskey, now Mrs. Zignetti of St. Louis, who had offered to testify against Dr. Cavaness but whom Art Margulis succeeded in excluding, although he did fail in his attempt to suppress any mention of the reckless-homicide convictions in 1972.

Margulis made a number of preliminary motions to bar certain evidence. He succeeded in having Charli's story of the gas burners turned on in the trailer suppressed as prejudicial and irrelevant, along with any references to Mark's death, to alleged arson and drug abuse by the doctor, and to specifically physical abuse of Marian. His motion to quash the search warrants obtained by Dave Barron—the ones resulting in the finding of the murder weapon and Sean's belongings—failed. Barron had made an error in indicating to the Saline County judge who issued the warrants that Dr. Cavaness had actually confessed to murder, when he had confessed only to shooting his son in the head. Judge Luten did not consider the error on Barron's part sufficiently grave to invalidate the warrants. Had the judge ruled otherwise, the murder weapon and Sean's clothing and wallet would have been inadmissible evidence because illegally obtained.

Barron's was the sort of trivial error—it was hardly surprising that someone would equate shooting one's son in the head with murder—that, with another judge in another state, could put a murder trial in jeopardy and result in higher-court reversals. But neither Judge Luten nor the Missouri Supreme Court had a history of upsetting a trial or a verdict on trivial grounds, believing rather that common sense ought to prevail in matters of justice. In this instance the key point was that the Saline County judge, based on the evidence then at hand, ought to have issued the warrants whether Dr. Cavaness had actually confessed to murder or not.

In a lengthy opening statement Steve Goldman described what the State's evidence would show, that John Dale Cavaness had murdered his son by coming up behind him, shooting him in the head once while he was standing and again after he had fallen to the ground. Goldman described how the doctor had taken the gun and Sean's belongings with him back to southern Illinois and hidden them. He said that the State would prove that the doctor was a man in desperate financial condition, who had for years been abusive and irresponsible toward his family, and who had murdered his son to collect a hundred and forty thousand dollars' worth of life insurance.

Margulis objected frequently during Goldman's presentation and lodged what were called continuing objections to the inclusion of such evidence as Marian's description of how Dale had told her in 1966 that he did not love her any longer. These objections would remain in the record as grounds for reversal on appeal, were Dale to be convicted; but during the trial Judge Luten overruled most of them. Margulis, as any experienced legal observer could see, was not overlooking anything that might help his client, was doing what any skilled defense attorney would do. But if Goldman could indeed prove to the jury's satisfaction all or most of what he outlined in his opening statement, Margulis was going to have to come up with new evidence to avoid a conviction.

Charli took the stand on the second day of the trial and described how Dale thought Sean was a hindrance to him and an embarrassment, how he had not wanted to pay for Sean's funeral, how he had denied having insurance on Sean and had suggested that the ashes go to a nonfamily member. She insisted that Sean had been looking forward to Christmas and had not seemed at all to have been in a suicidal frame of mind the last time that she had seen him.

Margulis did his best to rattle Charli but could not. He pressed her on the matter of the argument over the ashes. What was wrong with the doctor's suggestion that the ashes go to Tina Crowley? Margulis wanted to know. Didn't Tina love Sean?

"I think it is a very strange, unusual, weird request," Charli said sternly, not at all intimidated. "Tina had only known Sean four months. If you want to know my opinion, I am not going to give my brother-in-law's or any of my family's ashes to anyone."

"You were only a sister-in-law yourself?" Margulis asked.

"Exactly. But Dale asked my opinion and I told him. Would you give your loved one's ashes to someone?"

Kevin was also strong. He was able to convey in direct, clear language how his father, on the day before Sean's funeral, had called Sean an embarrassment.

Kevin tried to slip in the story about the gas in the trailer, but Margulis saw it coming and leaped in to object before Kevin could get the words out. When it was Margulis's turn to question Kevin, he surprised him by asking him whether he had ever been under psychiatric care. That information must have come from Dale, and Kevin answered truthfully that he had been depressed and had gone into a hospital briefly once, but for only a few days, less than a week. Steve Goldman objected to the irrelevance of this line of inquiry, but the judge let it stand. Margulis got Kevin to verify that Dale had given Sean checks for his rent and other small checks over the years, but Kevin countered this with several asides about Dale's contempt for Sean.

Marian's appearance this time was brief but damaging, in Goldman's view, to the defendant. Margulis thought that he could detect for the first time a resentment in Marian's voice, eyes and manner that bordered on all-out hatred for her ex-husband. Over Margulis's continuing objection she described Dale's rejection of her when she had been pregnant with Patrick and Dale's refusal to build them a new house when the place on Fourth Street burned down.

"He put us in a trailer," Marian said succinctly.

In St. Louis, she would call him, to try "to maintain communication between the father and the sons," with limited success. He was physically and verbally abusive to his family. "I don't know why he hates me," she quoted Sean as saying after he would talk to his father on the phone.

Sean had talked of suicide only once, Marian testified, when he was drunk, and in the morning he rejected the idea and could not remember having mentioned it.

Anticipating Dale's story of how he had shot Sean a second time to spare Marian the pain of her son's suicide, Steve Goldman asked her whether it made any sense to her that she would feel better if Sean had been murdered than if he had taken his own life.

"Heavens, no," Marian replied. "Who would?"

"I object to any further response," Margulis broke in.

"Sustained," said Judge Luten.

"I wish he would quit that," Marian said, referring to the defense attorney.

Margulis tried to imply, in questioning Marian, that Sean had been more suicidal than she would acknowledge and that Dale had been more generous to his sons than she or Kevin would admit. Had not Dale paid for Sean's tuition at a junior college in St. Louis?

"He paid for part of it," Marian said. "I paid for books and I paid for a lot of things."

Steve Goldman concluded the State's presentation of evidence on Saturday, November 16. He was satisfied that the prosecution witnesses had established the case against Dr. Cavaness, most tellingly through Dr. Turgeon's ballistics evidence, which more or less ruled out suicide; through the family's condemnation of the defendant; and through Detective Barron's straightforward presentation. Barron outlined the several lies Dale had told the police and said that, in his experienced view, Sean could not have committed suicide and that suicide had never seemed a possible cause of death.

To substantiate the doctor's peculiar behavior after Sean's death, Goldman called Peggy Ozment who, although she seemed nervous and a reluctant prosecution witness, said that Dale had appeared normal throughout the party and had been one of the last guests to leave. Had she known that Sean had died that morning and that Dale had seen his son die, she would, she admitted, have thought his behavior at the party odd.

A certified public accountant who had examined the doctor's financial situation detailed Dr. Cavaness's loans and notes due totaling nearly half a million dollars from various persons and institutions, including Medical Electronics, Ford Motor Credit, First State Bank, Credit Thrift of America, Illinois Industrial Development Authority, the Harrisburg National Bank, the Galatia Bank, the Farmers Home Administration, the Office of Economic Opportunity, and the General Motors Accounting Corporation. The C.P.A. estimated the doctor's net worth as minus two hundred thousand dollars. The yearly losses from his farming activities offset the income from his medical practice, and the doctor had reported net losses of approximately two hundred thousand dollars a year on his income tax for the past several years and therefore had no reason whatsoever to take out insurance policies on his sons as tax write-offs.

Art Margulis began his presentation of the defendant's evidence on Monday, November 18, and called Hap Dawson and a former manager of Hickory Handle to testify that Sean had been drinking heavily whenever he was in southern Illinois and that Dr. Cavaness had been worried about him.

"They were very tight, very close," Hap Dawson said. "Sean was always one of D.C.'s favorites."

Steve Goldman tore into Hap Dawson when he had a chance to cross-examine him. He asked him whether he had been drinking before he came to court or the night before, which Dawson denied. He asked whether he had been involved in shifting mortgaged cattle around from place to place to try to fool the Farmers Home Administration which, as the records showed, was threatening to foreclose on Hickory Handle. Dawson denied everything and said that the F.H.A. was trying to foreclose on every farmer in America. Goldman asked about the doctor's drinking habits, and Dawson replied in his drawl that Doc C. drank beer sometimes, sometimes vodka, and sometimes coffee, tea and milk. There was never an incident when Sean was thrown against the wall of a trailer.

Margulis called Harry Bramlet, Dale's insurance agent for the policies on Sean, who said that the policies had not been Dr. Cavaness's idea. Bramlet had talked the doctor into the policies, as a tax write-off and a sound investment, meeting with him on several occasions in late 1983 and early '84.

During cross-examination, Steve Goldman attempted to show that Bramlet was lying to protect the doctor, whom he had known since childhood. He got Bramlet to admit that write-offs were of no use to someone who was not paying any income tax, but Bramlet insisted that he had known nothing about the doctor's financial situation. Goldman asked Bramlet whether he had been a drinking buddy of the doctor's. How much did they drink together?

"Well," Bramlet said with a grin in his down-home way, "when we drank, we weren't just fooling around."

Whether or not to call a defendant to the stand to testify in his own defense is a dilemma faced by all criminal defense attorneys. Not to call the defendant can place suspicions in a juror's mind; to call him risks revealing facets of personality and inconsistencies of statement that could become factors swaying a jury toward conviction. In this instance Margulis's only choice was to let Dale Cavaness testify. The whole case, for better or for worse because of Dale's statements, rested on whether or not the jury believed his version of events. He was the only living witness to Sean's death. To keep him off the stand, to have him remain silent, would have been in effect to offer no defense at all, not a realistic alternative given the strength of the prosecution's case.

Dale looked as he had at the first trial, drawn, rumpled in an ill-fitting suit, anything but the picture of the competent, prosperous physician. He stated his name and accounted for his place of birth and higher education. Until their separation in 1971, he said, he and his wife and four sons had lived a wonderful life.

"It was a beautiful family," he said. "I mean, we had really everything anybody should need."

It was on him that the responsibility for disciplining the boys fell, Dale said, describing himself as "the enforcer." But Marian was an excellent housekeeper and there were no major problems of any kind until after the separation. After that, in St. Louis, Sean showed signs of destructive behavior and developed an alcohol problem by the time he was thirteen. When he quit high school, he had trouble finding and keeping jobs.

Dale admitted that he had always had "a cash-flow problem" but that the future of his farming operations looked very promising. In case anything happened to him, he had a policy on his own life for a hundred and ninety-eight thousand dollars, to be left in trust for the benefit of his sons, with Marian as the executor and trustee.

Margulis offered Dale's will and the policy on his own life in evidence.

Dale described paying Sean's rent and junior-college tuition. He had seen Sean once during 1984 in St. Louis, four weeks before his death, as he had originally told the police.

Dale described what he said had happened on the evening and morning of Sean's death, telling essentially the same story Dave Barron had heard on Christmas Eve—arriving at the apartment, spending time there with Sean, taking him out to Laclede's Landing until closing time, driving around for a while. They had not been drinking heavily, although Sean might have been drinking earlier that evening; Dale had no way of knowing.

He added that eventually they had headed west on what he thought was the highway to Arnold, Missouri, where he wanted to take a gun to be repaired. They pulled off on Lewis Road and onto Allen Road because Sean said he wanted to see the countryside, which looked like southern Illinois. Then Sean asked him to stop beside some hand-carved pillars because they looked like ladies' faces.

Dale then repeated his version of how he had given Sean the gun and how Sean had shot himself after saying "Tell Mom I'm sorry." He had then shot Sean again to preserve Marian's feelings by making it look like a homicide-robbery.

"What made you make that decision, Doctor?" Art Margulis asked him.

"It was—I'm sure that a lot of it was selfish," Dale said, "because if I didn't do that, as I saw it, I would have to go through this business, through the process of telling his mother even the final statement. She would have to go through the same kind of guilt that I was feeling. And the other way—it's almost as if it would go away. I guess it was a selfish form of denial, you know—if he was killed by somebody and you don't know who it is, at least it is gone. It is vanished."

He then wiped off Sean's hands, Dale said, took his wallet and things and headed for southern Illinois. He did not know why he had hidden the gun and the belongings. He had not been thinking clearly. He had been in shock.

When his chance came to cross-examine, Steve Goldman pounced.

"You just finished testifying a minute ago," Goldman said, his voice edged with sarcasm, "that this shooting of your son was partially self-serving for you. Do I understand that you are telling the jury that you shot Sean in the head again to make yourself feel better?"

Dale tried to take refuge in a professional analysis, speaking of himself in the third person, as if he had been present at the scene only as a kind of agent of fate, a victim of circumstance and psychologically determined reaction. No, he had not shot Sean in the head again to make himself feel better. The sequence of events had to be understood in another way.

"The human mind," Dale said, as if lecturing a medical student, "insulates itself in bizarre ways under stress. What I'm saying is that a denial is in some way an escape that would deny the fact that the thing ever happened. In that sense it would be self-serving."

"You knew that you were shooting your son in the head again, didn't you?"

"Well, obviously, you know that, but that's not the point."

Goldman believed that he could catch Dale in at least a dozen inconsistencies that would show the jury the doctor was lying. He went after them one by one, casting each accusation in the procedurally proper interrogative form. Dale maintained that Tina Crowley had requested Sean's ashes; she denied this under oath. He presented himself as not knowing what he was doing when he fired the second shot; his behavior indicated that he was thinking clearly in hiding the gun and his son's belongings and acting publicly as if nothing had happened during the following thirty-six hours.

Coming up to St. Louis on that Wednesday evening, Goldman said, Dale had not notified either Tina or Kevin of his arrival, although his purpose was supposedly to locate Sean; nor had he told anyone in southern Illinois, not even his live-in girlfriend, about his trip. What other reason would he have had for being secretive other than to carry out a premeditated, murderous mission?

He had been aware of Sean's drinking problem, yet he had encouraged Sean to drink—for what other reason than to render the poor young man insensible, so as to make him easier to kill, a lamb to the slaughter? His denial that much alcohol had been consumed that night was absurd, given Sean's 0.26 blood-alcohol level.

Dale had said that the west-county countryside looked like southern Illinois, yet he had turned off the interstate at a dioxin-contaminated site, a place that not only did not particularly resemble southern Illinois—unless grass and trees constituted a resemblance—but one that was bound to be deserted, because the area around it was sealed off. That Dale would choose this specific exit could hardly have been a coincidence; his action bore the marks of careful geographical research. And he was asking the jury to believe that he had handed his son a gun with a light trigger pull after a night of drinking. The jury could decide on the likelihood of this scenario.

Goldman, chilled by the impersonal way in which Dale had described the shooting, asked him to stand up and demonstrate the action to the jury, assuming that he would show matter-of-factly how he had made his "lucky" shot; but on the advice of counsel, Dale wisely declined to do so—a refusal eloquent in itself, Goldman believed.

He concluded his cross-examination by asking Dale whether he had thrown Sean and hit his head against a trailer wall in southern Illinois.

"Sean loves to be abused by me to his mother, and by his mother to me," Dale said dismissively, as if his dead son's feelings had been worthless all along. Since no one had accused Marian of violence, the statement was unresponsive, not to say enigmatic.

"Is that yes or no?" Goldman asked sharply.

"No."

Margulis called as his two final witnesses for the defense, a C.P.A. and a ballistics expert, realizing that the key points in the prosecution's evidence were Dale's financial condition and Dr. Turgeon's forensic analysis. The accountant, James T. Johnson of St. Louis, testified that the doctor had outside income which had been overlooked, including thirty thousand dollars a year in oil royalties from wells on the Galatia farm. He also stated that agreement had been reached in 1983 to sell Hickory Handle for over half a million dollars and that the doctor had outstanding accounts receivable from his medical practice of approximately a hundred thousand dollars. Johnson estimated the doctor's net worth at approximately a million one hundred thousand dollars.

But under Goldman's cross-examination, the accountant was made to waffle. He had not been aware of the latest foreclosure actions against the doctor by the F.H.A. and admitted that Dr. Cavaness had "a serious cash-flow problem." The sale of Hickory Handle had fallen through, Johnson agreed, except for a fifty-thousand-dollar down payment. Johnson admitted that he was not an expert on valuing land. He also agreed, under Goldman's questioning, that taking out large insurance policies as tax write-offs made no sense for a man in Dr. Cavaness's financial position.

Art Margulis called as the defense's ballistics expert a man in his mid-fifties named James Holt, who identified himself as a former member of the St. Louis County Police Department, at present a U.S. Army Intelligence officer. Holt had also testified at the first trial, and at the time Goldman had been pleased that Margulis had, apparently, been unable to find someone better qualified than Holt, who admitted on the stand to having had only limited experience with gunshot-wound analysis. Goldman's supposition was that Margulis must have tried to find someone with greater expertise to back up Dr. Cavaness's story of Sean's suicide but had been unable to get any widely respected and highly qualified pathologist to testify for the defense. The ballistics evidence was too strong; photographs and X rays of the wounds and blood-spatter patterns showed too clearly that Sean could not have shot himself. No respectable pathologist would be likely to reach the defense's conclusions.

Jack Nolen had also been curious about the weakness of the defense's ballistics testimony. On his own between trials Nolen did some checking. A source in Goldman's office revealed that Margulis and his assistants had indeed been dutiful in trying to find a highly regarded pathologist for their case and had been unable to do so. Nolen's information was that Margulis had contacted several well-known pathologists around the country; all had said that the prosecution's interpretation of the evidence was irrefutable. One pathologist, the chief medical examiner in a large southern city, had examined the photographs for about five minutes and had proclaimed simply, "He did it." Margulis was stuck with Holt.

In examining James Holt, Margulis cited *Gunshot Wounds*, a book by a Dr. Vincent DiMaio, which was regarded as a definitive text and which showed that, in suicides, two shots were often fired to the head when the first was not fatal. DiMaio also demonstrated that pulling the trigger with the thumb rather than with the index finger was not uncommon among suicides—a key point, since Sean would almost certainly have had to use his right thumb to pull the trigger had he inflicted either of the head wounds on himself.

Holt did his best to substantiate the defense's case, but under Goldman's cross-examination he wavered on several important points, notably as to the distance from which the shot to the back of the head had been fired: The amount of soot, searing and stippling indicated an extremely close shot, one nearly impossible for a person to inflict upon himself, even when firing with his thumb. Goldman, over Margulis's objections, also got Holt to admit that he had been transferred out of the ballistics section of the St. Louis County Police Department after he had testified at a trial that a semiautomatic weapon could not be fired with a clip out (it could, with a bullet still in the chamber); he could not recall another case, in which he had inaccurately testified that a bullet did not match a murder weapon.

Holt admitted that his training in the effects of bullets on bodies consisted in its entirety of one short course in forensic pathology at St. Louis University.

"And who taught it?" Goldman asked.

"Dr. George Gantner."

"Is he a pretty well-known pathologist, not only in this area but in the country?"

"Very well."

"Is his opinion very well respected by you?"

"Yes, it is."

"Do you think that he would know a little bit more about the pathology of that gunshot wound than you would?"

"He would know a tremendous amount more than I would."

In rebuttal, Steve Goldman called Dr. George Gantner to the stand.

25

DR. GEORGE GANTNER TOOK THE STAND ON TUESDAY, NOVEMBER 19, the fifth and final day of the trial. He was in his late fifties and identified himself in a resonant, self-confident voice as the chief medical examiner for both the county and the city of St. Louis, positions he had held since 1969 and 1977 respectively. He was, he said, the immediate past president of the American Academy of Forensic Science, an international organization; he was also professor of forensic and environmental pathology at St. Louis University, where he taught medical students, doctors in training as residents, and medical-legal investigators. He had written more than seventy articles published in medical journals and several books dealing with the medical-legal aspects of his profession.

Having reviewed the autopsy photographs and his associate Dr. Ronald Turgeon's report, Dr. Gantner stated that he agreed fully with Dr. Turgeon's conclusions, notably that the shot to the back of the head had been fired from within an inch of the surface of the skin, and that, based on the blood pattern on the left shoulder and arm, the victim had been standing when shot. The second shot, near the right ear, had been inflicted when the victim was

309

lying on the ground. The blood-alcohol count indicated that the victim had consumed a great deal of liquor and had a net level intake of twelve or thirteen drinks in him when he died. Sean's dexterity would have been seriously impaired, Dr. Gantner said, making it extremely unlikely that he would have been able to inflict a wound to the back of the head upon himself. Such a shot would have been nearly impossible to manage sober.

In cross-examining Dr. Gantner, Art Margulis tried, through the use of technical terms and the introduction of various alternative possible actions at the death scene, to shake the witness from his testimony. He was able to get Dr. Gantner to admit that either shot would have caused the victim to fall to the ground, but Dr. Gantner stood firm on all the points of his analysis. During this cross-examination, Dale, sitting at the defense table, grew obviously restless, scribbling notes and calling Margulis over to give him advice on what questions to ask. Margulis kept his composure, but relations between the defense counsel and the defendant appeared to be getting tense. Dr. Gantner had been on the stand for more than an hour when Margulis asked to approach the bench.

"Judge," Margulis said, outside the hearing of the jury, "Dr. Cavaness is unhappy and dissatisfied with the way I have asked the questions and, although he has written out questions for me which I have attempted to ask verbatim from his list, he is insisting that I have not asked the questions he wants. His question now is, can he ask the doctor questions?"

Margulis said that he had told his client that perhaps under the rules of the court he was entitled to ask Dr. Gantner questions. But he had advised Dr. Cavaness that this would not be in his best interests.

"His response to that," Margulis said, "is that I have not served him well, so he may as well go ahead, even if it looks bad. So I am requesting of you, on his demand, that he be allowed to ask Dr. Gantner questions."

Steve Goldman objected. To let Dr. Cavaness take over the questioning would turn the proceedings into a sham. The judge called a recess.

Margulis tried to talk Dale out of questioning Dr. Gantner, but Dale insisted. He did not care whether Margulis thought that this was a mistake and would look bad. Margulis had no choice but to ask the judge again to let Dale go ahead. At the bench, with the jury still out of the courtroom, Judge Luten listened as Dale explained his request:

"I am not criticizing my lawyer's presentation particularly," Dale said, "but I think that it may be possible that I could communicate with Dr. Gantner within the medical field a little better than he can."

"My position is," Steve Goldman objected, "that unless he wants to fire Mr. Margulis, which he can't do at this point anyway, I don't think that he has any real right to ask questions."

Judge Luten pressed Dale to clarify his position. Was he not satisfied with the inquiry by Mr. Margulis? Did he feel that his interests would be better served if he conducted some of the inquiry himself?

"Yes, sir," Dale replied. "I think that Dr. Gantner's evidence is so damaging, you know, without at least my attempt to—for further inquiry that, very honestly, I think I will be convicted."

Judge Luten agreed to let Dale cross-examine Dr. Gantner. With Margulis sitting at the defense table, Dale began by trying to explain why the court was permitting him to speak. The judge cut him off, saying that he had to stick to the interrogative form: He was not permitted to make statements and explanations.

From the beginning of his performance as his own counsel, Dale, in the opinion of every courtroom observer except perhaps his southern-Illinois supporters, did nothing but damage to his case. His manner, for one thing, was ice-cold; it was as if this had been a routine medical case, not one involving the death of his son. He handled and discussed the autopsy photographs of Sean's head and body without showing the slightest emotion, pointing out the wounds, the blood, the powder burns as if they were merely spots and colorings on a map. During a recess a friend of Margulis's who had been watching the proceedings out of curiosity rushed up to him in a hallway and told him that his client's performance was disastrous. He would have to get Dr. Cavaness to sit down and shut up. The jury was clearly disgusted with him.

"I can't control him," Margulis said. "I've tried. Believe me. I told the judge I'm totally against this. It's in the record."

Dale cited DiMaio's *Gunshot Wounds* in an effort to refute Dr. Gantner's conclusions about the closeness of the shot to the back of the head.

"You agree that you consider DiMaio an authority?" Dale asked.

"I went so far as to hire him," Dr. Gantner said, "to be the first chief medical examiner in the city of St. Louis, and he accepted. Then he decided to get married in Dallas and turned me down. So, yes, I consider him to be experienced in the field."

Dale was out of his league with Gantner, who had to correct him repeatedly on the proper use of technical vocabulary, going so far as to spell out words, such as "peri," meaning the area around a bullet hole, which Dale kept calling a halo. In Steve Goldman's view, Art Margulis had shown a greater competence in discussing the medical terminology of gunshot wounds than Dr. Cavaness exhibited. Dave Barron thought the same. What Art Margulis was thinking, they could only guess. Jack Nolen, watching from a back row, figured that Margulis was probably wishing that he had never taken this case. No one could control the doc, Nolen knew. He could see chickens coming home to roost all over the courtroom.

In a final effort, Dale tried to get Dr. Gantner to say that a close contact wound would leave metal fragments on the surface of the skin. Why were there no metal fragments in the area of the wound to the back of the head?

"And it is your opinion, then, that a near-contact wound would not leave any deposit of metallic fragments either from the bullet or the barrel?"

"Not necessarily, no," Dr. Gantner said. "In my opinion in this case, we have no evidence that it did."

"No more questions," Dale said, and he sat down.

In his closing argument, Steve Goldman went over all the evidence, putting particular stress on Dr. Gantner's credibility and describing Dale Cavaness as amoral:

"He is the kind of man who tried to impose his will onto others and treats them the way he wants to treat them, regardless of how they want to be treated. People expect that in a doctor to some degree. They expect a doctor to be authoritarian and a doctor to be smart, and he is that. He is smart. He is a smart doctor, but he is also a cold-blooded killer."

Goldman let the jury know how difficult it had been for Marian, Kevin and Charli to testify, to reveal to strangers their private tragedy. They had done so only for Sean's sake and to protect themselves from Dr. Cavaness's revenge. They wanted justice to be done.

"You are probably thinking," Goldman told the jury, "how can a man kill his own son, especially a doctor, who is supposed to save lives. Well, you know, as we go through life, we realize the older we get that people are often much more than they seem, and that certainly applies to doctors. Sean thought the world of him, and he is the one that ended that world."

Art Margulis in his closing argument spoke of the unthinkable nature of the crime with which Dr. Cavaness was charged and the impossibility of believing that any successful physician would kill his son for a hundred and forty thousand dollars, or for any amount of money. He reminded the jury of Sean's drinking and instability and said that the young man had been a prime candidate for suicide, which even Dr. Turgeon had stated under oath he could not "completely rule out" as the cause of death. And Dr. Cavaness would have known as an experienced surgeon that in any autopsy Sean's liver would have shown fatty tissue indicating alcoholism, thus invalidating the insurance policies.

At this point Steve Goldman dearly wished that he could bring up Mark's murder and show the jury the ghastly photographs of Mark's ravaged body. Goldman thought that it was likely that Dr. Cavaness had believed that Sean's body, left out in the country like Mark's, would also be eaten by animals, making an autopsy impossible. At any rate, Goldman understood, the insurance was still valid, since the cause of death had not been alcoholism, even though Sean had not admitted to his treatment for the problem when filling out the insurance application and his father had also failed to mention it.

Margulis, citing the judge's instructions to the jury, suggested that at most they could find the defendant guilty of involuntary manslaughter, in that he had admitted handing the gun to Sean, who, the evidence showed, was intoxicated. Beyond that, Margulis said, the prosecution's case was riddled with doubt.

Sean and his dad "had the best relationship of anyone in the family," Margulis said. Dr. Cavaness had paid Sean's rent and tuition and had sent him extra money. No one had been more concerned about his son's welfare.

Because, as in any criminal trial, the burden of proof was on the prosecution, Steve Goldman got the last word. His closing rebuttal argument was an impassioned plea for justice.

"If Dr. Cavaness shows anything about his feelings about Sean," Goldman said, "you can tell it when he was up here holding those

313

pictures of his dead son as if they're a bunch of playing cards. This is a big game to him. Think of him . . . on that night, December 13, when he snuck up here in the middle of the night and snuck up on his son and shot him in the back of the head. How he stood over him and shot him again in the ear. How Marian, his ex-wife, called him up and said, 'My God, our son is dead!' and he hung up on her."

Goldman told the jury that they would have to have the same courage as Marian and Kevin and Charli had had in testifying. They had to be able to tell John Dale Cavaness and all the John Dale Cavanesses that they cannot sacrifice their sons for insurance money or for any other motives.

Goldman's voice broke several times as he described how Sean had indeed idolized his father and how Dale had preyed at last upon those feelings.

"Sean never learned," Goldman said in conclusion, clearing his throat to keep his composure, his voice finally tremulous, his eyes glistening, "or rather, I guess, he learned too late, when he snuck up behind him, what his father was really like and what he really meant to his father.

"You are Sean's only chance for justice now. Thank you."

Marian, Kevin and Charli were in court for Goldman's closing argument, which moved them to tears and which Kevin said helped him to accept the awful necessity of having testified against his father. It had been a simple choice, really, difficult though it had been, between the murdered Sean and the murdering Dale. Not to have had the courage to testify would, as Steve Goldman said, have been to deny justice to the victim, not to speak of helping Dale go free to kill again. Kevin said that he hoped people would understand why he had had to do it.

"The people that matter will understand," Charli said. "We can' worry about the rest. They don't matter."

As for the verdict, they were not sure. Goldman and Dave Barron had warned them about the unpredictability of juries. But as Goldman had told the jury, if there was not already enough evidence in this case for a conviction, then no case could have enough.

Marian accompanied Kevin and Charli to their apartment t await the verdict, which they knew might take hours or even day to reach. The jury began deliberations at twenty minutes past four on Tuesday afternoon, one week to the day after their selection.

An hour and ten minutes later, the jury requested from Judge Luten further instruction as to the difference between first- and second-degree murder. The judge referred them to his original instructions, which defined the difference as that between premeditated murder and murder without deliberate premeditation.

At five minutes to seven, two hours and thirty-five minutes after they had begun deliberations, the jury returned with its verdict. The courtroom filled up again with the press and with Dale's supporters; Kevin, Charli and Marian remained at the apartment and were not aware that the jury had taken so little time to reach unanimous agreement.

The jury's foreman, Peter M. McLean, the twenty-six-year-old Hallmark employee, presented the verdict. The jury had found John Dale Cavaness guilty as charged.

Judge Luten asked each juror whether he or she agreed with the verdict; each replied in the affirmative.

Dale showed no emotion whatsoever as one juror after another reaffirmed his guilt in a steady, assertive voice. As was obvious from their manner, no jurors had doubted his guilt; the only discussion, and there had been little enough of that, had been on the question of premeditation. Dissent came from the rear of the courtroom in the form of murmurs from the visitors from Eldorado; other observers seemed pleased that justice had been done, among them two of the jurors from the first trial, who had come to see their work completed.

"It's a long time coming and I'm happy with the verdict," Steve Goldman told the press. Art Margulis expressed disappointment and looked pained when a reporter from the Kansas City *Star* said that Dr. Cavaness's southern-Illinois supporters were questioning his judgment in calling such an inexperienced ballistics expert to counter such distinguished State witnesses as Drs. Gantner and Turgeon. "I can't comment on that," Margulis had to say. "It would be unethical." He also had to make no comment when asked whether he had been paid in full. The story was, a reporter said, that the defense fund had dried up after reaching thirty-eight thousand dollars.

Margulis never did reveal whether he had been paid his full fee, but Jack Nolen, ever curious and resourceful, dug the story out from a couple of his private sources. Nolen heard that the doc, owing his attorney some twelve thousand dollars, had his supporters deliver to Margulis two expensive shotguns, one a Parker, which were supposed to be worth at least as much as the amount due. According to Nolen's informants, the guns were fakes, which Margulis would discover if and when he tried to sell them. One way or another, the doc had managed to screw even his attorney. There was no telling what else the doc might accomplish before this was all over.

The jury remained sequestered for another night. On the following day the penalty phase of the trial would take place. The jurors would have to decide whether Dr. Cavaness was to be punished by life imprisonment or by death.

Steve Goldman telephoned Kevin, Charli and Marian with the news. They were relieved, and they thanked him. Kevin was alarmed to learn that Goldman wanted him to testify in the penalty phase, in which the prosecutor intended to seek the death penalty, to disclose some incidents which had been excluded from the first part of the trial.

With Goldman requesting the death penalty, Kevin feared that for him to speak out again against his father, after guilt had been established and after he had already played, as he knew, a crucial role in Dale's conviction, would be like asking the jury to take revenge for him, for the family, for Sean. He was deeply uneasy about placing himself in that position. It was almost as if Goldman were asking him to become his own father's executioner.

But Goldman assured Kevin that all the evidence, not merely the family's testimony, had convicted his father. And the jury, not Kevin, would determine Dale's ultimate fate. Deciding on life or death was their civic responsibility, which they had agreed to carry out. They were a fine jury. They had understood the complex ballistics evidence perfectly well. Dr. Gantner's testimony, as well as Dale's self-incriminating performance in court, had been the crucial points. If so skillful a lawyer as Art Margulis could not get Dale off, nobody could have. Now all that Kevin had left to do was to supply the jury with a few more pieces of information so that they could make an intelligent and just decision. That was what the courts were for: to relieve victims and their families of the burden of carrying out justice.

Kevin agreed to take the stand once again. That night they talked of what they thought the jury would decide. They concluded that Dale's age—he was now sixty—would be taken into consideration and that he would be spared the death penalty. They agreed that they were satisfied with the conviction and being sure that Dale would be safely locked up forever.

"He won't stay in jail," Marian said. "He won't be able to stand being locked up. I know him. He'll kill himself."

In the hallway outside the courtroom after the verdict was announced, Detective Dave Barron encountered the Reverend Staley Langham, who was carrying his projector and slides and who expressed bitterness that Art Margulis had not permitted him to testify on the doctor's behalf. He had evidence that would have freed Dr. Dale. It was right there in those slides.

"There'll be a new trial," Reverend Langham told Barron, with some heat. "This one was a joke. It's a travesty. We all know Dr. Dale was innocent. That was a farce in there and a miscarriage of justice."

"Well, Rev," Barron said, leaning over Langham, "I know you're a man of the cloth, so you probably don't bet. But I'd like to bet you a dinner that there won't be any new trial. How about it?"

"I am not a betting man," Langham said.

"What makes you so sure there'll be a new trial?" Barron asked.

"We'll show this was a farce. Your people lied. You know that. And Margulis was incompetent. Having an incompetent attorney is grounds for a new trial."

"Oh, yeah?" Barron said, drawing closer, his voice rising. "Let me tell you something. If Art Margulis is incompetent, he sure as hell has fooled a lot of people and he sure gets paid a lot to be incompetent. Art Margulis is one of the best defense lawyers in St. Louis. There isn't any better. The one thing he won't do is turn a trial into a dog and pony show by putting jerks like you on the stand. He has too much respect for the court. Maybe that would work down where you come from, but we don't go for that kind of garbage in St. Louis."

Reverend Langham began shouting and waving his slides in the air: "Your evidence was phony! You lied! You perjured yourself! You falsified evidence!"

"Just a minute, Rev," Barron said. "If what you say is true, you're accusing me of a crime. Why don't you go upstairs and swear out a deposition if you believe it? And let me tell you something, Rev. If I ever hear you saying that again, I'll beat your ass in."

Reverend Langham retreated. He hurried out to join Bertis Herrmann and the other downcast, indignant supporters of the doc.

Whatever his opinion of the defense attorney, the Reverend Staley Langham was among eight character witnesses, including Bertis Herrmann and Emma Lou Mitchell, whom Margulis called to testify the next morning on Dr. Cavaness's behalf. Margulis's strategy was that the simple faith of these southern-Illinois people in their doctor, whose good deeds over the years they would recall, would be enough to persuade the jury to spare Dale's life. Like most people, Margulis assumed that Reverend Langham was an old friend of the doctor's. Why else would he have spent so much time defending him and helping to raise money for him, visiting him in prison, portraying him sympathetically to the press?

But when Margulis told Reverend Langham that he would at last have the opportunity to take the stand and to tell the jury about his long-term, intimate friendship with Dr. Cavaness, Langham, hanging his head, said that he was afraid that he could not do that. He had never known Dr. Cavaness well at all until he had gone to visit him in his jail cell after his arrest. He had merely known of him, who he was, but not to speak to him. He had seen the doctor at Pearce Hospital, of course, where like any minister he visited sick members of his congregation. It was more a matter of being familiar with the doctor's reputation, rather than a personal friendship.

"Oh, well," Margulis sighed, "we'll have to go with that, I guess."

The minister was the final character witness called by the defense. Reverend Langham, putting the best face on things without perjuring himself, said that he had lived in Eldorado for seven and a half years and that he had known Dr. Cavaness "just about that long, as far as the relationship at the hospital where he practiced." He said that he often visited the hospital and that Dr. Cavaness's reputation with his patients was "tremendous."

Goldman asked Langham whether he had heard that Dr. Cavaness had pushed another doctor out of a boat, had brought a gun to a physicians' meeting, was convicted of the reckless homicide of Donald McLaskey and his infant child, was convicted of medical fraud, and had been implicated in the selling of liquid morphine and Demerol to a convicted felon named Johnny Weingarten. To all of these Reverend Langham answered no, and that hearing about them now did not in one bit alter his high regard for Dr. Cavaness.

"Being a minister," Langham said, "I never accept gossip or hearsay, so from the evidence that I have, I love Dr. Cavaness as much right now as I did before you said these things."

When Steve Goldman called as the State's only witness during the penalty phase the defendant's son, Kevin Cavaness, Art Margulis feared the worst for his client. It was unprecedented in Margulis's more than twenty years' experience as a defense attorney to have a defendant's child perform such a role in the penalty phase of a trial. Margulis believed that the impact on the jury might prove fatal to Dr. Cavaness. Margulis had lost many cases and won many; he had never had a client sentenced to death.

All morning before taking the stand, Kevin had been on the verge of backing out and relinquishing this awful task, but the pictures he had seen of Sean's body, his bullet-torn head, his blood-soaked shirt—the thought that Dale had left him like Mark to rot or be savaged—kept coming into Kevin's mind. Finally he decided that for Mark's and Sean's sakes he had to go through with testifying again. His brothers would be standing with him in the witness box. He was their chance for redemption and for justice. His mother and his wife would be sitting there just behind the press, in the third row, plainly in his view. He could look at Marian and Charli and gain courage when he felt his father staring at him with murderous hatred in those hooded eyes.

Over Margulis's objections, Kevin, questioned by Goldman, said that Johnny Weingarten was the one-time son-in-law of Dr. Cavaness's girlfriend, Martha Culley. When he had asked his father about the arrest of Johnny Weingarten, Kevin said, Dale had threatened to kill him if he told anyone. Kevin then recounted Dale's story about the drugs in the safe.

"Whom did he say that he would kill when he was telling you this?" Goldman asked.

"Both Charli and me," Kevin said.

"What was your reaction to that?"

"At first," Kevin said, "I was kind of shocked, and then I thought, he doesn't really mean 'to kill.' But the way he said it, after I got to thinking about it, I do believe he meant it."

Margulis tried to soften this devastating testimony, which settled over the courtroom like a shroud.

"Kevin," Margulis said, "in your experience, isn't when you say something about 'I will kill you' a rather common expression of speech?"

"Not the way he expressed it," Kevin said.

"You said yourself that you concluded he probably didn't mean it, didn't you?"

"Well, I would like to hope he didn't."

There remained only the closing arguments by the defense and prosecution. Margulis emphasized the doctor's age and the fact that, in Missouri, there was no possibility of parole for a convicted capital murderer. That the doctor had undoubtedly served humanity in the past and saved many lives ought to weigh in the jury's decision, Margulis said:

"Clearly Dr. Cavaness is a valuable and a useful human being. There are a lot of services yet to be rendered."

Steve Goldman was relentless. Dr. Cavaness had forfeited his right to be treated like a normal human being. The jury was not being asked to play God. The doctor played God when he took the life of his son. Only God could sit in moral judgment. The jury was sitting only in legal judgment:

"This case cries out for the death penalty. Marian and Sean and Kevin deserve justice here. If people do not receive justice for a crime like this, they will seek it themselves in the streets."

Goldman asked the jurors to think about their own children and to place themselves in Marian's and in Kevin's position. The jury had done a fine and a courageous job so far, but they still had a job to complete. They should think of themselves as the representatives and the protectors of their fellow citizens in a state where the courts are friends of humanity:

"Your job is to raise once more the great protection that we have of the law, in St. Louis County, in Jackson County and everywhere in Missouri, where men and women and children seek to live safely and peacefully.

"Thank you."

The jury retired to their deliberations at eleven-thirty Wednesday morning. They returned after lunch with a verdict of death.

Dale tightned his lips but showed no other reaction. Marian bent over in her seat and cried; Kevin and Charli comforted her. They then made their way out of the courtroom, assailed by reporters' questions. Marian said that she was shocked by the death sentence for her ex-husband.

"I did love him once," she said. "I didn't expect this. It would have been enough to have him safely put away."

Kevin told the press that he would not wish death on anyone, but he was sure that his father felt no remorse for killing Sean. He had been suspicious, Kevin said, ever since Mark's death. He accepted the jury's decision, believing that they had done what was right:

"If I could be sure that he'd be safely locked up, that would be one thing. But as long as he's alive, I can't feel safe for myself or my family."

In the crowded corridor Art Margulis made his way through the reporters and came up to Kevin, looking him in the eye, extending his hand. Kevin took the lawyer's hand and wondered what this was all about. Margulis was not the person he expected to see after the trial. He did not feel hatred for the lawyer, but he hardly considered him a friend of the family.

"I hope things will be better for you from now on," Margulis said, and left.

Kevin, moved, was speechless, until he had to respond to more reporters' questions.

"I feel sad for him," Kevin said. "He is my father, whether I like it or not."

Asked if he thought his father was a Dr. Jekyll and Mr. Hyde, Kevin replied, "Yes, he was." Standing nearby with Jack Nolen and overhearing this exchange, Dave Barron commented that he thought Dr. Cavaness was Mr. Hyde all the way. Nolen agreed.

Both Kevin and Charli expressed to the reporters their disappointment and frustration at all the support Dale had received from the citizens of Eldorado.

"What bothers me," Charli said, "about the reaction of these people is that I grew up in Eldorado, I went to school in Eldorado with some of these people's children, and I worked in Eldorado at Pearce Hospital. I wonder, do people have blinders on? I heard one person say here today that no matter what someone told her about Dale it would not lower her opinion of him. What kind of reasoning is that?"

Dale's supporters assured the press that their loyalty remained firm. Martha Culley, who had made her first appearance in the courtroom that day because, she said, her high blood pressure prevented her from attending the entire trial, stated that Dale was "absolutely not" guilty of killing his son. She would visit him in prison as often as she could. Another woman, who had been Dr. Cavaness's patient for twenty years and who had written a letter to southern-Illinois papers denouncing the St. Louis police, revealed perhaps more than she knew by saying that "watching this trial was like watching a school play."

As Marian, Kevin and Charli were getting into their car, a woman who appeared to be in her sixties came up to them. She wanted to wish them well, she said, and to congratulate them on their courage and endurance. She was sure that justice had been done. She had gone to high school with Dale Cavaness, and she had always known that he was a bad person.

"Why is that?" Marian asked.

"Because once in high school my parents gave me a new watch, and Dale Cavaness asked to see it and he dropped it on the ground and stepped on it and crushed it."

The woman turned away and vanished before Marian had a chance to get her name.

26

IT WAS WITHIN JUDGE DREW LUTEN'S AUTHORITY TO OVERRULE the jury's recommendation of the death penalty and to lessen the sentence to life without parole. Art Margulis asked at the time of formal sentencing, on January 6, 1985, that the judge "show some mercy and some leniency in determining what sentence to impose."

Judge Luten saw no reason not to accept the jury's recommendation and uttered the fatal words:

"Therefore it is ordered and adjudged by the Court that said defendant, John D. Cavaness, be and is hereby sentenced to death, for the offense, murder first degree, a Class A felony; said sentence to be carried out at a time to be set by the Supreme Court of this State.

"Defendant is remanded to the custody of the Department of Justice Services of St. Louis County, Missouri, to be delivered by the Department of Justice to the warden of the State Penitentiary at Jefferson City on or before the 16th day of January, 1986, and there within the walls of the State Penitentiary, under the direction of said warden, he shall suffer death by the administration of lethal gas at a time to be set by the Supreme Court of this State, and said warden is directed to make return on this warrant to this Court showing the time, mode and manner in which this warrant was executed."

Appeal of a death sentence was automatic in Missouri as in all the other states. Art Margulis at this point withdrew from the case. The defense fund was exhausted, and Dale's supporters were publicly denouncing the defense attorney, accusing him of botching the job. Reverend Langham wrote to the judge and to other legal officials in St. Louis demanding a new trial, saying that he had explained new evidence to the defense attorney and could not understand "why Mr. Margulis abandoned his client." Langham signed his letters "Prayerfully yours."

At least one resident of Little Egypt, however, made a courageous attempt to heal a wounded, divided community. Erin Brothers was a young reporter for the Harrisburg *Daily Register* who was assigned to what was rather grandly called the "Eldorado Bureau" and who had personally covered the trial in St. Louis. In an editorial printed in large type, she confessed that, not having grown up in Eldorado, she did not know Dr. Cavaness and had never met him. (Dale had refused to give her an interview.) But the trial, she said, had left an indelible mark on her, as she was sure it had on the jury.

She praised Arthur Margulis for carrying out his difficult task. Both he and Steve Goldman "did unbelievable jobs of representing their sides, but Goldman's evidence prevailed." Given the evidence, Brothers said, the jury had made the right choice in convicting Dr. Cavaness; she was less sure about the death penalty.

Brothers offered understanding to the doctor's supporters. No man, she said, deserves to be entirely alone during his worst days. Justice had been done, but it was a sad day for everyone in the community, not a cause for rejoicing. As Kevin Cavaness had said, "He's still my father."

Brothers's article, a small masterpiece of tact, did much to enable people on opposite sides of the Cavaness fence to speak to one another again, especially in Harrisburg; in Eldorado, residents who would voice an opinion estimated that at least half the population still supported Dr. Cavaness. Jack Nolen put the number at more than half. He knew some of the supporters personally and liked many of them; they just had this fixation on the doc. It was almost like a religious cult.

Pursuing Dale's appeal fell to Beth Dockery, a young lawyer in the Office of the Public Defender in St. Louis who, in examining the trial transcript, admitted privately that no errors appeared to have been made by either the judge or the attorneys, who seemed to have done an admirable job with a difficult, emotion-fraught case. She was preparing her brief, however, when in April 1985, she received a telephone call from a man who identified himself as Howard Eisenberg, professor of law and director of the Legal Clinic at Southern Illinois University. Professor Eisenberg stated that he had been chief public defender for the state of Wisconsin from 1971 to 1978 and executive director of the National Legal Aid and Public Defenders Association in Washington, D.C., from 1978 to 1983, before assuming his position at S.I.U.

Professor Eisenberg said that he had been approached by a Reverend Staley R. Langham of Eldorado, who represented Dr. Cavaness's supporters, and asked to help with the appeal. He had agreed and had accepted advance expense money in the amount of a thousand dollars from Reverend Langham. He was not licensed to practice law in Missouri, but he proposed that he visit Dr. Cavaness in Jefferson City and prepare the brief for his appeal, which Dockery could then sign, as if it were her work. He had thirteen years' experience in these matters, and was glad to offer his help. He assured her that his interest in the case was purely intellectual and scholarly.

Beth Dockery replied that she would think the matter over. The more she thought about it, the more peculiar it seemed to her. She could not imagine, for one thing, how one would spend a thousand dollars on a trip to Jefferson City or what the purpose of such a visit would be. On an appeal it was not necessary to consult with the convicted prisoner; a brief courtesy visit was perhaps appropriate but not required; in the absence of new evidence, the trial transcript was all that was relevant.

Beth Dockery was not at all happy with the idea of putting her name under someone else's writing, as she understood Eisenberg to be suggesting. She could not accept that his involvement was a purely scholarly one: She suspected that what he had in mind was a "kamikaze defense," one in which the attorney deliberately performs incompetently so as to cause delay or, at best for his client, a reduction in sentence from death to life imprisonment. The tactic was unknown in Missouri but she was aware that at least one California lawyer had made a career out of it at both the trial and appellate levels.

Dockery telephoned Eisenberg and told him to get lost. When asked by a writer what he had to say about Beth Dockery's suspicions of his motives, Professor Eisenberg replied simply, "She is dead wrong." It was ridiculous for her to think that he was trying to set her up. He could not work with her, and he was getting off the case. He had given Reverend Langham back the thousand dollars.

For her part, Beth Dockery found that she could not work with Dr. Cavaness, who had refused to sign the forms necessary to declare his indigency and consequent eligibility to be defended at taxpayers' expense. She passed the case on to another assistant public defender, Deborah Doak, who agreed to argue the appeal with or without the proper forms.

At the state penitentiary at Jefferson City, a forbidding pile on the banks of the Missouri River which had been in continuous operation since the 1860s, Dale was death row inmate No. 40. He passed his time reading magazines—mostly medical and antiques journals—writing letters and making audio tapes for his putative biographer, Martha's relative from Oklahoma City. With the help of another inmate, a convicted narcotics dealer and killer who had made himself into something of a jailhouse lawyer, Dale sued the insurance company to recover the benefits he argued were due him on Sean's death. Like most death-row prisoners, who averaged about three pending lawsuits apiece, he filed other briefs, including one against a cattle company he claimed had cheated him several years before. Martha and Reverend Langham visited him about once a month; otherwise he kept mainly to himself, occasionally dispensing medical advice to other prisoners, who sometimes irritated him with their obtuseness.

These prisoners noted that Doc Cavaness, who insisted that he had been convicted because of the incompetence of his lawyer but refused to share the transcript of his trial with anyone, never accepted offers of the dope—usually marijuana or speed, sometimes morphine—smuggled into the prison or stolen from the infirmary. He even turned down offers of copies of *Playboy* or *Penthouse* magazines, saying that in these conditions a man had to use his willpower to control himself and that such material would only make him feel more frustrated.

With the trial over, Marian returned to Wausau to try to pick up again her new life with Les, but for several weeks she was barely ambulatory. She stayed in bed most of the day, a haunted creature, beaten down finally to despair. Although Les tried to tell her that it was unhealthy for her to do so, she kept looking at the family photographs she had managed to save from the fire at the house on Fourth Street—the Christmas snapshots of all the boys, of herself and Dale, pictures of Dale and herself in the wonderful days of courtship. She found in a shoebox his love letters to her when she was in New York and he in Baltimore. She did not reread them but put them into a manila envelope and mailed them to him at Jefferson City.

Les nursed her. He told her that she was a strong person; she had survived everything else, and she would come through this. He called her Skip, treated her depression as if it were merely a convalescence. He was most concerned about her when she collapsed weeping and cried absurdly that Sean's death had been her fault.

By the summer of 1986 Marian had more or less recovered. It took little to start her crying, but she was determined to go on, to set an example for Patrick and for Kevin. Nothing she could feel or do would make the tragedy grow or shrink by an inch or an ounce; better to defy fate and live. Les was so happy to have his gal, as he said, back on her feet that he decided they needed to celebrate. She had always wanted to see France. They made a tour of the Rhône Valley, enjoyed the beauties of the Côte d'Or.

Kevin too found himself on an emotional rack, wondering whether at some obscure point in the past he had done something, or failed to do something, that had goaded his father into wrath. At other times he felt consumed with anger at his father, vowed to witness his execution, then changed his mind, cursed his father not only for what he had done but for what he was still doing to the family, simply by being alive or by having existed at all.

"We thought it was all over," Kevin said to Charli, "but the son of a bitch is still there. He's still haunting us. He'll never die, even if they kill him."

By June of 1986, Charli knew that she was pregnant again. Kevin prayed aloud that his father's curse would not affect this baby as it had Kelly Ann, whose grave they visited in September to mark the first anniversary of her death.

Just after seven on the morning of Monday, November 17, 1986, at the state penitentiary at Jefferson City, a prison guard was making his morning rounds when he approached a cell and noticed through the bars that inmate No. 40, Dr. John Dale Cavaness, appeared to be hanging from the cell door. The guard unlocked and with some difficulty managed to shove open the door. He found that Dr. Cavaness was indeed hanging from the door by means of three brown electrical extension cords which had been tied together and looped at one end with a slipknot. Dr. Cavaness appeared to be dead. The guard called for medical assistance.

The guard took down the body and attendants arrived to administer CPR. Other prison officials entered the cell and took photographs of the scene. Dr. Richard Bowers pronounced Dr. Cavaness dead at seven minutes past eight. The death was ruled a suicide. It was noted on the official report that the prisoner had greased the slipknot with Vaseline to make it close rapidly. The suicide had been an act of remarkable will, since the deceased must have raised his feet off the floor while hanging in order to cause the knot to tighten around his throat; and, before passing out, he could have stood upright to halt the process.

Inside Dr. Cavaness's locker prison officials found a suicide note and eleven large and small envelopes containing legal papers and personal letters and another note stating that he wanted all his personal property to go to his girlfriend, Martha Culley.

The suicide note, neatly typewritten, double-spaced, was addressed to "The Missouri State Prison Administration" and became the final item in Dale's official file. "I want to make it clear," the note began, "that this final act has nothing to do with my care or treatment while confined to this institution." Guards and other personnel had been considerate and respectful of him, Dale wrote. He could handle the confinement and depression but, he continued:

I am burdened by the problems that it creates for the ones I care most deeply about and feel that time will resolve that in my absence. I intend to attempt to pursue my exoneration but frankly am aware of the long and stressful legal processes that that would require and my situation is much like that of a patient found to have a malignancy. If the initial treatment is bungled, the patient has nothing to look forward to except a lifetime of agony, even if life is sustained. The same end result occurs when the legal approach to a capital crime is poorly carried out and I am much too aware of the prognosis in both cases. . . .

Dale praised again the attitude toward him of prison officials and concluded:

Please see that my personal belongings are turned over to Rev. Staley Langham or some other person designated by my attorney T. R. Murphy and notify one of the people I designate, other than Martha Culley, so that she may be spared the emotional stress of what I'm sure we all know will be a shock.

Nowhere in the suicide note nor in any of the other letters and documents did Dale mention Kevin, Patrick, Marian, or his dead sons. When in the following weeks his will was filed, Martha Culley was listed as the sole beneficiary. She was also listed as the sole beneficiary of the one-hundred-and-ninety-eight-thousand-dollar policy that he had taken out on his own life: He had changed the beneficiary from his sons, with Marian as trustee, to Martha after his conviction. A clause saying that the policy was invalid if the insured committed suicide had expired on the day before Dale killed himself.

On Wednesday, November 19, an editorial appeared in the Harrisburg *Daily Register* under the headline LET IT REST. The "strange, even bizarre" story of Dr. John Dale Cavaness had come to an end, the editorial said, "punctuated sadly and abruptly by his own hand." The case had polarized Eldorado and Harrisburg. There had been no middle ground: "One either believed whole-heartedly in [his] innocence or believed just as whole-heartedly that he was guilty." The story had dissolved long friendships, left some people hurt and others angry and "almost everyone puzzled." It was unfortunate that the case would continue to be discussed for years to come, "because it's over now. We should let it rest."

329

Some old-timers and scholars of the Charlie Birger legend in Little Egypt recalled that the same newspaper had expressed almost identical sentiments fifty-eight years before, upon the occasion of the hanging of that gangster.

About one hundred invited guests showed up for a memorial service in honor of Dr. Cavaness, held later that month at the First Presbyterian Church in Eldorado, organized by Reverend Langham and Martha Culley. It was said that Dale himself had given, among the papers found in his cell, instructions for the service and for the guest list which, needless to say, did not include any family members. Pat and Betty Ray Sullivan received an invitation but discovered that they had to be out of town.

Three ministers in addition to Reverend Langham officiated at the service, which began with a tape recording of the Harrisburg High School choir performing "I Will Not Leave You Comfortless" and continued with the singing of "Onward, Christian Soldiers" and "Amazing Grace," the recitation of the Twenty-third Psalm, the reading of Rudyard Kipling's poem "If" and Helen Keller's homily "Life Is Good" and concluded with the singing of "The Battle Hymn of the Republic."

His soul was marching on. When, several weeks later, Dr. Cavaness's will was entered in probate, a local man said that he planned to buy the Hickory Handle farm and to erect there a concrete cross in memory of the doctor.

About a month after the suicide Dave Barron visited Kevin at his house to hand over a box of Dale's belongings—stuff found in the Oldsmobile Toronado, some shotgun parts, a wallet, a car maintenance manual—and to see how Kevin and Charli were getting on. They had moved to a bigger place in anticipation of the new baby. Charli's pregnancy seemed to be proceeding without complications.

On top of a cardboard box that sat on the hi-fi next to the bust of Ernest Hemingway, Barron noticed a plastic bag filled with what looked like plant food.

"He just came in the mail yesterday," Kevin said. "Want to see him?"

The bag was filled with Dale's ashes which, to Kevin's shock after weeks of trying to find out what had happened to his father's remains, prison officials had sent him, as the next of kin. Now he didn't know what to do with them. They were spooking him, he said.

Barron, who had never before seen what undertakers called "cremains," examined the bag and, shuddering, noticed that bits of teeth and bone dotted the ashes.

"I tell you what," Barron said. "This stuff's got a lot of calcium in it. It would probably harden up pretty good. What do you say we mix it up with some cement and take it over to Jeff City to the gas chamber? We could make a step out of it, a little step up to the gas chamber, so every guy who goes in there has to step on him. We could call it the Dr. Cavaness Memorial Step."

Kevin said that it wasn't such a bad idea. But he said that he had decided that he had better not mess with his father's ghost. He had better try to put the old man to rest. He was thinking of driving down to southern Illinois and sprinkling the ashes on the Hickory Handle farm.

"There's a nest of copperheads down there," Kevin said. "I could throw him in with the copperheads but I'm afraid he might come back as a snake and bite me."

Kevin thought he would simply spread the ashes on the land:

"I could ask Jack Nolen to ride shotgun when I go down there. Every time I'm in Egypt, I can feel the cross hairs on the back of my neck."

Dave Barron could tell that Kevin's feelings about Dale were complex. Barron regretted, a little, having made the suggestion about the memorial step. That was how he felt about the doc; but Kevin had filial loyalties that went beyond and above and beneath what you could type out in a police report. You could not dispense with your father. Kevin was trying to act tough, was tough, but he was marked. He wanted to do what was right, whatever that meant; but he was branded, in a way, his father's son. It was beyond fathoming. Barron could not help thinking of his adopted son.

Barron and his wife had the nine-year-old boy in the house now. The adoption people had explained that he would try to test them, because he had never been wanted before; no one had ever loved him.

Dave Barron saw Kevin as an older version of the adopted boy.

Lost. Wondering whether everybody was as hateful as his father. Wondering about his father. Lucky to have Charli, Marian. A strong young man but one brutally tested by life.

Just last week the pond near the Barrons' house had frozen over. Dave had forbidden his daughters and the adopted boy to skate on the pond: The ice was always too thin, even in the dead of winter.

But the boy had gone out on the ice. Dave ordered him back to shore. The boy retreated to his room and threw a fit.

"I'm leaving," the boy said when Dave came into his room.

"You are?" Dave asked him. "Where are you going? Where will you live?"

"On the street!" the boy said.

"Really?" Dave said. "You're sure you don't want to live in this nice warm house?"

"No!" said the boy.

"What about the rash on your face?" Dave Barron said. "It's almost gone now. Who's going to put medicine on it for you every night if you live on the street?"

"Can I borrow your suitcase?" Dave Barron's adopted son said.

"No," Dave said. "You can't borrow my suitcase. We want you to stay here. We love you."

"I'm going!" the boy said.

"Are you sure?"

"Well," the boy said, "I'll decide later."

"Okay."

Dave Barron withdrew from Kevin's house, respectful, understanding that Kevin himself would have to figure out what to do with the ashes. Barron accepted that he could not solve a mystery beyond law.

On February 24, 1987, Charli gave birth to a healthy baby girl. They named her Shannon, in keeping with the tradition of Irish names in the Cavaness clan; but she looked like Charli, had her large, round brown eyes. Kevin was glad that she was a girl and that she resembled Charli. She might break the cycle. Kevin was wary of the Cavaness genes, for a generation or two anyway.

* * *

On a gray, misty day in March, Kevin drove down to southern Illinois with his father's ashes beside him in the car, along with the few things from the Toronado that Dave Barron had given him. He met Jack Nolen at the courthouse in Shawnee Square. He transferred everything to Nolen's Buick. Nolen headed for Route 34 and the Handle.

Unarmed, Kevin did not feel safe in Little Egypt, even with Detective Nolen by his side. He understood now what a loyal friend Nolen had been to the family and how much he had wanted to arrest Mark's killer; and Kevin would not have undertaken this mission without Nolen's company. But Dale's friends were everywhere. They did not care about his mother or Charli or Shannon or Patrick or Mark or Sean. They might have heard he was coming and be waiting for him at the farm. The bend in the road before Herod would be the perfect place for an ambush. The idea of cross hairs on the back of his neck haunted him. Dale had shot Sean from behind.

On the far side of Harrisburg on Route 34, beyond the gas stations and the Huck's Convenience Food Store, Jack Nolen pulled up, at Kevin's request, at T. R. Murphy's house. Kevin did not wish to give Murphy the time of day, but he thought he might as well turn over Dale's things to him. Nolen agreed to take them into the house.

"I've got Kevin Cavaness with me," Nolen said to Murphy. "He wanted you to have this stuff of Dale's. We're going to take a look at Hickory Handle. Old time's sake."

"You can't go up there," Murphy said. "We're not through probate yet. You can't go up there without permission."

"Is that right?" Nolen said. "Well, what do you know. I'll tell you something. I don't know how to get in touch with the owner, do you?"

Murphy said nothing. Nolen walked out, cheerful as a dog at dawn.

At the Handle in the afternoon mist, in the wet, darkening light, Jack Nolen stood beside his car; Kevin, a large, slow-moving form, made his way up the hill from the barn, carrying the bag of ashes.

Kevin did not go to the top of the hill, to the crest where the old graveyard had been, to where you could look out over the valley toward the Shawnee hills and the Ohio, to where he an Sean had sown Mark's ashes ten years before. He paused instea at a low knoll. He tilted the bag, keeping his hands well back, nc wishing to touch his father's ashes. He let them pour out in a slo stream, spreading them evenly on the earth.

—Southern Illinois, St. Louis, Tulsa, 1986–198

Acknowledgments

I WISH TO THANK MARIAN GREEN AND KEVIN AND CHARLI
Cavaness for their candor and tireless assistance. I am also grateful
to Patrick Cavaness for his reminiscences and to Les Green for his
hospitality.

About one week before his suicide, I made a formal request
through the Office of the Public Defender to interview John Dale
Cavaness at the State Penitentiary at Jefferson City, Missouri, although I did not expect him to reveal any more to me than he had
to others. I visited the prison in 1987 to talk to guards and inmates.
I am grateful to death-row inmate Doyle J. Williams for his detailed
account of the doctor's behavior in prison.

In southern Illinois and in St. Louis, Jack T. Nolen, Dave Barron,
Steve Goldman, Art Margulis, Eddie Miller, Pann and Lou Beck,
Pat and Betty Ray Sullivan, Greg Sullivan, Sam Yarbrough, Dorothy Zignetti, Beth Dockery, Howard Eisenberg, Erin Brothers;
and, in Florida, Eddie Bell; and, in southern Missouri, Marilyn
and Chuck Leonard were of invaluable assistance.

In Tulsa I wish to thank Professor James G. Watson for his help
with nineteenth-century historical and literary background; Dr. J.

ACKNOWLEDGMENTS

Paschal Twyman, president of the University of Tulsa, for his knowledge of bovine genetics; Roger Atwood, M.D., and Donald Brawner, M.D., for medical expertise. My thanks also to Justice Ronald M. George of the California Court of Appeal for guiding me through legal thickets.

Many people in Eldorado, Harrisburg and McLeansboro and a few in St. Louis who talked and wrote to me about Dr. Cavaness preferred to remain anonymous. I must thank them collectively here for much valuable information and insight.

All of the persons and incidents in this book are actual and, to the best of my knowledge, accurately portrayed, based on interviews and on materials noted below, under "Sources." The following names represent actual people but have been changed for reasons of discretion: Chet Williams, Jim Eldridge, Frank Stoat, Johnny Weingarten, Grolsch, "the Panther."

My literary agent, Robert Gottlieb, vice-president of the William Morris Agency, has been a wonderful help throughout with his enthusiasm, good humor, optimism, diplomacy and intelligence.

I have been blessed with a distinguished, superb editor, Harvey Ginsberg, vice-president and senior editor at William Morrow, who brought to the manuscript his experience, literary taste and story sense. I came to trust his judgment—for me a novel phenomenon—although such lapses as may remain in the text are my own.

The dedication of this book to my wife, Suzanne Beesley O'Brien, is an expression of gratitude for her energetic and resourceful work as my research assistant and confidante. Without her I would not have been able to obtain some information, nor as effectively to conduct several interviews and to evaluate source material. She acted also to rebuff distractions and interruptions.

Sources

The people named above have been my principal sources. Characterizations of the persons and dramatizations of the incidents in this book are based on interviews and on various documents, including trial transcripts and evidence in Cause No. 518664, *State of Missouri* v. *John Dale Cavaness*, Eileen Jones, C.C.R., Official Reporter; other court and police documents; correspondence; press files and videotapes of television news broadcasts; school records; historical documents, journals and books.

For the earlier parts of the story, those dealing with the history of southern Illinois and the circumstances of Cavaness's youth, I have consulted books, journals and documents of which I was made aware first through the help of Dr. Rennard Strickland, dean of the College of Law, Southern Illinois University, and most extensively with the help and guidance of Gary DeNeal of Herod, Illinois. Mr. DeNeal is a poet, fiction writer, essayist and historian who with his wife, Judy, edits and publishes *Springhouse*, a bimonthly journal which is a treasure-trove of Egyptian lore and reference. Gary DeNeal was selfless and tireless in alerting me to historical materials; neither he nor his wife holds any opinions about the Cavaness case but assisted me out of scholarly love for their native place.

Some readers, I suspect, will be as captivated as I have been by the ambiance of Little Egypt. For them I append the following informal bibliographical commentary, keyed in sequence to my early chapters and offered in the spirit of Gary and Judy DeNeal as a guide to a fascinating, little-known part of America.

John W. Allen, *Legends & Lore of Southern Illinois* and *It Happened in Southern Illinois* (Johnston City, Illinois, 1963 and 1968), provide good accounts of the origins of the name Egypt and of other place names as well as succinct accounts of most of the historical and legendary figures prominent in the region's history.

For the backgrounds of Eldorado and Harrisburg, see *Saline County: A Century of History, 1847–1947* (Utica, Kentucky, 1947), essays by various hands covering such matters as Indians, pioneer life, courts, religion, schools, business, coal mining, etc. One learns here that the pronunciation of Eldorado as "Elder-RAY-dough" derives from its founding in 1858 by Judge Samuel Elder and his kin, who originally named the place Elderedo; the railroad changed the spelling on the station in the late 1870s.

Ethnic and geographical origins of the people of Egypt have been documented extensively, but the most colorful account is in Milo Erwin, *The History of Williamson County* (Marion, Illinois, 1876). Erwin, a local lawyer with a flamboyant literary style, produced what is in my opinion a quirky, unknown delight. See also "Why Egypt?," by John J. Dunphy and "Egypt vs. Arkansas," by Brann the Iconoclast, both in *Springhouse* (Vol. I, No. 3, March–April 1984).

The best account of the Herrin Massacre is in Paul M. Angle, *Bloody Williamson* (New York, 1952), a magnificent book by a distinguished historian; Angle also narrates the Bloody Vendetta, the Klan war, and the career of Charlie Birger. For an argument defending the actions of the Herrin mob, see "The Other Side of Herrin," a pamphlet (n.d.) published by the Illinois Mine Workers; for management's side, see "The Herrin Conspiracy," a pamphlet issued by the National Coal Association (Washington, D.C., n.d.). See also *The Herrin Massacre*, by Chatland Parker, published by the Williamson County Historical Society (Marion, Illinois, 1925). *Oldham Paisley*, (Marion, Illinois, 1974) by Margaret N. O'Shea, gives a vivid account of the life of the region's most respected newspaper publisher and editor, 1915–70, and his struggles to cope with the various waves of violence.

The best account of the Harpes and of other outlaws resident at Cave-in-Rock is Otto A. Rothert's *The Outlaws of Cave-in-Rock* (New York: 1924), which documents many of the brothers' crimes; see also Paul I. Wellman, *Spawn of Evil* (New York, 1964).

For Charlie Birger, the definitive source is Gary DeNeal's *A Knight of Another Sort: Prohibition Days and Charlie Birger* (Danville, Illinois, 1981), a thoroughly researched and fascinating biography, much of it based on interviews with surviving gangsters and law-enforcement figures. John Bartlow Martin's accounts of wars between the Birger and Shelton gangs appear in his *Butcher's Dozen and Other Murders* (New York, 1950). See also Angle, *Bloody Williamson*, cited above.

For a detailed portrait of Little Egypt during the Depression, see Malcolm Brown and John N. Webb, *Seven Stranded Coal Towns* (Washington, D.C., 1941). For postwar southern Illinois, see Baker Brownell, *The Other Illinois* (New York, 1959).

For moving personal accounts of life in Little Egypt during the Depression, see Robert J. Hastings, *A Nickel's Worth of Skim Milk* and *A Penny's Worth of Minced Ham* (Carbondale, Illinois, 1972 and 1986). *A History of the Baptist Hour Association* (Harrisburg, Illinois, 1957) gives an account of the growth of the program and offers a portrait of the religious character of the region.

For Billy Potts, see Ronald L. Nelson, "In Search of Billy Potts," *Springhouse* (Vol. II, No. 3, May–June 1985), and the same author's follow-up article in the July–August issue. I have written a prose narrative of the story in *Springhouse* (Vol. IV, No. 3, May–June 1987) in which I have combined various accounts including Robert Penn Warren's "The Ballad of Billie Potts."

For Crenshaw's Hickory Hill, now known as the Old Slave House, see *Illiniwĕk* (Vol. X, No. 3, May–June 1972), a thorough documentation of the history of the salt works and the activities at the mansion, which is now a museum.

For James Ford, see W. D. Snively, Jr., and Louanna Furbee, *Satan's Ferryman: A True Tale of the Old Frontier* (New York, 1968). Charles Neely's *Tales and Songs of Southern Illinois* and Richard Dorson's *Buying the Wind* (Menasha, Wisconsin, 1938; Chicago, 1964) are sources of regional folklore and song.

The origin and meaning of Dale Cavaness's favorite term, "Rudie," is obscure; Kevin Cavaness suggests the derivation I have included in the text; etymological sources affirm the connection between "rude" and "rowdy" with specific reference to "Illinois Rowdies" of frontier days who frightened visiting Englishmen by bringing long rifles to church (see the *Oxford English Dictionary*). A senior resident of Evansville, Indiana, however, assures me that to anyone within a two-hundred-mile radius of Evansville, which would include Eldorado, the term "Rudy" means male homosexual, deriving from the first name of a deceased homosexual necrophiliac undertaker, whose activities became legendary in a region known for its attachment to the morbid and the gothic. It seems doubtful, however, that Dale Cavaness meant the term in this way.

My account of the 1937 Ohio River flood derives from newspapers and from *Rudy's Life in Shawneetown, 1928–1980* (Shawneetown, Illinois, 1980), by Rudy Phillips, King of the Hoboes, a vivid portrayal of Shawneetown life.

An amusing account of the modern history of McLeansboro appears in H. Allen Smith's *Lo, the Former Egyptian* (New York, 1952).

For the flavor of daily life in Egypt from the 1950s to the present, see Gary DeNeal's frequent essays in *Springhouse* and *Illinois* magazines.

77600